FUTURE
English for Results

5

Contributing Authors

Lynn Bonesteel

Arlen Gargagliano

Jeanne Lambert

Series Consultants

Beatriz B. Díaz

Ronna Magy

Federico Salas-Isnardi

Future 5
English for Results

Pearson Education, 221 River Street, Hoboken, NJ 07030 USA

Staff credits: The people who made up the *Future* team, representing editorial,
production, design, manufacturing, and marketing, are Pietro Alongi, Rhea Banker,
Peter Benson, Nancy Blodget, Elizabeth Carlson, Jennifer Castro, Tracey Munz Cataldo,
Natalia Cebulska, Aerin Csigay, Mindy DePalma, Dave Dickey, Gina DiLillo, Warren
Fischbach, Pam Fishman, Nancy Flaggman, Irene Frankel, Shelley Gazes, Gosia Jaros-
White, Mike Kemper, Niki Lee, Melissa Leyva, Stefan Machura, Amy McCormick, Linda
Moser, Liza Pleva, Joan Poole, Sherry Preiss, Stella Reilly, Mary Rich, Lindsay Richman,
Barbara Sabella, Katarzyna Starzynska-Kosciuszko, Loretta Steeves, Kim Steiner,
Alexandra Suarez, Katherine Sullivan, Paula Van Ells, and Marian Wassner.

Cover design: Rhea Banker
Cover photo: Kathy Lamm/Getty Images
Text design: Elizabeth Carlson
Text composition: Word & Image Design Studio, Inc.
Text font: Minion Pro

Library of Congress Cataloging-in-Publication Data
A catalog record for the print edition is available from the Library of Congress.

Printed in the United States of America
ISBN 13: 9780134696188 (Student Book with MyEnglishLab)
ISBN 10: 0134696182 (Student Book with MyEnglishLab)
1 17

ISBN 13: 9780134659510 (Student Book with Essential Online Resources)
ISBN 10: 0134659511 (Student Book with Essential Online Resources)
1 17

Contents

To the Teacher

Welcome to *Future*
English for Results

Future is a six-level, four-skills course for adults and young adults correlated to state and national standards. *Future* supports Workforce Innovation and Opportunity Act (WIOA) goals and prepares adults for College and Career Readiness (CCRS), English Language Proficiencies (ELP), job skills, standardized tests, and EL-Civics. It incorporates research-based teaching strategies, corpus-informed language, and the best of modern technology.

KEY FEATURES

Future provides everything your students need in one integrated program.

In developing the course, we listened to what teachers asked for and we responded, providing six levels, more meaningful content, a thorough treatment of grammar, explicit skills development, abundant practice, multiple options for state-of-the-art assessment, and innovative components.

Future serves students' real-life needs.

We began constructing the instructional syllabus for *Future* by identifying what is most critical to students' success in their personal and family lives, in the workplace, as members of a community, and in their academic pursuits. *Future* provides outstanding coverage of life-skills competencies, basing language teaching on actual situations that students are likely to encounter and equipping them with the skills they need to achieve their goals. The grammar and other language elements taught in each lesson grow out of these situations and thus are practiced in realistic contexts, enabling students to use language meaningfully, from the beginning.

Future grows with your students.

Future takes students from absolute beginner level through low-advanced proficiency in English, addressing students' abilities and learning priorities at each level. As the levels progress, the curricular content and unit structure change accordingly, with the upper levels incorporating more academic skills, more advanced content standards, and more content-rich texts.

Future is fun!

Humor is built into each unit of *Future*. Many of the conversations, and especially the listenings, are designed to have an amusing twist at the end, giving students an extra reason to listen—something to anticipate with pleasure and to then take great satisfaction in once it is understood. In addition, many activities have students interacting in pairs and groups. Not only does this make classroom time more enjoyable, it also creates an atmosphere conducive to learning in which learners are relaxed, highly motivated, and at their most receptive.

Future puts the best of 21st-century technology in the hands of students and teachers.

In addition to its expertly developed print materials and audio components, *Future* goes a step further.

- Every **Student Book** comes with **Essential Online Resources** and optional **MyEnglishLab** for use at home, in the lab, or wherever students have access to a computer. The online resources can be assigned by teachers and used both by students who wish to extend their practice beyond the classroom and by those who need to "make up" what they missed in class.
- The **Tests and Test Prep** book comes with the *Future* **Exam**View® *Assessment Suite*, enabling teachers to print ready-made tests, customize these tests, or create their own tests for life skills, grammar, vocabulary, listening, and reading.
- The **Companion Website** provides a variety of teaching support, including a PDF of the Teacher's Edition and Lesson Planner notes for each unit in the Student Book.

Future provides all the assessment tools you need.

- The **Placement Test** evaluates students' proficiency in all skill areas, allowing teachers and program administrators to easily assign students to the right classes.
- The **Tests and Test Prep** book for each level provides:
  - **Printed unit tests** with accompanying audio CD. These unit tests use standardized testing formats, giving students practice "bubbling-in" responses as required for CASAS and other standardized tests. In addition, reproducible test prep worksheets and practice tests (in the online resources) provide invaluable help to students unfamiliar with such test formats.
  - The *Future* **Exam**View® *Assessment Suite* is a powerful program that allows teachers to create their own unique tests or to print or customize already prepared tests at three levels: pre-level, at-level, and above-level.
- **Performance-based assessment:** Lessons in the Student Book end with a "practical assessment" activity such as Role Play, Make It Personal, or Show What You Know. Each unit culminates with both a role-play activity and a problem-solving activity, which require students to demonstrate their oral competence in a holistic way. The **Teacher's Edition and Lesson Planner** provides speaking rubrics to make it easy for teachers to evaluate students' oral proficiency.
- **Self-assessment:** For optimal learning to take place, students need to be involved in setting goals and in

monitoring their own progress. *Future* has addressed this in numerous ways. In the Student Book, checkboxes at the end of lessons invite students to evaluate their mastery of the material. End-of-unit reviews allow students to see their progress in grammar and writing. After completing each unit, students go back to the goals for the unit and reflect on their achievement. In addition, the Essential Online Resources and MyEnglishLab provide students with continuous feedback (and opportunities for self-correction) as they work through each lesson. The Workbook contains the answer keys, so that students can check their own work outside of class.

Future addresses multilevel classes and diverse learning styles.

Using research-based teaching strategies, *Future* provides teachers with creative solutions for all stages of lesson planning and implementation, allowing them to meet the needs of all their students.

- The **Multilevel Communicative Activities Book** provides an array of reproducible activities and games that engage students through different modalities. Teachers' notes provide multilevel options for pre-level and above-level students, as well as extension activities for additional speaking and writing practice.
- The **Teacher's Edition and Lesson Planner** offers pre-level and above-level variations for every lesson plan, as well as numerous optional and extension activities designed to reach students at all levels.
- The **Transparencies and Reproducible Vocabulary Cards** include picture and word cards that will help kinesthetic and visual learners acquire and learn new vocabulary. Teachers' notes include ideas for multilevel classes.
- The **Essential Online Resources** included with the Student Book have extraordinary tools for individualizing instruction, as well as providing immediate feedback. All new reading and writing printable activities support College and Career Readiness goals (for levels 1–5). Multiple life-skills and listening activities with listen, record, and compare functions allow students to practice these skills outside of class. In addition, the audio files for the book are available in the Essential Online Resources, enabling students to listen to any of the material that accompanies the text.
- The **MyEnglishLab** option includes everything in the Essential Online Resources and much more. Readings with interactive activities and feedback (for all units in levels 1–5) support College and Career Readiness skills. Grammar Coach video presentations and additional online interactive activities for all of the grammar lessons give students extra grammar practice.

- The **Workbook with Audio**, similarly, allows students to devote their time to the lessons and specific skill areas that they need to work on most. In addition, students can replay the audio portions they want to listen to as many times as necessary, choosing to focus on the connections between the written and spoken word, listening for grammar, pronunciation, and/or listening for general comprehension.

Future's persistence curriculum motivates students to continue their education.

Recent research about persistence has given us insights into how to keep students coming to class and how to keep them learning when they can't attend. Recognizing that there are many forces operating in students' lives—family, jobs, childcare, health—that may make it difficult for them to come to class, programs need to help students:
- Identify their educational goals.
- Believe that they can successfully achieve them.
- Develop a commitment to their own education.
- Identify forces that can interfere with school attendance.
- Develop strategies that will help them try to stay in school in spite of obstacles.

Future addresses all of these areas with its persistence curriculum. Activities found throughout the book and specific persistence activities in the back of the book help students build community, set goals, develop better study skills, and feel a sense of achievement. In addition, the Essential Online Resources and MyEnglishLab are unique in their ability to ensure that even those students unable to attend class are able to make up what they missed and thus persist in their studies.

Future supports busy teachers by providing all the materials teachers need, plus teacher support.

The **Student Book, Workbook with Audio, online resources, Multilevel Communicative Activities Book**, and **Transparencies and Reproducible Vocabulary Cards** were designed to provide teachers with everything they need in the way of ready-to-use classroom and homework materials so they can concentrate on responding to their students' needs.

Future provides ample practice with flexible options to best fit the needs of each class.

The Student Book provides 60–100 hours of instruction. It can be supplemented in class by using:
- Teacher's Edition and Lesson Planner expansion ideas
- Transparencies and Reproducible Vocabulary Cards
- Workbook exercises
- Multilevel Communicative Activities

- Tests
- Essential Online Resources activities, as well as Student Book audio
- MyEnglishLab activities
- Activities on the Companion Website (futureenglishforresults.com)

TEACHING MULTILEVEL CLASSES

Teaching tips for pair and group work

Using pair and group work in an ESL classroom has many proven benefits. It creates an atmosphere of liveliness, builds community, and allows students to practice speaking in a low-risk environment. Many of the activities in *Future* are pair and small-group activities. Here are some tips for managing these activities:

- Limit small groups to three or four students per group (unless an activity specifically calls for larger groups). This maximizes student participation.
- Change partners for different activities. This gives students a chance to work with many others in the class and keeps them from feeling "stuck."
- If possible, give students a place to put their coats when they enter the classroom. This allows them to move around freely without worrying about returning to their own seats.
- Move around the classroom as students are working to make sure they are on task and to monitor their work.
- As you walk around, try to remain unobtrusive, so students continue to participate actively, without feeling they are being evaluated.
- Keep track of language points students are having difficulty with. After the activity, teach a mini-lesson to the entire class addressing those issues. This helps students who are having trouble without singling them out.

Pairs and groups in the multilevel classroom

Adult education ESL classrooms are by nature multilevel. This is true even if students have been given a placement test. Many factors—including a student's age, educational background, and literacy level—contribute to his or her ability level. Also, the same student may be at level in one skill, but pre-level or above-level in another.

When grouping students for a task, keep the following points in mind:

- *Like-ability* groups (in which students have the same ability level) help ensure that all students participate equally, without one student dominating the activity.
- *Cross-ability* groups (in which students have different ability levels) are beneficial to pre-level students who need the support of their at- or above-level classmates. The higher-level students benefit from "teaching" their lower-level classmates.

For example, when students are practicing a straightforward conversation substitution exercise, like-ability pairings are helpful. The activity can be tailored to different ability levels, and both students can participate equally. When students are completing the more complex task of creating their own conversations, cross-ability pairings are helpful. The higher-level student can support and give ideas to the lower-level student.

The *Future* Teacher's Edition and Lesson Planner, the Teacher's Notes in the Multilevel Communicative Activities Book, and the Teacher's Notes in the Transparencies and Reproducible Vocabulary Cards all provide specific suggestions for when to put students in like-ability versus cross-ability groups, and how to tailor activities to different ability levels.

Level	Description	CASAS Scale Scores
Intro	True Beginning	Below 180
1	Low Beginning	181–190
2	High Beginning	191–200
3	Low Intermediate	201–210
4	High Intermediate	211–220
5	Low Advanced	221–235

Unit Opener

Each unit starts with a full-page photo that introduces the themes of the unit.

Are You Safe?

4

Preview

What natural disaster is about to happen? What would you do to stay safe?

A **Preview question** engages students and sets the context for the unit.

UNIT GOALS

☐ Talk about being safe in natural disasters and emergencies

☐ Talk about keeping latchkey kids safe

☐ Identify home safety measures

☐ Learn about workers' rights to a safe workplace

☐ Identify workplace safety measures

A **list of goals** summarizes the key competencies presented in the unit.

UNIT 4 **65**

Reading

High-interest articles introduce students to cultural concepts and useful, topical information with a focus on preparing students for academic and other real-life reading tasks.

Before You Read exercises activate students' background knowledge and build other **pre-reading skills**.

Comprehension questions check understanding of the article and build reading skills.

Essential **reading skills**, such as summarizing, visualizing, and identifying the main idea, are explicitly taught and practiced.

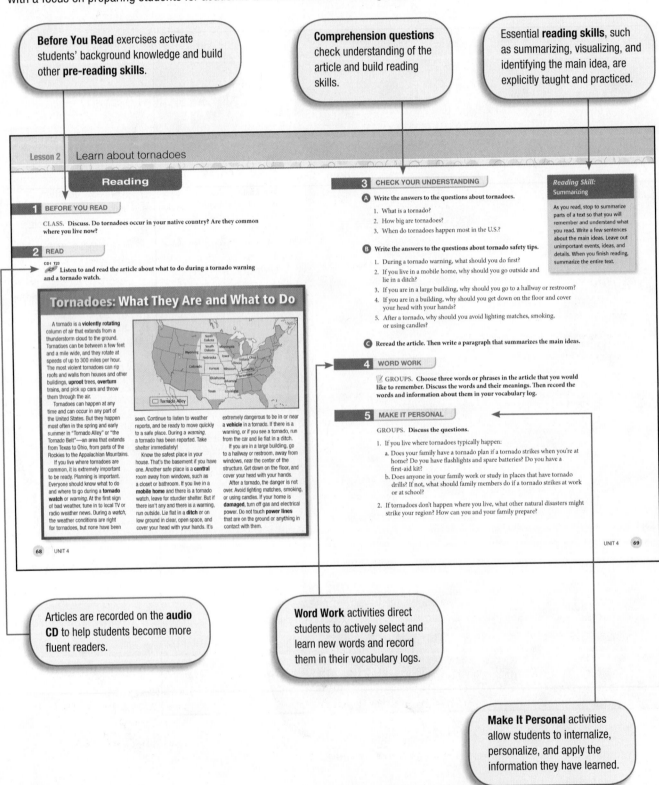

Articles are recorded on the **audio CD** to help students become more fluent readers.

Word Work activities direct students to actively select and learn new words and record them in their vocabulary logs.

Make It Personal activities allow students to internalize, personalize, and apply the information they have learned.

Grammar

Each unit presents one or two grammar points in a logical, systematic grammar syllabus.

Grammar charts clearly present the target grammar.

Grammar Watch notes call attention to specific aspects of the grammar point.

Contextualized grammar practice progresses from controlled to open-ended exercises.

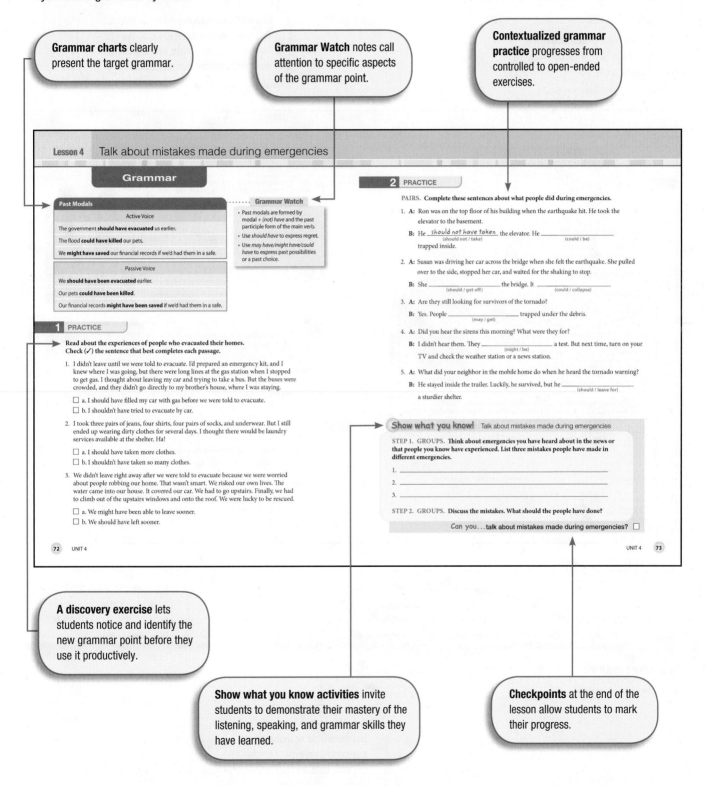

A discovery exercise lets students notice and identify the new grammar point before they use it productively.

Show what you know activities invite students to demonstrate their mastery of the listening, speaking, and grammar skills they have learned.

Checkpoints at the end of the lesson allow students to mark their progress.

Listening and Speaking

Listening lessons present topical information and the key vocabulary and competencies of the unit.

Before You Listen activities introduce new language and cultural concepts.

Listening comprehension questions focus first on the main ideas of the listening and culminate with inference questions and oral language activities.

Lesson 5 Talk about keeping latchkey kids safe

Listening and Speaking

1 BEFORE YOU LISTEN

A CLASS. Discuss the questions.

1. In your home country, is it common for children to spend time alone, without their parents or others looking after them?

2. At what age do you think a child can be responsible for taking care of himself or herself? At what age do you think a child can be responsible for taking care of younger siblings? Explain.

3. If you have children, where do they go after school?

B Read the information about latchkey children.

"Latchkey children" or "latchkey kids" refers to children who spend time home alone without parents or others to supervise them. Some people believe that the term became widely used during World War II, when many fathers were away fighting the war and many mothers went to work in the factories. Today, there are still many latchkey children, and their numbers are rising. In some cases, children want to go home after school, and they feel they are too old to have a baby-sitter. Older children may pressure parents to allow them to go home after school, even when child care or after-school programs are available. However, many parents of latchkey children do not have a choice: They simply can't afford to pay for child care and have no other options.

C GROUPS. Latchkey children can get into different kinds of trouble when they are home alone. Look at the categories in the chart. Can you think of examples? Write at least one example for each category.

Pressure from Friends to Break Rules	Accidents and Emergencies
Strangers	Emotional and Psychological Issues

2 LISTEN

CD1 T27

A Tania is a single mother who doesn't get home until after 6:00. Her 12-year-old son, Greg, is home alone after school. Listen to her talk with her neighbor Nick about the things she is worried about. Write the problems and the solutions her neighbor suggests.

Possible Problems	Possible Solutions
1. What if strangers call?	
2.	
3.	
4.	
5.	

CD1 T27

B Read the information in the Communication Skill box. Then listen again. Write the phrase Nick uses to offer each suggestion.

Suggestion 1: _Why don't you_

Suggestion 2: _____

Suggestion 3: _____

Suggestion 4: _____

Suggestion 5: _____

Communication Skill:
Making Suggestions

You can begin a suggestion with these phrases:

Why don't you (+ verb)?
Have you thought about (+ gerund)?
Maybe you could (+ verb).
If I were you, I'd (+ verb).
Could you (+ verb)?

3 CONVERSATION

ROLE PLAY. PAIRS. Work with a partner who was not in your group in Exercise 1C. Student A is the parent and Student B is the neighbor.

STEP 1. Select a problem to work on from the chart in Exercise 1C.

STEP 2. Create a conversation like the one between Tania and her neighbor. Use expressions from the Communication Skill box. Write the conversation down.

STEP 3. Practice the conversation. Use gestures and appropriate emotion.

STEP 4. Perform the role play in front of the class.

Students apply **critical thinking skills** in discussions about the topic.

Corpus-informed **model conversations** use target grammar and competencies to model spoken language.

A **problem-solving activity, personalized activity,** or **supported role-play** reinforces the concepts and language learned in the lesson.

A **communication skill**, such as alternative ways to make suggestions, is modeled and practiced in each unit.

Life Skills

Life Skills lessons in each unit focus on functional language, practical skills, and authentic printed materials, such as websites, schedules, maps, catalogs, labels, and signs.

Civics, life skills, and **cultural information** related to life in the U.S. are introduced in context.

Critical thinking skills are introduced and practiced in real-life contexts.

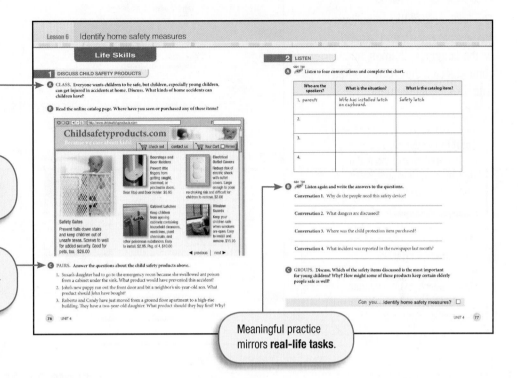

Meaningful practice mirrors **real-life tasks**.

Writing

Writing instruction is process-based, leading students to write well-organized short essays or letters about familiar topics. Each unit focuses on key features of a specific genre, such as instructions, letters to the editor, or autobiographical essays.

The **Before You Write** section presents the genre and includes a **writing tip** to help students structure, unify, and clarify their academic writing.

Think on Paper presents writing strategies and **graphic organizers** that students can use to plan and structure their writing.

Students perform a **prewriting activity** to gather information and ideas on the topic.

Students are directed to read and analyze a student **writing model**, which illustrates the features of the genre and the writing tip.

Self-editing checklists help students revise, edit, and proofread their work to be sure that they have implemented the Writing Tip and other new writing concepts.

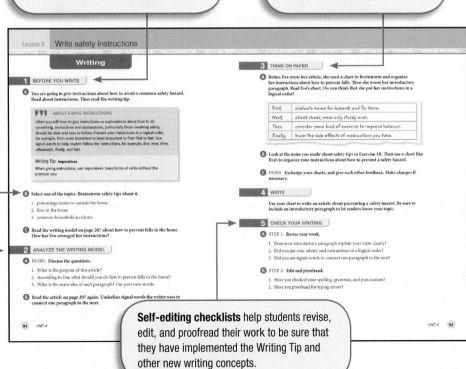

Review & Expand

The final page of the unit allows students to review and expand on the language, themes, and competencies they have worked with throughout the unit.

Act It Out activities assign different sections of the unit to students to review and present to a partner or group.

Problem-solving tasks encourage critical thinking and allow students to demonstrate understanding of topics in real-life situations.

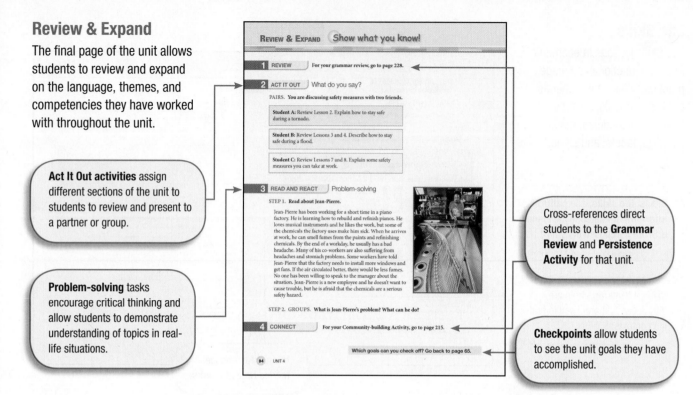

Cross-references direct students to the **Grammar Review** and **Persistence Activity** for that unit.

Checkpoints allow students to see the unit goals they have accomplished.

Grammar Review

Grammar Review allows students to check their mastery of the unit grammar.

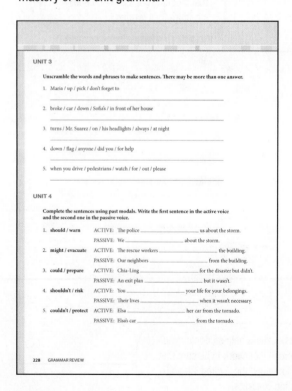

Persistence Activities

Persistence activities build community in the classroom, help students set personal and language learning goals, and encourage students to develop good study skills and habits.

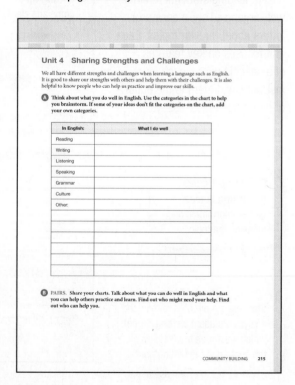

MyEnglishLab

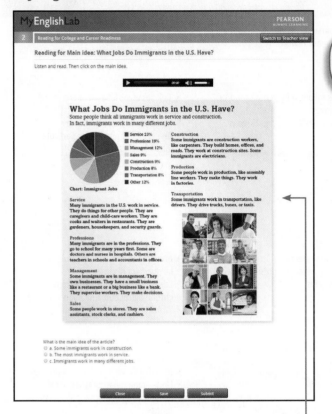

MyEnglishLab delivers rich online content to engage and motivate **students**.

Grammar Coach videos give additional grammar presentations and practice.

MyEnglishLab delivers innovative teaching tools and useful resources to **teachers**.

MyEnglishLab also provides students with:
- rich interactive practice in listening, speaking, vocabulary building, and life skills
- immediate and meaningful feedback on wrong answers
- grade reports that display performance and time on task

Reading and writing lessons, based on College and Career Readiness Standards (CCRS), develop essential skills for academic and career readiness.

With **MyEnglishLab**, teachers can:
- view student scores by unit and activity
- monitor student progress on any activity or test
- analyze class data to determine steps for remediation and support

Scope and Sequence

UNIT	LISTENING AND SPEAKING	GRAMMAR	LIFE SKILLS	
Pre-Unit **Getting Started** *page 2*	• Ask for personal information • Give personal information	• Grammar terms review • Verb tense review		

1
Setting Goals, Pursuing Dreams
page 5
	• Describe personality traits
	• Listen to several career counseling sessions and take notes
	• Discuss long-term career goals
	• Talk about a career path
	• Talk about SMART goals
	• *Communication Skill:* Using examples
	• *Presentation Skills:*
	  ◦ Make eye contact
	  ◦ Explain and refer to your chart
	  ◦ Ask for suggestions
		• Verbs followed by gerunds and/or infinitives
		• Gerunds following prepositions
			• Talk about job-related interests and abilities
			• Complete an interests survey
			• Analyze skills needed for particular jobs	

2 **Getting a Job** *page 25*	• Talk about interview do's and don'ts • Listen to a career counselor's advice about interviewing • Listen to and critique job applicants' responses to interview questions • Listen to and role-play a job interview • *Communication Skill:* Asking questions	• Present perfect • Present perfect vs. present perfect continuous	• Analyze the content, structure, and language of résumés • Learn the difference between a chronological and a functional résumé • Write a chronological résumé	
3 **Road Trip** *page 45*	• Listen to and take notes as a driving instructor talks about what to do in case of an accident • Talk about driving laws and customs • *Communication Skill:* Taking part in discussions	• Inseparable and separable phrasal verbs • *Grammar Watch:* Gerunds and infinitives in general statements	• Identify car parts and related problems • Understand different types of car insurance, including special insurance terms • Use online traffic information, including a detour map • Interpret Internet maps and directions	
4 **Are You Safe?** *page 65*	• Listen to a story of survival • Retell a news story about an earthquake • Listen to a news report about Hurricane Katrina • Discuss safety and evacuation procedures • Listen to and take part in discussions about child safety • *Communication Skill:* Making suggestions	• Past modals	• Identify safety measures that can prevent accidents at home and work • Use an online catalog page to learn about child safety products • Interpret information about workplace safety measures	
5 **Advancing on the Job** *page 85*	• Listen to a performance review • Talk about how to respond to constructive criticism • Listen to discussions about job-training opportunities • Use a company Intranet site to role-play a conversation about on-the-job training • Talk about factors that influence job promotions • Discuss job-performance evaluations • *Communication Skill:* Clarifying	• Clauses with *although* and *unless*	• Use a course catalog to complete a course schedule	

READING	WRITING	PROBLEM SOLVING	PERSISTENCE
• Learn to use a glossary • Develop vocabulary learning skills	• Take notes		• Community building • Orientation to book
• Read about doing job research • Read about setting goals and achieving what you want • Read about overcoming an obstacle • *Reading Skills:* ◦ Highlighting/Underlining key information ◦ Previewing	• Use word webs to gather and organize information • Write a descriptive essay about your interests, skills, and goals • *Writing Tip:* Topic sentences	• Suggest ways for someone to achieve a long-term career goal despite obstacles	• *Study Skills:* Exploring Your Expectations
• Read about preparing for a job search • Read about tricky interview questions and how to answer them • *Reading Skills:* ◦ Using prior knowledge ◦ Comparing and contrasting	• Use a T-chart to list job requirements and those skills and traits that make you a good candidate for a job • Write a cover letter for a résumé • *Writing Tip*: Using language from a job ad in a cover letter	• Give advice to someone who is nervous about a job interview	• *Community Building:* Speaking English Well
• Read about what to do if your car breaks down • Read about what to do if the police stop you • Read and interpret Internet driving directions • *Reading Skills:* ◦ Paraphrasing ◦ Understanding sequence	• Use a chart to brainstorm and organize an argument • Write a letter to the editor about whether people should be allowed to use cell phones while driving • *Writing Tip:* Supporting details and examples	• Suggest ways to improve someone's daily drive to work so that the person can be more punctual	• *Study Skills:* The Importance of Reading
• Read about tornadoes, including safety measures you can take • Read about workers' rights to a safe workplace • *Reading Skills:* ◦ Summarizing ◦ Monitoring comprehension	• Use a chart to brainstorm and organize instructions • Write an essay that gives instructions about how to avoid a common safety hazard • *Writing Tip:* Imperatives	• Advise someone about how to handle a workplace safety issue	• *Community Building:* Sharing Strengths and Challenges
• Read about factors that influence promotion • Read a job-performance review • Read about *I* and *You* statements • Read about sports idioms used in the workplace • *Reading Skills:* ◦ Identifying the main idea ◦ Scanning	• Use an outline to organize a self-evaluation • Write a self-evaluation about your performance at work or school • *Writing Tip:* Using good examples	• Give advice to someone who is upset by negative comments on a performance review	• *Study Skills:* Building Your Vocabulary All the Time

Text in red = Civics and American culture

UNIT	LISTENING AND SPEAKING	GRAMMAR	LIFE SKILLS	
6 **Health** *page 105*	• Listen to a conversation about a medical problem • Talk about medical specialists and the conditions they treat • Describe medical problems • Listen to a presentation and take notes • Discuss diabetes • Ask and answer questions about health • *Communication Skill:* Giving advice	• Embedded *Wh-* questions • Embedded *Yes/No* questions	• Identify side effects of medications • Identify how to take medications properly	
7 **Citizenship** *page 125*	• Discuss how a bill becomes a law • Listen to a lecture on naturalization and take notes • Discuss becoming a U.S. citizen • *Communication Skill:* Exchanging opinions	• *Grammar Watch:* Passive with *get* • The past perfect	• Learn about different kinds of maps • Interpret a historical map of the U.S. • Identify the special features of a map	
8 **Knowing the Law** *page 145*	• Listen to a lecture on the rights of people accused of crimes and take notes • Discuss the *Miranda* warning • Listen to a lecture on types of crimes • Talk about one's opinions • *Communication Skill:* Qualifying opinions	• Future real conditional	• Recognize sexual harassment in the workplace • Understand sexual harassment laws	
9 **Saving the Planet** *page 165*	• Listen to an interview about a carpooling program • Discuss carpooling • Discuss tips for greening your community • Talk about doing your share for the environment • Listen to a conversation about recycling • *Communication Skill:* Expressing comparison and contrast	• The past subjunctive with *wish* • The past unreal conditional	• Discuss recycling rules • Interpret a recycling calendar • Identify items that are recyclable	
10 **Technology** *page 185*	• Listen to a lecture on the history of the Internet and take notes • Talk about the growth of the Internet • Listen to a discussion on how the Internet is affecting communication • Discuss the pros and cons of the Internet • Listen to a conversation about the language of text messaging • Discuss text messaging as a way of communicating • *Communication Skill:* Expressing agreement and disagreement	• Adjective clauses	• Understand how to use an instruction manual	

READING	WRITING	PROBLEM SOLVING	PERSISTENCE

• Read about preparing for a doctor appointment
• Identify the main idea
• Read about first aid and emergency procedures
• Read message board posts
• Read about preventive health screenings
• *Reading Skills:*
  ◦ Visualizing
  ◦ Recognizing cause and effect
	• Use a chart to organize ideas
	• Write a persuasive essay for or against smoking bans in public places
	• *Writing Tip:* Introductory paragraphs
		• Suggest ways a parent can help an inactive, overweight child control diabetes	• *Study Skills:* Studyng in the U.S.

• Read about the beginnings of the United States
• Read about the organization of the U.S. government
• Read about individual rights in the Constitution
• Read about the benefits of U.S. citizenship
• *Reading Skills:*
  ◦ Using a T-chart to take notes
  ◦ Using text structure and formatting
	• Use a T-chart to brainstorm and organize ideas
	• Write a formal e-mail to an elected official about a problem that concerns you
	• *Writing Tip:* Using a problem/solution structure
		• Give advice about ways the U.S. legal system can be used to improve construction safety measures	• *Study Skills:* Writing Strategies

• Read about the right to vote
• Read about child abuse laws
• Read about sexual harassment
• Read about traffic tickets and traffic court
• Read about the importance of paying fines
• *Reading Skills:*
  ◦ Distinguishing fact from opinion
  ◦ Making inferences
	• Use a Venn diagram to organize points of comparison and constrast
	• Write an essay comparing and contrasting the legal systems in your home country and the U.S.
	• *Writing Tip:* Showing similarities and differences
		• Suggest a method of dealing with suspected child abuse	• *Study Skills:* Reading Skills/Strategies

• Read about ways to protect the environment and save money
• Read a blog about one student's experience with recycling
• Read about how daily life is changing our world
• Read about the "greening" of Greensburg, Kansas
• *Reading Skills:*
  ◦ Understanding the style and structure of blogs (web-logs)
  ◦ Using visuals
	• Use a chart to arrange events in a logical order
	• Write a personal narrative about how you have tried to help the environment
	• *Writing Tip:* Using time order
		• Suggest ways an office manager can "green" an office	• *Study Skills:* Becoming a Lifelong Learner

• Read about virtual driving
• Read about computer training
• Read about the history of the Internet
• *Reading Skills:*
  ◦ Identifying an author's purpose
  ◦ Using a timeline
	• Use a chart to structure an autobiographical essay
	• Write an autobiographical essay about a challenge you faced
	• *Writing Tip:* Using concrete examples and sensory details
		• Give advice to a new employee who is struggling to learn about unfamiliar computer equipment and procedures	• *Goal Setting:* Moving Forward

Text in red = Civics and American culture

Correlations

UNIT	CASAS Reading Basic Skill Content Standards	CASAS Listening Basic Skill Content Standards	
1	**U1:** 1.1; 1.2; 1.3; 1.4; 2.2; 3.2; **L1:** 3.4; **L2:** 2.8; **L4:** 2.7; 3.5; 7.2; **L6:** 6.2; 6.6; **L7:** 4.8; **L8:** 3.3; **SWYK Review and Expand:** 3.3	**U1:** 2.3; **L2:** 3.1; **L3:** 3.1; 4.7; 5.8; 5.9; 6.5; **L6:** 5.8; **L7:** 6.5; **L8:** 5.8; **SWYK Review and Expand:** 5.6	
2	**U2:** 1.1; 1.2; 1.3; 1.4; 2.2; 3.2; **L1:** 3.4; **L2:** 1.6; **L3:** 3.6; **L4:** 3.12; **L5:** 3.4; 7.3; **L6:** 3.9; **L9:** 3.4; 4.8; **SWYK Review and Expand:** 3.3	**U2:** 2.3; **L1:** 5.8; **L4:** 5.8; **L5:** 5.6; **L6:** 3.9; 4.2; **L7:** 4.6; **L8:** 3.9; 4.2; **SWYK Review and Expand:** 5.6	
3	**U3:** 1.1; 1.2; 1.3; 1.4; 2.2; 3.2; **L1:** 3.1; 4.1; 5.1; **L2:** 3.4; 6.4; 7.6; **L5:** 3.4; 3.13; **L6:** 3.3; 7.4; **L7:** 3.4; **L8:** 4.9; **L9:** 3.3; **SWYK Review and Expand:** 3.3	**U3:** 2.3; **L1:** 2.4; 2.9; 4.2; **L2:** 5.5; 6.1; **L4:** 5.5; 5.8; **L5:** 2.9; 4.2; **L6:** 4.7; **SWYK Review and Expand:** 5.6	
4	**U4:** 1.1; 1.2; 1.3; 1.4; 2.2; 3.2; **L1:** 3.5; 7.4; **L2:** 3.5; 7.7; **L3:** 3.3; **L5:** 3.3; **L6:** 3.3; 3.12; **L7:** 3.5; 5.5; **L8:** 3.2; **L9:** 3.4; **SWYK Review and Expand:** 3.3	**U4:** 2.3; **L1:** 4.6; **L2:** 5.6; **L3:** 4.11; 5.8; **L4:** 3.1; **L5:** 4.6; **L6:** 4.2; **L7:** 5.6; **SWYK Review and Expand:** 5.6	
5	**U5:** 1.1; 1.2; 1.3; 1.4; 2.2; 3.2; **L1:** 3.5; 7.2; **L2:** 3.4; 4.1; 6.2; 6.6; **L5:** 3.4; 4.1; 4.3; **L6:** 3.4; 4.2; 4.3; 4.8; **L7:** 3.2; **L8:** 3.4; 3.12; 3.15; **L9:** 3.3; **SWYK Review and Expand:** 3.3	**U5:** 2.3; **L1:** 5.9; 6.1; **L3:** 2.4; 4.6; 5.8; 6.7; **L5:** 4.6; **L7:** 4.3; **L8:** 2.3; **SWYK Review and Expand:** 5.6	
6	**U6:** 1.1; 1.2; 1.3; 1.4; 2.2; 3.2; **L1:** 6.5; 7.2; **L3:** 4.10; 3.5; **L4:** 3.7; **L5:** 3.3; **L7:** 3.5; 6.5; **L9:** 3.3; **SWYK Review and Expand:** 3.3	**U6:** 2.3; **L1:** 5.6; 6.1; **L2:** 2.9; 4.2; **L3:** 6.5; **L4:** 5.6; **L5:** 4.6; **L6:** 3.6; 3.14; **L7:** 5.6; **L8:** 5.8; **SWYK Review and Expand:** 5.6; 6.6	
7	**U7:** 1.1; 1.2; 1.3; 1.4; 2.2; 3.2; **L1:** 3.5; **L2:** 4.1; 4.3; **L3:** 3.5; **L4:** 3.5; **L5:** 2.12; **L6:** 3.5; 4.10; 7.2; **L8:** 4.9; **L9:** 3.4; **SWYK Review and Expand:** 3.3	**U7:** 2.3; **L1:** 4.2; 5.9; 6.2; **L3:** 5.9; **L4:** 5.9; **L5:** 4.11; **L6:** 5.9; 6.1; **L7:** 5.10; **SWYK Review and Expand:** 5.6	
8	**U8:** 1.1; 1.2; 1.3; 1.4; 2.2; 3.2; **L1:** 2.12; 3.2; 5.5; **L2:** 3.4; **L3:** 3.5; 7.10; **L4:** 3.5; **L5:** 3.5; **L6:** 3.5; 7.8; **L7:** 5.5; **L8:** 3.5; **L9:** 3.4; **SWYK Review and Expand:** 3.3	**U8:** 2.3; **L1:** 5.9; **L2:** 3.13; **L3:** 5.8; 6.11; **L5:** 5.8; **L6:** 5.8; 6.10; **L7:** 5.8; 6.10; **L8:** 5.8; **SWYK Review and Expand:** 5.6	
9	**U9:** 1.1; 1.2; 1.3; 1.4; 2.2; 3.2; **L1:** 3.5; **L2:** 3.3; 4.3; 4.8; **L3:** 3.4; **L4:** 3.5; **L5:** 3.5; 4.8; **L8:** 3.5; 3.12; 4.10; **L9:** 3.4; **SWYK Review and Expand:** 3.3	**U9:** 2.3; **L1:** 5.8; **L3:** 5.8; **L4:** 5.8; **L5:** 5.8; **L6:** 4.6; **L7:** 3.13; **L8:** 5.8; **SWYK Review and Expand:** 3.6	
10	**U10:** 1.1; 1.2; 1.3; 1.4; 2.2; 3.2; **L1:** 2.11; 2.12; 3.5; **L2:** 3.7; 4.9; **L4:** 3.5; 7.11; **L5:** 3.9; **L6:** 2.7; **L7:** 3.5; 4.3; **L8:** 3.3; **L9:** 3.4; 4.8; **SWYK Review and Expand:** 3.3	**U10:** 2.3; **L1:** 5.8; **L3:** 5.8; **L4:** 5.8; **L6:** 5.8; **L7:** 5.8; **L8:** 4.6; **SWYK Review and Expand:** 5.6	

CASAS Competencies	Unit CCR Standards
U1: 0.1.2; 0.1.5; 0.1.7; 0.2.1; 0.2.4; **L1:** 0.2.1; 0.2.4; 4.1.3; 4.1.8; 4.1.9; **L2:** 4.1.9; **L3:** 4.1.9; **L4:** 4.1.7; **L5:** 4.1.9; **L6:** 7.1.1; **L7:** 7.1.1; 7.1.2; **L8:** 7.1.3; **L9:** 0.2.1; 4.1.9; **SWYK Review and Expand:** 4.1.9; 7.1.1	RI/RL.7.1, RI/RL.6.4, W/WHST.6-8.2.a, W/WHST.6-8.2.b, W/WHST.6-8.2.c, W/WHST.6-8.2.d, W/WHST.6-8.2.e, W/WHST.6-8.2.f, W/WHST.6-8.4, W/WHST.6-8.5, W.7.7, W/WHST.6-8.9.b, SL.8.1.a, SL.8.1.b, SL.8.1.c, SL.8.1.d, SL.8.4, SL.8.5, SL.8.6, SL.8.6, L.6.1.f, L.8.1.f, L.6.1.i, L.8.1.i, L.6.3.a, L.8.3.a, L.6.3.b, L.8.3.b, L.6.3.c, L.8.3.c, L.6.4.a, L.6.4.d, L.8.6
U2: 0.1.2; 0.1.5; 0.1.7; 0.2.1; 0.2.4; **L1:** 4.1.3; 4.1.5; **L2:** 4.1.2; **L3:** 0.2.2; 4.1.2; **L4:** 4.1.5; 4.1.7; **L5:** 4.1.5; 4.1.7; **L7:** 4.1.5; 4.1.7; **L9:** 4.1.2; 4.1.8; **SWYK Review and Expand:** 4.12; 4.15; 4.17	RI/RL.7.1, RI/RL.6.4, RI.8.9, W/WHST.6-8.2.a, W/WHST.6-8.2.b, W/WHST.6-8.2.c, W/WHST.6-8.2.d, W/WHST.6-8.2.e, W/WHST.6-8.2.f, W/WHST.6-8.4, W/WHST.6-8.5, W.7.7, W/WHST.6-8.9.b, SL.8.1.a, SL.8.1.b, SL.8.1.c, SL.8.1.d, SL.8.3, SL.8.6, L.6.1.i, L.8.1.i, L.6.1.k, L.8.1.k, L.6.1.k, L.8.1.k, L.6.3.a, L.8.3.a, L.6.3.b, L.8.3.b, L.6.3.c, L.8.3.c, L.6.4.a, L.6.4.d, L.8.6
U3: 0.1.2; 0.1.5; 0.1.7; 0.2.1; 0.2.4; **L1:** 1.9.9; **L2:** 1.9.7; **L3:** 1.9.7; **L4:** 1.9.7; **L5:** 1.9.8; **L6:** 1.9.7; **L7:** 2.2.5; **L8:** 2.2.5; **SWYK Review and Expand:** 1.9.7; 7.3.1; 7.3.2	RI/RL.7.1, RST.6-8.3, RI/RL.6.4, RI.6.7, W.7.1.a, W.7.1.b, W.7.1.c, W.7.1.d, W.7.1.e, W/WHST.6-8.4, W/WHST.6-8.5, W.7.7, W/WHST.6-8.9.b, SL.8.1.a, SL.8.1.b, SL.8.1.c, SL.8.1.d, SL.8.2, SL.8.3, SL.8.6, L.6.1.f, L.8.1.f, L.6.1.i, L.8.1.i, L.6.1.k, L.8.1.k, L.6.3.a, L.8.3.a, L.6.3.b, L.8.3.b, L.6.3.c, L.8.3.c, L.6.4.a, L.6.4.d, L.8.6
U4: 0.1.2; 0.1.5; 0.1.7; 0.2.1; 0.2.4; **L2:** 3.4.8; **L3:** 3.4.8; **L4:** 3.4.8; **L6:** 3.4.2; **L7:** 3.4.2; **L8:** 4.3.2; **SWYK Review and Expand:** 3.4.8; 4.3.2	RI/RL.7.1, RST.6-8.1, RI/RL.6.4, RI.6.7, RST.6-8.7, W/WHST.6-8.2.a, W/WHST.6-8.2.b, W/WHST.6-8.2.c, W/WHST.6-8.2.d, W/WHST.6-8.2.e, W/WHST.6-8.2.f, W/WHST.6-8.4, W/WHST.6-8.5, W.7.7, W/WHST.6-8.9.b, SL.8.1.a, SL.8.1.b, SL.8.1.c, SL.8.1.d, SL.8.4, SL.8.6, L.6.1.i, L.8.1.i, L.6.1.k, L.8.1.k, L.6.3.a, L.8.3.a, L.6.3.b, L.8.3.b, L.6.3.c, L.8.3.c, L.6.4.a, L.6.4.d, L.8.6
U5: 0.1.2; 0.1.5; 0.1.7; 0.2.1; 0.2.4; **L1:** 4.4.1; 4.4.2; 4.4.7; **L2:** 4.4.3; 4.4.4; **L3:** 0.1.6; 4.6.1; 4.8.2; **L4:** 4.4.2; 4.4.4; 4.6.1; **L5:** 4.4.5; **L6:** 2.8.3; 4.4.5; 4.4.8; 7.1.2; 7.1.3; **SWYK Review and Expand:** 4.4.2; 4.4.4; 7.3.1	RI/RL.7.1, RI/RL.6.2, RST.6-8.2, RI/RL.6.4, RI.6.7, RST.6-8.7, W/WHST.6-8.2.a, W/WHST.6-8.2.b, W/WHST.6-8.2.c, W/WHST.6-8.2.d, W/WHST.6-8.2.e, W/WHST.6-8.2.f, W/WHST.6-8.4, W/WHST.6-8.5, W.7.7, W/WHST.6-8.9.b, SL.8.1.a, SL.8.1.b, SL.8.1.c, SL.8.1.d, SL.8.2, SL.8.3, SL.8.4, SL.8.6, L.6.1.j, L.8.1.j, L.6.1.k, L.8.1.k, L.6.1.l, L.8.1.l, L.6.2.a, L.8.2.a, L.6.3.a, L.8.3.a, L.6.3.b, L.8.3.b, L.6.3.c, L.8.3.c, L.6.4.a, L.6.4.d, L.8.6
U6: 0.1.2; 0.1.5; 0.1.7; 0.2.1; 0.2.4; **L1:** 3.1.3; **L2:** 3.6.4; **L3:** 3.3.1; 3.3.2; **L4:** 3.4.3; **L6:** 3.6.4; **L7:** 0.1.4; 3.5.9; **L8:** 3.6.3; **L9:** 3.4.5; **SWYK Review and Expand:** 3.1.2; 3.3.1; 3.5.9	RI/RL.7.1, RI/RL.6.2, RST.6-8.2, RI/RL.6.4, W.7.1.a, W.7.1.b, W.7.1.c, W.7.1.d, W.7.1.e, W/WHST.6-8.4, W/WHST.6-8.5, W.7.7, W/WHST.6-8.9.b, SL.8.1.a, SL.8.1.b, SL.8.1.d, SL.8.2, SL.8.6, L.6.1.k, L.8.1.k, L.6.3.a, L.8.3.a, L.6.3.b, L.8.3.b, L.6.3.c, L.8.3.c, L.6.4.a, L.6.4.d, L.8.6
U7: 0.1.2; 0.1.5; 0.1.7; 0.2.1; 0.2.4; **L1:** 5.2.1; **L2:** 5.2.1; **L3:** 5.2.1; 5.2.2; 5.5.2; 5.5.3; 5.5.4; **L4:** 5.2.2; 5.3.2; **L5:** 5.5.2; 5.5.4; **L6:** 5.3.6; **L7:** 0.1.3; 5.3.6; **L8:** 5.2.1; **L9:** 7.3.1; 7.3.2; **SWYK Review and Expand:** 5.2.2; 5.3.6; 5.5.2; 5.5.3; 5.5.4	RI/RL.7.1, RI/RL.6.4, RI.6.5, RI.7.5, W.7.1.a, W.7.1.b, W.7.1.c, W.7.1.d, W.7.1.e, W/WHST.6-8.4, W/WHST.6-8.5, W.7.7, W/WHST.6-8.9.b, SL.8.1.a, SL.8.1.b, SL.8.1.c, SL.8.1.d, SL.8.2, SL.8.3, SL.8.6, L.6.1.g, L.8.1.g, L.6.1.i, L.8.1.i, L.6.1.k, L.8.1.k, L.6.3.a, L.8.3.a, L.6.3.b, L.8.3.b, L.6.3.c, L.8.3.c, L.6.4.a, L.6.4.d, L.8.6
U8: 0.1.2; 0.1.5; 0.1.7; 0.2.1; 0.2.4; **L1:** 5.3.2; 7.4.5; **L2:** 5.3.2; 5.3.7; **L3:** 5.1.1; 5.6.3; **L4:** 4.2.6; 5.3.8; **L5:** 5.3.8; 5.3.9; **L6:** 5.3.7; **L7:** 5.3.7; 7.4.5; **L8:** 5.3.7; **L9:** 7.2.3; 7.2.6; **SWYK Review and Expand:** 4.2.6; 5.3.2; 5.6.3	RI/RL.7.1, RI.8.3, RH.6-8.3, RI/RL.6.4, RI.6.5, RI.7.5, RI.6.7, RST.6-8.7, W/WHST.6-8.2.a, W/WHST.6-8.2.b, W/WHST.6-8.2.c, W/WHST.6-8.2.d, W/WHST.6-8.2.e, W/WHST.6-8.2.f, W/WHST.6-8.4, W/WHST.6-8.5, W.7.7, W/WHST.6-8.9.b, SL.8.1.a, SL.8.1.b, SL.8.1.c, SL.8.1.d, SL.8.6, L.6.1.h, L.8.1.h, L.6.1.j, L.8.1.j, L.6.1.k, L.8.1.k, L.6.1.l, L.8.1.l, L.6.2.a, L.8.2.a, L.6.3.a, L.8.3.a, L.6.3.b, L.8.3.b, L.6.3.c, L.8.3.c, L.6.4.a, L.6.4.d, L.8.6
U9: 0.1.2; 0.1.5; 0.1.7; 0.2.1; 0.2.4; **L1:** 5.7.1; **L2:** 5.7.1; **L3:** 5.7.1; 7.2.2; 7.3.3; 7.4.2; **L4:** 5.7.1; **L5:** 5.7.1; 7.2.2; **L7:** 5.7.1; **L8:** 5.7.1; **L9:** 5.7.1; 7.2.6; **SWYK Review and Expand:** 5.7.1	RI/RL.7.1, RST.6-8.1, RI.8.3, RI/RL.6.4, RI.6.5, RI.7.5, RI.6.7, RST.6-8.7, RI.8.8, W/WHST.6-8.3, W/WHST.6-8.4, W/WHST.6-8.5, W.7.7, W/WHST.6-8.9.b, SL.8.1.a, SL.8.1.b, SL.8.1.c, SL.8.1.d, SL.8.2, SL.8.4, SL.8.6, L.6.1.h, L.8.1.h, L.6.1.i, L.8.1.i, L.6.1.j, L.8.1.j, L.6.1.k, L.8.1.k, L.6.1.l, L.8.1.l, L.6.3.a, L.8.3.a, L.6.3.b, L.8.3.b, L.6.3.c, L.8.3.c, L.6.4.a, L.6.4.d, L.8.6
U10: 0.1.2; 0.1.5; 0.1.7; 0.2.1; 0.2.4; **L1:** 7.7.1; 7.7.3; **L2:** 7.7.6; **L3:** 7.7.1; 7.7.3; **L4:** 7.7.1; **L5:** 7.7.1; **L6:** 7.7.3; 7.7.4; 7.7.5; **L7:** 6.7.1; 7.7.1; 7.7.3; **L8:** 7.7.1; **SWYK Review and Expand:** 7.7.1	RI/RL.7.1, RI.8.3, RST.6-8.3, RI/RL.6.4, RI.7.5, RI.8.6, RH.6-8.6, RI.6.7, RST.6-8.7, W/WHST.6-8.3, W/WHST.6-8.4, W/WHST.6-8.5, W.7.7, W/WHST.6-8.9.b, SL.8.1.a, SL.8.1.b, SL.8.1.c, SL.8.1.d, SL.8.2, SL.8.3, SL.8.6, L.6.1.a, L.8.1.a, L.6.1.c, L.8.1.c, L.6.1.j, L.8.1.j, L.6.1.k, L.8.1.k, L.6.1.l, L.8.1.l, L.6.3.a, L.8.3.a, L.6.3.b, L.8.3.b, L.6.3.c, L.8.3.c, L.6.4.a, L.6.4.b, L.6.4.c, L.6.4.d, L.8.6

About the Series Consultants and Authors

SERIES CONSULTANTS

Dr. Beatriz B. Díaz has taught ESL for more than three decades in Miami. She has a master's degree in TESOL and a doctorate in education from Nova Southeastern University. She has given trainings and numerous presentations at international, national, state, and local conferences throughout the United States, the Caribbean, and South America. Dr. Díaz is the district supervisor for the Miami-Dade County Public Schools Adult ESOL Program, one of the largest in the United States.

Ronna Magy has worked as an ESL classroom teacher and teacher-trainer for nearly three decades. Most recently, she has worked as the ESL Teacher Adviser in charge of site-based professional development for the Division of Adult and Career Education of the Los Angeles Unified School District. She has trained teachers of adult English language learners in many areas, including lesson planning, learner persistence and goal setting, and cooperative learning. A frequent presenter at local, state and national, and international conferences, Ms. Magy is the author of adult ESL publications on life skills and test preparation, U.S. citizenship, reading and writing, and workplace English. She holds a master's degree in social welfare from the University of California at Berkeley.

Federico Salas-Isnardi has worked for 20 years in the field of adult education as an ESL and GED instructor, professional development specialist, curriculum writer, and program administrator. He has trained teachers of adult English language learners for over 15 years on topics ranging from language acquisition and communicative competence to classroom management and individualized professional development planning. Mr. Salas-Isnardi has been a contributing writer or consultant for a number of ESL publications, and he has co-authored curriculum for site-based workforce ESL and Spanish classes. He holds a master's degree in applied linguistics from the University of Houston and has completed a number of certificates in educational leadership.

AUTHORS

Lynn Bonesteel has been teaching ESL since 1988. She is currently a full-time senior lecturer at Boston University Center for English Language and Orientation Programs (CELOP). Ms. Bonesteel is also the author of *Password 3: A Reading and Vocabulary Text*, and co-author of *Center Stage: Express Yourself in English 2, 3, and 4* (Pearson Longman).

Arlen Gargagliano has been an ESL adult school teacher and program coordinator for over 20 years. Ms. Gargagliano was most recently the coordinator for Westchester Community College's library program and is currently a teacher in that same program. She has written two student textbooks on the topic of writing, as well as the corresponding teacher's books, and regularly facilitates workshops on the subject of teaching writing to adults. She also writes cookbooks, teaches cooking, and is a regular culinary guest on Spanish-language television.

Jeanne Lambert has worked in the field of adult ESL as an instructor, program coordinator, and curriculum developer for over 12 years. She began her career in Adult Education in Tampa. In New York City, she has worked in ESL programs for The City University of New York (CUNY) and the Brooklyn Public Library. She has presented at conferences in the areas of writing, grammar, and civics-based ESL instruction and has developed a curriculum for CUNY with an emphasis on American History. Ms. Lambert holds a master's degree in writing from Brooklyn College of The City University of New York. She currently works as an ESL materials writer and teaches an ESL Practicum for undergraduates at the New School University in New York City.

Acknowledgments

The author and publisher would like to extend special thanks to our Series Consultants whose insights, experience, and expertise shaped the course and guided us throughout its development.

Beatriz B. Díaz Miami-Dade County Public Schools, Miami, FL

Ronna Magy Los Angeles Unified School District, Los Angeles, CA

Federico Salas-Isnardi Texas LEARNS, Houston, TX

We would also like to express our gratitude to the following individuals. Their kind assistance was indispensable to the creation of this program.

Consultants

Wendy J. Allison Seminole Community College, Sanford, FL

Claudia Carco Westchester Community College, Valhalla, NY

Maria J. Cesnik Ysleta Community Learning Center, El Paso, TX

Edwidge Crevecoeur-Bryant University of Florida, Gainesville, FL

Ann Marie Holzknecht Damrau San Diego Community College, San Diego, CA

Peggy Datz Berkeley Adult School, Berkeley, CA

MaryAnn Florez D.C. Learns, Washington, D.C.

Portia LaFerla Torrance Adult School, Torrance, CA

Eileen McKee Westchester Community College, Valhalla, NY

Julie Meuret Downey Adult School, Downey, CA

Sue Pace Santa Ana College School of Continuing Education, Santa Ana, CA

Howard Pomann Union County College, Elizabeth, NJ

Mary Ray Fairfax County Public Schools, Falls Church, VA

Gema Santos Miami-Dade County Public Schools, Miami, FL

Edith Uber Santa Clara Adult Education, Santa Clara, CA

Theresa Warren East Side Adult Education, San Jose, CA

Piloters

MariCarmen Acosta American High School, Adult ESOL, Hialeah, FL

Resurrección Ángeles Metropolitan Skills Center, Los Angeles, CA

Linda Bolognesi Fairfax County Public Schools, Adult and Community Education, Falls Church, VA

Patricia Boquiren Metropolitan Skills Center, Los Angeles, CA

Paul Buczko Pacoima Skills Center, Pacoima, CA

Matthew Horowitz Metropolitan Skills Center, Los Angeles, CA

Gabriel de la Hoz The English Center, Miami, FL

Cam-Tu Huynh Los Angeles Unified School District, Los Angeles, CA

Jorge Islas Whitewater Unified School District, Adult Education, Whitewater, WI

Lisa Johnson City College of San Francisco, San Francisco, CA

Loreto Kaplan Collier County Public Schools Adult ESOL Program, Naples, FL

Teressa Kitchen Collier County Public Schools Adult ESOL Program, Naples, FL

Anjie Martin Whitewater Unified School District, Adult Education, Whitewater, WI

Elida Matthews College of the Mainland, Texas City, TX

Penny Negron College of the Mainland, Texas City, TX

Manuel Pando Coral Park High School, Miami, FL

Susan Ritter Evans Community Adult School, Los Angeles, CA

Susan Ross Torrance Adult School, Torrance, CA

Beatrice Shields Fairfax County Public Schools, Adult and Community Education, Falls Church, VA

Oscar Solís Coral Park High School, Miami, FL

Wanda W. Weaver Literacy Council of Prince George's County, Hyattsville, MD

Reviewers

Lisa Agao Fresno Adult School, Fresno, CA

Carol Antuñano The English Center, Miami, FL

Euphronia Awakuni Evans Community Adult School, Los Angeles, CA

Jack Bailey Santa Barbara Adult Education, Santa Barbara, CA

Megan Belgarde-Carroll Evans Community Adult School, Los Angeles, CA

Robert Breitbard District School Board of Collier County, Naples, FL

Diane Burke Evans Community Adult School, Los Angeles, CA

José A. Carmona Embry-Riddle Aeronautical University, Daytona Beach, FL

Donna Case Bell Community Adult School, Huntington Park, CA

Veronique Colas Los Angeles Technology Center, Los Angles, CA

Carolyn Corrie Metropolitan Skills Center, Los Angeles, CA

Marti Estrin Santa Rosa Junior College, Sebastopol, CA

Sheila Friedman Metropolitan Skills Center, Los Angeles, CA

José Gonzalez Spanish Education Development Center, Washington, D.C.

Allene G. Grognet Vice President (Emeritus), Center for Applied Linguistics

J. Quinn Harmon-Kelley Venice Community Adult School, Los Angeles, CA

Edwina Hoffman Miami-Dade County Public Schools, Coral Gables, FL

Eduardo Honold Far West Project GREAT, El Paso, TX

Leigh Jacoby Los Angeles Community Adult School, Los Angeles, CA

Fayne Johnson Broward County Public Schools, Ft. Lauderdale, FL

Loreto Kaplan, Collier County Public Schools Adult ESOL Program, Naples, FL

Synthia LaFontaine Collier County Public Schools, Naples, FL

Gretchen Lammers-Ghereben Martinez Adult Education, Martinez, CA

Susan Lanzano Editorial Consultant, Briarcliff Manor, NY

Karen Mauer ESL Express, Euless, TX

Rita McSorley North East Independent School District, San Antonio, TX

Alice-Ann Menjivar Carlos Rosario International Public Charter School, Washington, D.C.

Sue Pace Santa Ana College School of Continuing Education, Santa Ana, CA

Isabel Perez American High School, Hialeah, FL

Howard Pomann Union County College, Elizabeth, NJ

Lesly Prudent Miami-Dade County Public Schools, Miami, FL

Valentina Purtell North Orange County Community College District, Anaheim, CA

Barbara Raifsnider San Diego Community College, San Diego, CA

Mary Ray Fairfax County Adult ESOL, Falls Church, VA

Laurie Shapero Miami-Dade Community College, Miami, FL

Felissa Taylor Nause Austin, TX

Merari Weber Metropolitan Skills Center, Los Angeles, CA

Meintje Westerbeek Baltimore City Community College, Baltimore, MD

Thanks also to **MaryAnn Florez**, D.C. Learns, for the Persistence Activities.

Pre-Unit

Getting Started

Welcome to Class

1 LEARN ABOUT YOUR BOOK

A CLASS. **Turn to page iii. Write the answers to the questions.**

1. What information is on this page?
2. How many units are in this book?
3. Which unit is about health?
4. Which two units are about work?

B PAIRS. **Where will you find the following? Locate each section. Write the page number.**

Grammar Review _____   Persistence Activities _____   Glossary _____

Grammar Reference _____   Audio Script _____   Index _____

2 REVIEW GRAMMAR TERMS

A **English grammar has eight parts of speech. Read the definitions. Fill in the blanks with the correct part of speech from the box.**

| adjective | adverb | conjunction | interjection |
| noun | preposition | pronoun | verb |

_____verb_____ a word or group of words that describes an action, experience, or state of being; for example: *work, is feeling, was*

_____ a word or group of words that represents a person, place, thing, quality, action, or idea; for example: *John, teacher, school, book, happiness, study skills*

_____ a word that describes or adds to the meaning of a verb, adjective, another adverb, or a sentence; for example: *slowly, very*

_____ a word or phrase that is used to express surprise, shock, or pain; for example, *Ouch! Wow!*

_____ a word that is used instead of a noun; for example: *she, us, mine*

_____ a word that describes a noun or pronoun; for example: *new, easy, our*

_____ a word or group of words that is used before a noun or pronoun to show place, time, direction; for example, *in, at, through*

_____ a word that connects parts of sentences, phrases, or clauses; for example, *and, but, while*

3 LEARN ABOUT THE GLOSSARY

A Look at the article on the bottom of page 16. Find the words in bold. The words are in bold because they are in the glossary in the back of the book. Find the glossary. Write the page number it starts on and the one it ends on: _____-_____

B GROUPS. Look at the example below of the word *occupation* from the glossary. Compare it to the dictionary entry for the same word from the *Longman Dictionary of American English*. Discuss the questions.

Glossary

occupation *n.* job or profession

Dictionary

oc·cu·pa·tion /ˌakyəˈpeiʃən/ n. **1** [C] *formal* a job or profession [➡ **employment, work**]: *the occupations available to women* **2** [U] the act of entering a place and getting control of it, especially by military force [➡ **occupy**]: *the German occupation of France in the war* **3** [U] *formal* a way of spending your time

1. What information about *occupation* does the glossary provide?
2. Why are there three definitions for *occupation* in the dictionary, but only one definition in the glossary?
3. What does *n.* mean?

4 LEARN ABOUT WORD WORK

A GROUPS. Discuss. Current research on language learning shows that the more times you come into contact with a new word, the more likely you are to remember that word. Do you agree? Is this true for you?

B GROUPS. Look at the Word Work activity on page 35. The directions tell you to write words you want to remember in your vocabulary log. Select the words that interest you. Here are some specific suggestions:

1. Use a separate notebook, a section of your notebook, or a computer file for your vocabulary log.
2. For each word you want to learn, include the following information:
   - new word
   - the place where you saw or heard it
   - the sentence the word was in
   - the definition or translation of the word

Example:

Word	Place I saw or read it	Sentence
environment	Future 5, page 6	I need to have a quiet work environment.

<u>Definition:</u> the situations, people, etc., that influence the way in which people live and work

3. Every week, review the words you want to remember.

STEP 1. PAIRS. **Introduce yourselves.**

STEP 2. PAIRS. **Take turns. Interview your partner. Take notes.**

Where did you grow up? _____

What was your hometown like? _____

When did you come to the U.S.? _____

Did you come here alone or with your family? _____

What do you like to do on the weekend? _____

What kinds of food do you like? _____

Do you have any special talents? _____

Have you studied English before? _____

How long have you been a student in this school? _____

Why are you studying English now? _____

Are you taking any other classes? _____

What will you do when you finish this class? _____

Do you work? What do you do? _____

Are you going to change careers in the next five years? _____

STEP 3. CLASS. **Introduce your partner to the class. Give your partner's name and say one or two things you learned about him or her.**

This is Nidia Alfonso. She's a medical receptionist now. She wants to be an X-ray technician.

6 REVIEW VERB TENSES

GROUPS. **Look at the questions in the interview above. Find one example of each of the following verb tenses and write the question on the line.**

Simple present   *What do you like to do on the weekend?*

Simple past   _____

Future   _____

Present perfect   _____

Present continuous   _____

Setting Goals, Pursuing Dreams

1

Preview

What would your dream job be? What steps would you take to reach that goal?

UNIT GOALS

- [ ] Identify and talk about job-related interests and abilities

- [ ] Describe personality traits

- [ ] Discuss how to find job information

- [ ] Talk about abilities and plans

- [ ] Talk about long-term career goals

- [ ] Overcome obstacles to achieving your goals

Life Skills

1 TAKE A SURVEY

A CLASS. Discuss. What kinds of things do you enjoy doing in your free time? What kinds of things do you enjoy doing at work or in class?

B Read the statements from a survey. Are they true for you? Check (✓) *yes* or *no*.

http://www.thingsilike.us

Interests Survey

		Yes	No
1	I enjoy working with my hands.	☐	☐
2	I like helping other people.	☐	☐
3	I like to design, create, or invent things.	☐	☐
4	I enjoy working with tools and machines.	☐	☐
5	I enjoy being with people all day.	☐	☐
6	I don't mind doing simple paperwork.	☐	☐
7	I like to solve puzzles.	☐	☐
8	I enjoy hearing other people's opinions.	☐	☐
9	I can easily follow written instructions.	☐	☐
10	I need to have a quiet work environment.	☐	☐
11	I enjoy math.	☐	☐
12	I enjoy physical activity.	☐	☐
13	I prefer to work without supervision.	☐	☐
14	I like to produce things.	☐	☐
15	I enjoy working with a team.	☐	☐
16	I want to work outdoors.	☐	☐

C PAIRS. Compare your responses.

2 PRACTICE

A Read the job descriptions on page 7. Select a job for each person, based on his or her *yes* responses to the Interests Survey.

Ramiro: Questions 1, 4, 9, 12, 14   Job: ___*cabinetmaker*___

Mary: Questions 3, 7, 8, 11, 15   Job: _____

Soon-Young: Questions 2, 5, 6, 12, 13   Job: _____

Cabinetmaker

Responsibilities: Read blueprints and instructions to make and install cabinets. Use hand tools, power tools, and other machines. Measure cabinet parts. Instruct lower-level personnel.
Qualifications: High school diploma or GED. Three years' experience.

LPN (Licensed Practitioner Nurse)

Job description: Assist nurses and physicians with patients' personal care, daily activities, and emotional support. Communicate with patients' families. Complete forms, reports, records. Should be compassionate and patient.
Requirements: LPN license and minimum 6 months' experience. Must have ability to set priorities, make judgments, and work independently without supervision.

Graphic Designer

Responsibilities: Creative, artistic person able to come up with design proposals for print advertisements with team of designers. Present ideas to customers and be able to revise designs to fit customer needs. Must be able to work under pressure and meet deadlines.
Requirements: Bachelor's or associate degree in related field. Experience with design software, interest in technology, strong communication and problem-solving skills.

B PAIRS. Which of the jobs above would you enjoy the most? Why?

C GROUPS. Discuss. Look at the types of skills and the examples. Which skills are most important for each job listed in Exercise A? Why?

Skills	Examples
Communication skills	Write messages, understand spoken and written instructions, listen well, speak clearly
Interpersonal skills	Get along with others; cooperate with, guide, or teach others; resolve conflicts; negotiate
Problem-solving skills	Plan (for example, budget, schedule), solve technical or practical problems, use math
Lifelong learning skills	Take responsibility for learning new skills, use communication and information technology

A: *Which types of skills are important for the cabinetmaker?*
B: *Interpersonal skills are important because the cabinetmaker has to teach others.*
C: *I think problem-solving skills are also important because the cabinetmaker needs to measure and fix things that aren't working correctly.*

D GROUPS. Discuss the questions.

1. If you could have any job you wanted, what would it be?
2. How is this job a good match for your interests?
3. How will good communication, interpersonal, problem-solving, and lifelong learning skills help you in this job?

Can you...talk about job-related interests and abilities? ☐

Grammar

Verbs Followed by Gerunds and/or Infinitives

Verb + Gerund	Verb + Infinitive
I **enjoy working** with my hands.	I **need to have** a quiet work environment.
I **don't mind doing** simple paperwork.	I **want to work** outdoors.
Verb + Gerund or Infinitive	
I **like solving** puzzles.	I **like to solve** puzzles.
I **prefer working** without supervision.	I **prefer to work** without supervision.

Grammar Watch

- A gerund is the *-ing* form of a verb and is used as a noun.
- An infinitive is *to* + the base form of a verb.
- Some verbs are followed only by a gerund or only by an infinitive.
- Some verbs are followed by either a gerund or an infinitive.

For a list of verbs followed only by a gerund, only by an infinitive, or by either, see page 223.

1   PRACTICE

A Look at the Interests Survey on page 6. Underline the gerunds and circle the infinitives.

B Complete the sentences with a gerund or an infinitive. Some sentences have two correct answers. Use the list on page 223 to help you.

1. I enjoy ____listening____ to music while I work.
   (listen)

2. I plan _____ learning about new technology.
   (continue)

3. Angela doesn't like _____ in her second language because it's so difficult.
   (write)

4. Phuong plans _____ some classes at the community college.
   (take)

5. Do you mind _____ with sick people?
   (work)

6. I don't have good communication skills, so I hate _____.
   (negotiate)

7. Ibrahim has good problem-solving skills, so he agreed _____ a schedule.
   (create)

8. I don't mind _____ criticism from my supervisor.
   (receive)

Complete the conversation with the gerund or infinitive form of the words in the box. There may be more than one correct answer.

be	find	live	meet	use
do	have	make	move	work

A: I've decided I want ____to be____ a dental technician.
1.

B: Really? What does a dental technician do?

A: Basically, a dental technician makes false teeth.

B: And you really think you'd like _____ that?
2.

A: Absolutely. I enjoy _____ with my hands. And I like _____ tools
3.   4.

and _____ things.
5.

B: Do you need _____ a degree or certification?
6.

A: I'm not sure. I need _____ with our career counselor. I have an appointment
7.

next week. I'll find out then. What about you? Any plans?

B: Well, I'm considering _____ to Fairbanks. My only brother lives there. I want
8.

_____ near my family. But I'll need _____ work before I move.
9.   10.

Show what you know! Identify job-related interests and abilities

PAIRS. Check (✓) *Like, Don't mind,* or *Don't like* in the chart. Then talk about each activity.

A: *I like using computers because it's easy for me. I use my computer every day at home. How about you?*

B: *Actually, I don't mind using computers, but it's difficult for me. I want to improve my skills, so I go to the computer lab every day.*

Activity	Like	Don't mind	Don't like
Use computers			
Teach others			
Solve problems			
Talk on the phone			
Work with tools and machines			

Can you... identify job-related interests and abilities? ☐

Listening and Speaking

1 BEFORE YOU LISTEN

A **CLASS.** When you look for a job, you need to consider your interests and abilities. What else do you need to think about?

B **PAIRS.** Match the adjectives that describe personality traits with the correct definitions.

___c___ 1. cooperative   a. does not lie, cheat, or steal; sincere

_____ 2. honest   b. outgoing and friendly

_____ 3. extroverted   c. willing to work with others; helpful

_____ 4. intuitive   d. usually positive about things

_____ 5. optimistic   e. able to make judgments and decisions based on feelings rather than facts

C **GROUPS.** Compare your answers. Discuss. What kind of person do you think most employers want to hire? Explain.

2 LISTEN

A **PAIRS.** Look at the picture of Ruben talking to his career counselor. Predict: What questions will the counselor ask? Take notes.

B CD1 T2   Listen. Were your predictions correct?

C CD1 T2   Listen again. Answer the questions.

1. What job does Ruben have now?

   _____

2. What job does he think he's interested in?

   _____

3. Why is he considering this job?

   _____

4. What are some things he is good at?

   _____

A In the next part of the conversation, Ruben uses the adjectives from Exercise 1B to describe himself. Before you listen, complete the descriptions with the correct adjective.

1. I'm (a/an) _____honest_____ person. For example, sometimes customers leave things in the restaurant—like purses or wallets or cell phones. I always try to find the owner.

2. I'm (a/an) _____ person. If another waiter is busy and I'm not, I pour water and coffee for his customers.

3. I'm (a/an) _____ person. I'm always friendly with new staff. I try to teach them everything they need to know.

4. I'm (a/an) _____ person. I don't know what career I want, but I believe it's waiting for me. And I believe I'll find it.

5. I'm (a/an) _____ person. When I find the job that's right for me, I'll just know.

CD1 T3

B 💿 Listen and check your answers.

4 MAKE IT PERSONAL

STEP 1. Use the personality traits web to describe the kind of person you are. Fill in adjectives and examples.

STEP 2. GROUPS. Use your personality traits web and the adjectives in Exercise 1B to ask and answer questions about the kind of person you are. Be sure to give examples to support your answers.

> **Communication Skill:**
> Using Examples
>
> Using examples when you speak can help you get your meaning across to the listener. When you listen, examples can help you understand a speaker's main points.

A: *What kind of person are you? Are you extroverted?*
B: *I think so. I like being with other people and I make new friends easily.*
C: *No. I'm pretty shy. I'm nervous when I meet people, and I like to spend time alone.*

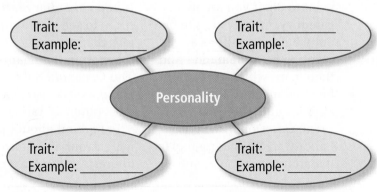

Trait: _____
Example: _____

Trait: _____
Example: _____

Personality

Trait: _____
Example: _____

Trait: _____
Example: _____

Reading

1 BEFORE YOU READ

CLASS. What jobs would you like to know more about? What are some ways that you could find information about them?

2 READ

CD1 T4

Ali Sheronick is a career counselor. Listen to and read his career advice newsletter.

The U.S. Department of Labor is a federal organization that publishes a resource called the *Occupational Outlook Handbook (OOH)*. This is available online and describes hundreds of jobs and gives the *outlook*, or *prediction*, about the future for those jobs. It provides information about whether an occupation will grow or become less important in the future *(projections)*. It also gives information on salaries and job requirements.

Sheronick's Career Advice

Ali Sheronick, Career Advisor

Some people decide on the job they want at a young age. I would never **discourage** people from following their dreams. But millions of people don't really know what they want to do. If you are in this **category**, my advice is to find out what **occupations** are going to be **in demand**—and then learn which ones might be good matches for your abilities and interests.

The U.S. Department of Labor website is a great place to find information about

jobs. On the homepage, look under *Top 20 Items*. If you click on *Occupational Outlook Handbook*, you can search for a specific occupation, such as "nurse." You will see information about training and education requirements, how much the job pays, what workers do, **working conditions**, and the demand for the job in the next few years. This information is available for hundreds of jobs! Back on the homepage, look under "agencies" and then *Bureau of Labor* **Statistics** *(BLS)* to see information on jobs that are expected to grow the most in the near future. The *Occupational Outlook Handbook* is also available in most public libraries.

To find out about jobs that match your abilities and interests, talk with a career

counselor. A counselor can probably help by arranging personality or **aptitude tests** to match you to specific jobs. A counselor may also help you get informational interviews. These are not job interviews. They simply give you a chance to talk with someone who has the job you are interested in or with someone who supervises people with such jobs. These interviews are a great way to learn about working conditions and job duties. Many informational interviews are done by phone, but in some cases you can actually go to the workplace.

Always remember to prepare for any phone interviews or meetings by thinking of questions to ask. And always remember to send a thank-you note to anyone who meets or talks with you. Good luck!

A PAIRS. Read the newsletter again. Find the information below and highlight or underline it in the newsletter. Then check your answers with a partner.

- the website the writer refers you to
- key words you can use when you look for information on the website
- two things a career counselor might be able to help you with

> **Reading Skill:**
> Highlighting or Underlining Key Information
>
> As you read, highlight or underline main points or information that is especially useful for you. Generally, you should not highlight more than 10 percent of a text.

B Write the answers to the questions.

1. Where can you find the *Occupational Outlook Handbook*?

   _____

2. What information does the *Occupational Outlook Handbook* give about specific jobs?

   _____

3. Where can you look to find out which jobs are expected to grow in the future?

   _____

4 WORD WORK

✐ GROUPS. Choose three words or phrases in the newsletter that you would like to remember. Discuss the words and their meanings. Then record the words and information about them in your vocabulary log.

Show what you know! Discuss how to find job information

GROUPS. Discuss the questions.

1. What are some jobs you think will be in demand over the next ten years?
2. Why do you think they will be in demand?
3. Are you interested in any of them? If yes, which ones?
4. What jobs would you like to read about in the *Occupational Outlook Handbook*?
5. What information would you want to know about these jobs?

Can you...discuss how to find job information? ☐

UNIT 1 **13**

Grammar

Gerunds Following Prepositions

A counselor can help **by arranging** personality or aptitude tests.

Prepare **by thinking** of questions to ask.

Grammar Watch

- A gerund is the only form of a verb that can follow a preposition.
- Sample prepositions are *about*, *at*, *by*, *for*, *in*, and *of*.

1 **PRACTICE**

A Read the career advice article on page 12 again. Find two more examples of prepositions followed by gerunds and underline them.

ONE-STOP CAREER CENTER

B Complete the paragraphs about Andrea with the correct prepositions below and the gerund form of the verbs. Some prepositions may be used more than once.

> about   at   for   in

   Andrea is looking for a job. She met with a counselor at the One-Stop Career Center in her county and took a series of aptitude tests to find out what skills she is strong or weak in.

   Andrea's tests showed that she is good ____*at solving*____ problems.
(solve)
She's great at math. Andrea is good _____ with people. She's interested
(work)
_____ about new technology. Surprisingly, she did not do well in
(learn)
communication skills, but this may simply be because she needs improvement

_____.
(write)
   Andrea likes variety, and she likes to be free to move around. She wouldn't be

interested _____ at a desk all day.
(sit)
   After Andrea got her test results, she had some informational interviews. After each

interview, she wrote notes thanking the interviewers _____ with her. Now
(talk)
Andrea is thinking _____ an engineer.
(be)

Read about what five people plan to do to get jobs or better jobs. Then write sentences about them, using *by* and a gerund.

Gina is going to improve her math skills by taking classes at the community college.

I want to improve my math skills. I'm going to take classes at the community college.

1

Gina

I want to improve my image at work. I'm going to wear better clothes.

2

Todd

I want to learn Spanish. I plan to get a tutor.

3

Khenan

I want to learn more about work as a physician's assistant. I plan to go on an informational interview.

4

Ilya

I want to find out about employment resources. I'm going to meet with the librarian at the public library.

5

Mei-Feng

Show what you know!   Talk about abilities and plans

STEP 1. **Use a gerund and information about yourself to complete each sentence.**

1. I'm good at _____.

2. I'm not good at _____.

3. As a child, I was interested in _____.

4. I've never been interested in _____.

5. I'm going to improve my English by _____.

6. I'd like to be better at _____.

STEP 2. GROUPS. **Discuss your answers. Then talk about the kinds of jobs you might be interested in and how you might find out more about them.**

Can you...talk about abilities and plans? ☐

Reading

1 BEFORE YOU READ

CLASS. Discuss. What do you want in the future? Talk about what you want to *be*, to *have*, and to *do*.

2 READ

CD1 T5

Preview the article. Check (✓) the statement that best describes it. Then listen to and read the article more thoroughly.

☐ 1. The article discusses the importance of having clear goals.

☐ 2. The article presents arguments for choosing goals that serve others.

☐ 3. The article discusses the difficulties of achieving goals in the film industry.

> *Reading Skill:*
> Previewing
>
> Good readers preview a text before reading it: They look at photos, illustrations, graphs, or charts. They look over the text quickly to get the main idea, paying special attention to the title and subtitles, and the first and last sentence in each paragraph.

Getting What You Want

What do you want? **Financial security**? Your own home? A successful career? Whatever it is, without a clear goal, you probably won't get it. A goal is a **commitment** to getting what you want. There are two parts to setting a goal. First, visualize the **outcome** you desire —see it clearly in your **imagination**. Then write the outcome you will achieve and the date by which you will achieve it. Make your goal **measurable**. "To get in shape" is not a measurable goal. "To lose 20 pounds by next April" is. You can stand on a scale in April and know if you have succeeded.

A Clear Vision

Many people have discovered the power of goal setting. Bruce Lee was one such person. As a child, Bruce

Lee wasn't strong or healthy, and as a young man, he struggled against **numerous obstacles** in the U.S. film industry, including **racial prejudice**. But Lee went on to achieve great

success in **martial arts** and action movies. It is reported that Lee wrote himself a letter in 1970. He wrote that, by 1980, he would be the best-known Asian movie star in the U.S. and that he would earn $10 million. Lee tirelessly pursued his goal. Sadly, he died before the 1973 release of Enter the Dragon, which finally made him a superstar. But Lee achieved his goal seven years early.

Turn *Your* Dreams into Goals

Not all of us have $10 million goals, but we can all learn from Bruce Lee's example. Like Lee, we can write our goals down on paper. Like Lee, we can make our goals measurable. We can work hard, keeping our goals clearly in mind. And hopefully, like Lee, we'll succeed.

CHECK YOUR UNDERSTANDING

Write the answers to the questions.

1. Visualizing is an important part of goal setting. What is another important part?
2. Were Bruce Lee's goals measurable? Explain.

4 **WORD WORK**

A **Find these words in the article. Then use them to complete the sentences.**

> commitment   financial security   obstacles   outcome

1. I don't need to be rich, but ___financial security___ is important to me.

2. Achieving your goals isn't easy. You will always face _____.

3. I've made a(n) _____ to come to class every day.

4. When you are involved in a disagreement with someone, try to think of a(n)

   _____ that would make both of you happy.

B ☑ **GROUPS.** **Choose three words or phrases in the article that you would like to remember. Discuss the words and their meanings. Then record the words and information about them in your vocabulary log.**

Show what you know! Learn about setting goals

STEP 1. **Write three more things in each column in the chart. Then check (✓) one thing you want most.**

	TO BE	TO HAVE	TO DO
1.	an engineer	a house	speak three languages
2.			
3.			
4.			

STEP 2. **Write a clear and measurable goal for your choice.**

Can you...learn about setting goals? ☐

Listening and Speaking

1 BEFORE YOU LISTEN

GROUPS. Talk about your long-term career goals. What do you want to be doing 10 or 15 years from now? What steps will you have to take to achieve your goals? (If you are retired, or if you don't plan to work, talk about other personal goals.)

2 LISTEN

CD1 T6

A Ruben is talking to his career counselor again. Listen to the first part of the conversation. Write the four things he has done so far.

1. _____

2. _____

3. _____

4. _____

CD1 T7

B Listen to the rest of the conversation and complete the flowchart for one possible career path for Ruben.

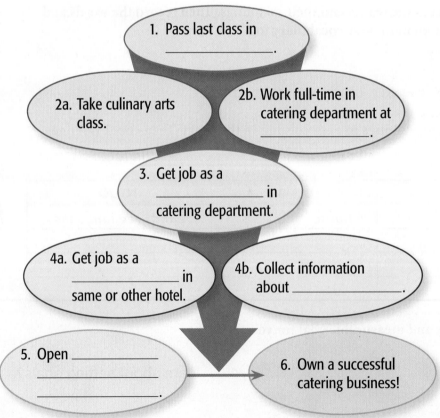

1. Pass last class in _____.

2a. Take culinary arts class.

2b. Work full-time in catering department at _____.

3. Get job as a _____ in catering department.

4a. Get job as a _____ in same or other hotel.

4b. Collect information about _____.

5. Open _____ _____.

6. Own a successful catering business!

3 PRACTICE

A Goals that are most likely to be achieved are called SMART goals. Read the chart below.

SMART goals are:	
Specific	It is easy to see exactly what job the person wants, where he or she wants it, and the salary he or she expects.
Measurable	There is a way to see that the goal has been reached. For example, the person could show pay stubs. These would indicate what the job is, where it is, and what the salary is.
Achievable	It's achievable if it's possible for the goal-setter.
Relevant	It's relevant if it meets the needs of the goal-setter. If the person is a good match for the job, the goal is relevant.
Time bound	There is a specific date tied to the goal.

B PAIRS. Which of these goals is a SMART goal? Why?

1. I'll have a good job in the future.
2. I will have a job as an X-ray technician, with an income of over $50,000 per year, in the Houston area, by 2012.

C SAME PAIRS. Discuss. How can Ruben revise his long-term goal, of owning a catering business, to make it a SMART goal?

4 MAKE IT PERSONAL

STEP 1. Write a SMART ten-year career goal in your notebook.

STEP 2. PAIRS. Read your goal to your partner. Discuss how you will achieve your goal.

STEP 3. Create a flowchart for your career path. Use the flowchart for Ruben's career path as a model.

STEP 4. GROUPS. Present your SMART goal and career path to your group. Follow the steps in the presentation skills box.

Presentation Skills

- Make eye contact, hold up your flowchart, point to your final goal, and read it. Explain how it is a SMART goal.

- Explain your flowchart, step by step. Refer to your chart, but don't read from it. Look at other group members as much as possible.

- Ask if there are any questions or suggestions for improving your flowchart for your career path.

Overcome obstacles to achieving your goals

Reading

1 BEFORE YOU READ

GROUPS. Discuss the questions.

1. Why is mastering English a first step toward achieving a career goal for many students?
2. Why do students need to persist, or not give up, in order to succeed?
3. How can students find ways to study even when it's impossible to come to class?
4. How can students return to class after taking time off and complete a program?

2 READ

CD1 T8

Listen to and read the essay about how one student overcame an obstacle to her studies.

A Solution to My Problem by Alicia Lopez

I am really happy to be back in class. Last term, I dropped out because I had **transportation** problems. Our class was from 7:00 to 9:00 P.M. The last bus from our school was at 9:00. I don't have a car or a driver's license. I tried to leave class early, but sometimes I missed the bus, and that was a big problem. Twice, I had to call my cousin to come pick me up, and he doesn't live near either my house or the school. And when I left in time to catch the bus, I always missed the end of class and our homework assignment. I became discouraged, and I stopped coming to school.

But I really wanted to come back. One day a friend suggested that I ask one of my classmates for a ride. I told her that this was a good idea, but actually I wasn't **comfortable** with it. Then I started to think of other ways to solve my problem. I put up some signs in our school, saying that I was looking for someone to share a ride with. I included my phone number and the nights I had class.

I also realized that if transportation was a problem for me, it was probably also a problem for other students. So I talked with our school counselor and we came up with a plan. I wrote an article for our school newspaper, **informing** students that a new Ride **Referral** Program was starting. Students who needed rides could sign up on a list in the counselor's office. Students who were willing to give rides **in exchange** for part of the cost of gas could put their names on another list. The students from the two lists could contact each other to work out **arrangements**. I was lucky. A student in my neighborhood contacted me. Now she gives me a ride to class, and I help pay for gas.

3 CHECK YOUR UNDERSTANDING

Write the answers to the questions.

1. What was Alicia's obstacle, and how did she overcome it?

2. Do you think Alicia's response to her obstacle was a good one? Can you think of any other way she could have solved her problem?

4 WORD WORK

 **GROUPS.** Choose three words or phrases in the essay that you would like to remember. Discuss the words and their meanings. Then record the words and information about them in your vocabulary log.

Show what you know! Overcome obstacles to achieving your goals

STEP 1. Think about obstacles to your own persistence. Rank the obstacles below from 1 to 6 (1 = most difficult; 6 = least difficult).

_____ work schedule / lack of time

_____ transportation problems

_____ lack of support from family members or friends

_____ no child care available when you need to come to class

_____ lack of money

_____ lack of confidence or feeling discouraged

STEP 2. GROUPS. Compare your answers in Step 1. Discuss these and other obstacles and offer one another possible solutions.

STEP 3. Think of a goal that you are trying to achieve right now or that you will try to achieve in the future. Think about possible obstacles.

STEP 4. GROUPS. Talk about your goals and possible obstacles. Present two suggestions for overcoming each obstacle.

Can you... overcome obstacles to achieving your goals? ☐

Writing

1 BEFORE YOU WRITE

A You are going to write a descriptive essay about your interests, skills, and goals. Read about descriptive essays. Then read the writing tip.

FYI   ABOUT DESCRIPTIVE ESSAYS

A descriptive essay includes specific details to help readers picture a person, place, or thing. Like other types of essays, it usually contains an introduction, one or more body paragraphs, and a conclusion.

Writing Tip: Topic Sentences

In an academic essay, each paragraph should have a topic sentence. A topic sentence gives the main idea about the topic of the paragraph. All the other sentences in the paragraph support the topic sentence—they give more information about it. The topic sentence is usually the first sentence in a paragraph, but not always; sometimes it occurs in other places.

B Ask yourself these questions. Record your responses.

1. What things interest me the most? Give examples.
2. What skills do I have? Describe them in detail.
3. What is my SMART career goal?
4. What am I doing now (what studies or work)?
5. How do I plan to achieve my goal?

C Read the writing model on page 205. What things does Andrea like to do?

2 ANALYZE THE WRITING MODEL

A PAIRS. Discuss the questions.

1. What are Andrea's main interests?
2. What are two adjectives she uses to describe herself?
3. What is her career goal?

B Read the writing model on page 205 again. Underline the topic sentence in each paragraph.

3 THINK ON PAPER

A Read the word webs Andrea made before she wrote her descriptive essay.

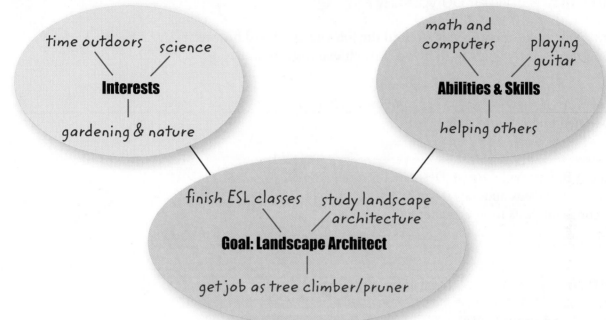

B Review the notes you made about your interests, skills, and goals in Exercise 1B. Then use word webs like Andrea's to brainstorm and organize ideas for your essay.

4 WRITE

Use your word webs to write a descriptive essay about your interests, skills, and goals. Be sure to include a topic sentence for each paragraph.

5 CHECK YOUR WRITING

A STEP 1. Revise your work.

1. Have you written three paragraphs—one for each circle in your word web?
2. Does each paragraph have a topic sentence?
3. Have you used specific details to describe yourself and your goals?

B STEP 2. Edit and proofread.

1. Have you checked your grammar, spelling, and punctuation?
2. Have you proofread for typing errors?

1 REVIEW For your grammar review, go to page 226.

2 ACT IT OUT What do you say?

PAIRS. You are discussing ways to find the job you want and how to set long-term career goals so that you can achieve your dreams.

> **Student A:** Review Lesson 1. Explain how to identify job-related interests and skills.

> **Student B:** Review Lesson 4. Describe the *Occupational Outlook Handbook* and how it can be used to match someone's interests to a particular job.

3 READ AND REACT Problem-solving

STEP 1. Read about Lydia.

Lydia has two children and a secure job at a health-care agency, but she doesn't really enjoy the work she's doing. She likes math and is very good with computers. She longs to go to college and get a degree in computer technology. When she told her husband about her desire to go back to school and change jobs, he discouraged her. He said that changing careers would be too risky financially. He reminded her that they have two children to support. Lydia can understand his fears, but she wants a job that is satisfying. She would really like to work in the Information Technology (IT) department of a big company some day.

STEP 2. GROUPS. What is Lydia's problem? What can she do?

4 CONNECT For your Study Skills Activity, go to page 212.

Which goals can you check off? Go back to page 5.

Getting a Job

Preview

How do people usually find jobs in your home country? Is job-hunting different in your home country from the way it is in the U.S.? Explain.

UNIT GOALS

- ☐ Prepare for a job search

- ☐ Analyze and write a chronological résumé

- ☐ Talk about interview do's and don'ts

- ☐ Prepare for a job interview

- ☐ Talk about your education and work experience

Reading

1 BEFORE YOU READ

CLASS. Discuss. When you search for a job, how do you prepare? Talk about your personal experiences of looking for work.

2 READ

CD1 T9

Listen to and read the online article. How did your prior knowledge help you read the article?

Reading Skill:
Using Prior Knowledge

Before you read a text, ask yourself, "What do I already know about this topic?" Connecting the text to your prior knowledge will help you understand and remember what you read. Also, identifying what you already know may help you realize what you *don't* know. This prepares you to look for new information as you read.

http://www.seekjobs.tv

seekjobs.tv

home
employment opportunities
articles
résumé
create your own profile

Preparing for Your Job Search

Imagine that you want to get a new job—either your first job or a better job. Here are some things you can do months before you start to actually apply for jobs.

1. **Identify public and private agencies that can help you.** Look in the yellow pages under "**Employment Agencies**" to find private agencies. (Private agencies charge a fee. Sometimes they only charge the fee after finding you a job. Sometimes the employer pays the fee.) Look in the state government section of your phone book for public employment agencies. Government pages are usually blue. (Public agencies do not charge a fee.) Keep a list of the names and phone numbers of the agencies.

2. **List names of people who might help you.** If you belong to an organization (a school, community, or religious organization), include the names of members who could help you. For example, someone might be able to introduce you to an employee at a business you're interested in, or could help you write your résumé, or could help you practice answering interview questions.

3. **Make a file of documents.** Include, for example, diplomas, certificates, and **reference letters** from your teachers or employers. You may not need all of these, but collect as many as possible.

4. **Research companies you are interested in.** Find information on their websites, contact their **Human Resource (HR) Departments** to request information, or ask your career counselor or librarian for help finding information.

5. Read about interview skills and **prepare answers to common interview questions.**

If you follow this advice, you'll be prepared when you apply for jobs.

Complete the sentences. Look back at the article on page 26 to find the information.

1. There are private and public employment _____agencies_____ to help you find jobs.

2. If you are a member of a community _____, there may be another member who could help you find a job.

3. You should keep _____, such as diplomas and training certificates, to show to employers.

4. One way to find information about a company is to go to its _____ on the Internet.

📝 **GROUPS. Choose three words or phrases in the article that you would like to remember. Discuss the words and their meanings. Then record the words and information about them in your vocabulary log.**

Show what you know! Prepare for a job search

PAIRS. Discuss the questions.

1. What advice in the article would be easy for you to follow? Why?
2. What advice in the article would be difficult for you to follow? Why?
3. Have you already done any of the things in the article? If so, which ones?
4. Are there any suggestions in the article that you could follow at this time? If so, which ones?

Can you... prepare for a job search? ☐

Life Skills

1 ANALYZE RÉSUMÉS

CLASS. Look at the résumé on page 29. Discuss the questions.

1. Do jobs in your home country require résumés? If so, what kinds of jobs?

2. Do you need a résumé for the kind of job you have or are interested in getting in the U.S.?

3. Where can you get help with writing a résumé?

2 PRACTICE

A Read the model résumé on page 29. What kinds of information about yourself should you include in a résumé? Check (✓) the items.

- ☐ 1. work experience
- ☐ 2. job desired
- ☐ 3. age
- ☐ 4. height, weight, and hair color
- ☐ 5. job skills
- ☐ 6. names of references
- ☐ 7. contact information
- ☐ 8. educational background

B PAIRS. Compare answers.

C Notice that in a résumé you don't need to write complete sentences. Compare these sentences to the information in the résumé on page 29. Cross out the words that do not appear in the résumé.

1. ~~I am~~ seeking ~~a~~ full-time, entry-level accounting position.

2. I attended Hillsborough Community College.

3. I took ESL, academic, and computing classes.

4. I am responsible for balancing cash registers and for recording sales.

5. I close the store two nights a week.

6. I shelved items in the deli.

7. I assisted with ordering and receiving.

8. I can type 70 words per minute.

D Read about types of résumés. Which type of résumé did Iris write? (See page 222 for an example of the other type of résumé.)

A **chronological résumé** emphasizes your work history. It lists information about your work experience and education in reverse chronological (time) order.

A **functional résumé** focuses on your skills, not specific jobs. It lists similar skills and abilities together and explains how you used them in previous jobs. People without any previous employment in the field for which they are interviewing should consider using a functional résumé. So should people with gaps in their work history.

Iris Martinez
115 Hammond Avenue, Largo, Florida 33773
Home phone: (727) 555-3296, Cell phone: (727) 555-4860, E-mail: irism@umail.com

Position Desired	Seeking full-time, entry-level accounting position	
Education	2008–present	**Hillsborough Community College, Tampa** One-year course in Accounting Operations Classes: clerical skills, computing, human relations, technical math, accounting
	2007–2008	**Kingly Adult High School, Largo** Classes: ESL, academic, computing
	2007	**Technical bachelor's degree, El Salvador** (equivalent to technical high school degree in U.S.)
Experience	2008–present	**Robertson's Supermarket, Largo** Assistant Manager Responsible for balancing cash registers and for recording sales. Assist manager with other tasks. Help at cash registers and at food counter. Close store two nights a week.
	2007–2008	**Publix, Seminole** Stockperson Shelved items in deli. Assisted with ordering and receiving.
Skills	Type 70 words per minute. Experience with Excel, Word, Access, and QuickBooks. Bilingual in Spanish and English. Excellent interpersonal skills.	
References	Provided upon request	
Transcripts	Provided upon request	

3 MAKE IT PERSONAL

GROUPS. Discuss. Which kind of résumé would be best for you to write? Why?

Can you...analyze résumés? ☐

Life Skills

1 PREPARE TO WRITE A RÉSUMÉ

CLASS. Read the information on résumé tips. Is any information surprising to you? Explain.

Résumé Tips:

- Be brief and clear. Try not to write more than one page.

- Never lie or misrepresent yourself in your résumé. Many employers check the information.

- If you don't know the address of a previous employer, you can check the yellow pages or look online, or you can call and ask for it. If you don't remember your employment dates, you can call your previous employer's Human Resources (HR) Department and ask.

- There shouldn't be any mistakes in your résumé. Check your spelling, grammar, and punctuation. Always have someone proofread your work. People usually have to write several drafts.

- Use high-quality paper. The paper should be white or off-white.

2 PRACTICE

STEP 1. Complete the form on page 31 to organize your information.

STEP 2. PAIRS. Exchange your completed forms. Ask each other questions to clarify details or to provide more information for your résumés.

STEP 3. Write or type your résumé. (All résumés must be typed, but if you are working in class and do not have access to a computer, you can write the first draft by hand.) Use your form and Iris's résumé on page 29 to help you.

STEP 4. PAIRS. Read your partner's résumé. Ask questions or make suggestions to improve the résumé.

STEP 5. Revise your résumé. See how much you can improve it. Then have your partner look at your revisions.

Personal information

Full name: _____

Address: _____

Phone number(s): _____

E-mail address (if you have one): _____

Work history

Employer 1

Name and city or town of Employer 1 (current or most recent): _____

_____

Year you started employment: _____ Position: _____

Responsibilities: _____

_____

Year employment ended if you're not still working: _____

Employer 2

Name and city and town of Employer 2: _____

_____

Year you started employment: _____ Position: _____

Responsibilities: _____

_____

Year employment ended: _____

Educational information

Name and city or town of current or most recent school or program: _____

_____

Degrees, certificates, types of courses: _____

_____

Additional information

Skills, interests, activities, and volunteer work: _____

_____

_____

Can you...write a chronological résumé? ☐

Talk about interview do's and don'ts

Listening and Speaking

1 BEFORE YOU LISTEN

GROUPS. Someone you know is going for a job interview. What advice would you give him or her? Suggest at least one idea for each category. Take notes.

1. Physical appearance

   You should dress appropriately for the job you are interviewing for.

2. Body language

   _____

3. Voice

   _____

4. Proper way to address interviewer

   _____

5. Other

   _____

2 LISTEN

CD1 T10

A 💿 An employment counselor is giving a talk about job interviewing. Listen. What are some of the do's and don'ts he talks about? Take notes.

1. Physical appearance

   _____

2. Body language

   _____

3. Voice

   _____

4. Proper way to address interviewer

   _____

B **GROUPS.** Compare your ideas in Exercise 1 with the employment counselor's ideas. Which ones were the same?

C **GROUPS.** Discuss the questions.

1. Were any of the tips in the counselor's talk new to you? Which ones?

2. Which tips do you think will be easy for you to remember or follow? Which tips do you think will be difficult?

D 💿 Now listen to four job applicants answer interview questions. What mistake does each person make?

1. Beatriz: _____

2. Said: _____

3. Bruno: _____

4. Shin-Hae: _____

3 PRACTICE

PAIRS. Look at the pictures of Fabio and Gosia at their job interviews. Consider the jobs that they are interviewing for. What did they do correctly? What mistakes did they make?

Fabio: Computer Technician   Gosia: Office Assistant

4 MAKE IT PERSONAL

GROUPS. Talk about experiences you've had at job interviews. Discuss the questions.

1. Did you make any mistakes?

2. Are you worried about making mistakes in future interviews?

3. What can you do to avoid such mistakes?

4. A "first impression" is someone's first judgment or idea about another person. What do you do to make a good first impression when you meet people?

Reading

1 BEFORE YOU READ

A **CLASS.** Interviewers often ask applicants general questions. Look at the three questions in the article. Why do you think interviewers ask these kinds of questions?

B Read the article. Which tip do you find most helpful?

Three Commonly Asked Interview Questions

QUESTION 1. Can you tell me a little about yourself?

TIP: The interviewer wants to know… your skills and qualifications, not about your personal life or your problems. If you have not worked before, describe classes you have taken or are taking and how they have prepared you for the job.

QUESTION 2. What is your greatest strength?

TIP: The interviewer wants to know… a strength that will be useful in the job you're applying for. If possible, give an example of how this strength has been useful in another job.

QUESTION 3. What is your greatest weakness?

TIP: The interviewer wants to know … that you are aware of your weaknesses and that you are addressing them. You should mention a work-related weakness that *used to be* a problem and describe the steps you've taken to correct it.

Reading Skill: Comparing and Contrasting

Making comparisons and contrasts helps you understand a text better. When you compare, you notice how things are similar. When you contrast, you look at how they are different.

2 READ

CD1 T12

Listen to and read the interview questions and answers. How are Eva's and Nabil's responses different?

Interviewer: Can you tell me a little about yourself?

Eva: I'd really like to stay in school, but I need to work full-time. My husband works, but he doesn't make enough to pay our rent and other bills, and we need to buy a car. Our children need clothes and **supplies** for school. I really need this job, and I'll work very hard if I get it.

Nabil: I've worked in a department store for two years. I started as a part-time employee because I was in school. A few months ago my supervisor offered me a full-time position. But I was still taking classes, so I couldn't take the job. Now I've completed my program in **retail** management, and I'm ready for the full-time responsibilities of an assistant manager.

Interviewer: What is your greatest strength?

Eva: My greatest strength is my commitment to service. For example, in my job, I understand that all of my behavior and actions have an **impact** on the **customer**. If I see something on the floor, I pick it up. If a co-worker needs help, I help. And, of course, I'm polite to customers.

Nabil: Well, I'm optimistic. I don't get discouraged when bad things happen. For example, my father has been ill for many months, but I encourage him and try to be cheerful.

Interviewer: What is your greatest weakness?

Eva: Well, I'm so focused on doing good work that I might seem too **ambitious**. Some people in my department had that **impression**. I realized that I needed to do more to contribute to the success of my co-workers. Since then, I've constantly looked for ways to help them.

Nabil: My greatest weakness is my temper. Sometimes I get angry when computers **crash**. And sometimes I lose my temper if people pressure me when I already have a lot of stress.

3 CHECK YOUR UNDERSTANDING

GROUPS. Discuss. Who do you think gave the best answer for each interview question? What's wrong with the other answer for each question?

4 WORD WORK

GROUPS. Choose three words or phrases in the interview that you would like to remember. Discuss the words and their meanings. Then record the words and information about them in your vocabulary log.

Show what you know! Respond to interview questions

STEP 1. Think of a job you would like to have. How would you answer the three interview questions if you were interviewed for this job? Write a short answer for each question.

STEP 2. ROLE PLAY. PAIRS. Role-play part of a job interview. Use the responses you wrote in Step 1 and answer your partner's questions. Then switch roles.

Can you...respond to interview questions? ☐

Grammar

Present Perfect

I**'ve completed** my program in retail management.

My father **has been** ill *for* many months.

Since then, I**'ve looked** for ways to help them.

Use the present perfect:

- to talk about an indefinite time in the past.
- to talk about things that happen during a time period that isn't finished.
- with *for* or *since* to talk about things that began in the past and continue to the present. We use *for* with periods of time, for example, *for three weeks, for two months, for over an hour*. We use *since* with specific times in the past, for example, *since last May, since I started this job*.

1   PRACTICE

A **Read the example sentences in the chart and answer the questions.**

1. Which sentence or sentences talk about an indefinite time in the past?
2. Which sentence or sentences talk about things that began in the past and continue to the present?

B **Read about Iris. Underline the verbs in the present perfect.**

Iris <u>has</u> carefully <u>prepared</u> for her interview. She has researched the company, and she has prepared answers to common interview questions. She has written a résumé and cover letter, and she has made copies of both. Iris has never had an interview at a big company before, but she feels confident.

C **Complete the paragraph about Iris. Write the present perfect form of the verbs in parentheses.**

As for her qualifications, Iris is in good shape. She _____ her
                                                                (not / complete)
program yet, but she will very soon. She _____ most of her classes,
                                                      (finish)
and she _____ well on her tests. Iris _____ part-time
              (do)   (work)
for quite a while, and her supervisor will give her a great reference. So Iris has a good

chance of getting the job she wants.

A STEP 1. Write *Have you . . . ?* questions using the words below.

1. talk with a career counselor

   Have you talked with a career counselor?

2. write a résumé

   _____

3. go on any job interviews since you came to the U.S.

   _____

4. use the Internet to look for employment ads or postings

   _____

5. experience any obstacles to reaching your career goals

   _____

6. talk with others who have the kind of job you want

   _____

7. change jobs in the last five years

   _____

B STEP 2. CLASS. Walk around the class. Ask and answer the questions you wrote in Step 1. When you answer, offer some additional information. When someone answers *yes*, write his or her name in the box at the right of the question in Step 1.

A: *Have you ever talked with a career counselor?*
B: *Yes, I have. I talked with Mr. Goodman. He was very helpful.*
                    OR
   No, I haven't. I should do that soon.

Show what you know!   Prepare for a job interview

STEP 1. GROUPS. Discuss. What has your experience been with job interviews in the U.S.? Who has had the most experience?

STEP 2. CLASS. Report to the class about your group's job interview experience.

Can you... prepare for a job interview? ☐

Listening and Speaking

1   BEFORE YOU LISTEN

CLASS. **What is the correct etiquette, or rules for polite behavior, at a job interview?**

1. At an interview, when do you take a seat?
2. Should you accept an offer of coffee or tea?
3. If the interviewer asks if you have any questions, what questions, if any, should you ask?
4. What should you say at the end of the interview?

2   LISTEN

CD1 T13

A   Iris went on a job interview. Listen and answer the questions.

1. Did Iris take a seat?
2. Did she accept an offer of coffee or tea?
3. What did she say when the interviewer asked if she had any questions?
4. What did she say at the end of the interview?

B   PAIRS. Compare answers. Did Iris do the right things?

CD1 T14

C   Liam went on a job interview. Listen. What are at least four things that Liam did wrong? Take notes.

3   CONVERSATION

ROLE PLAY. PAIRS. **Student A, you are Liam. Student B, you are the interviewer. Review the audio script of Liam's interview on page 234. Then redo Liam's interview so that he makes a better impression. Ask open-ended questions.**

> *Communication Skill:*
> Asking Questions
>
> A job interview is a two-way conversation. Asking questions helps you find out information and carry on a lively conversation. Ask open-ended questions that begin with the words *Who, What, Where, When, Why,* and *How.* This way you will receive more than a *yes/no* response. For example, you might ask: *What would my typical workday be like in this job?*

PAIRS.   Here are a few more tips and example responses for questions in a job interview. Match the questions with the tips. Write the correct letter on the line before the tip.

Questions

a. Can you describe how you handled a difficult situation at work?

b. May we contact your references?

c. How do you handle stress on the job?

d. What do you know about our company?

e. Why are you leaving your current employer?

f. How do you respond to criticism?

Tips

___d___ 1.   Always have an answer to this question. Research the company before your interview.

_____ 2.   Never say anything negative about your current or past employer. Say something positive, such as "I'm ready to take on more responsibilities, but there are no opportunities for advancement right now."

_____ 3.   You should not lie, but make your answer as positive as you can. "I try to relax outside of work by doing things with my family or listening to music."

_____ 4.   The interviewer wants to hear that you can handle criticism and learn from it. You can honestly say, "I listen to it carefully and I ask what I can do to improve."

_____ 5.   The answer must always be "yes."

_____ 6.   You should prepare an answer for this kind of question and be able to describe the situation.

5   **MAKE IT PERSONAL**

STEP 1.   How confident are you that you could answer questions at a job interview? Rate yourself from 1 to 5 (1 = very confident; 5 = not at all confident).

STEP 2.   GROUPS.   Discuss reasons for your rating with your group. How could you gain confidence? Give each other suggestions.

Grammar

Present Perfect vs. Present Perfect Continuous

Present Perfect	Present Perfect Continuous
Iris **has done** a lot of research.	Iris **has been doing** a lot of research.
I**'ve taken** courses at Hillsborough Community College.	I**'ve been taking** courses at Hillsborough Community College.
Iris **has worked** evenings as an assistant manager for a year.	Iris **has been working** evenings as an assistant manager for a year.
I**'ve made** an effort to greet everyone at the beginning of my shift since I realized this.	I**'ve been making** an effort to greet everyone at the beginning of my shift since I realized this.

Grammar Watch

- The present perfect focuses on the completion of an action. It describes an action that is finished.
- The present perfect continuous emphasizes the continuation of an action into the present and possibly the future. It focuses on an action in progress.

1 PRACTICE

CD1 T15

Listen to and complete the sentences. Then check (✓) *Continuing Action* or *Completed Action*.

	Continuing Action	Completed Action
1. I've __been working on__ my résumé.	✓	☐
2. I've _____ night classes.	☐	☐
3. My friend has _____ my résumé.	☐	☐
4. I've _____ for full-time jobs.	☐	☐
5. Miriam has _____ classes in landscape design.	☐	☐
6. Sheena has _____ all of her classes for her degree.	☐	☐
7. We've _____ all day for our math exam.	☐	☐
8. She's finally _____ her applications for college.	☐	☐

A First, use the words in the chart to write questions in the present perfect continuous. Then walk around and ask your classmates the questions. Write the name of a classmate who answers *yes*.

Have you . . . ?	Name
learn new work skills this year	
use English outside of class as much as possible	
work for a temp agency	
learn a new computer skill	
look for a new job	
try to correct a work-related weakness	

B PAIRS. Talk about two things you have done this year. Use the present perfect continuous. Ask and answer questions about them.

A: *I've been learning a new computer skill.*
B: *Really? What?*
A: *I've been learning how to download and send photos. I want to exchange pictures with my family back in Ecuador.*

Show what you know! Talk about your education and work experience

STEP 1. ROLE PLAY. PAIRS. Describe a job you're interested in, and then plan a role play of a job interview. Use the résumés you wrote on page 30.

Interviewee: Sell yourself—eagerly tell about the things you have done and have been doing that will make you a good employee. Use the correct body language, speak clearly and in a positive tone of voice, and maintain good posture and eye contact.

Interviewer: Remember to ask about strengths and weaknesses.

STEP 2. PAIRS. Practice, and then perform your role play for the class.

Can you . . . talk about your education and work experience? ☐

Writing

1 BEFORE YOU WRITE

A You are going to write a cover letter for a résumé to a potential employer. Read about cover letters. Then read the writing tip.

> **FYI**   ABOUT COVER LETTERS
>
> A cover letter briefly highlights the key points of your résumé. It describes your qualifications for a job, your interest in the position, and your positive personality traits. Like all formal letters, cover letters should be typed, follow a standard format, and be polite in tone. Employers receive many applications and résumés for a single position. The purpose of a cover letter is to attract the attention and interest of the person who has to skim material from potential applicants.
>
> **Writing Tip:** Using language from the job ad in the cover letter
>
> You want your cover letter to show that you are the match the employer is looking for. So read the job ad carefully and use some of the same language in your cover letter.

B Look at the résumé you wrote on page 30 again. Underline key points about your job qualifications and personality traits that you might want to highlight in a cover letter.

C Read the job ad and the writing model for a cover letter on pages 205–206. How does Iris show that she would be a good match for the job?

2 ANALYZE THE WRITING MODEL

A PAIRS. Discuss the questions.

1. What aspects of Iris's educational background does she highlight?

2. What personality traits does she mention?

B Read the writing model on page 206 again. Underline language in the cover letter that matches the requirements in the job ad.

3 THINK ON PAPER

A Read the T-chart Iris Martinez made before she wrote her cover letter. In the first column, she listed requirements for the entry-level accounting job at Megametro Media. In the second column, she listed those skills and traits that make her a good candidate for the job.

Entry-Level Accountant: Job Requirements	My Skills/Traits/ Experience
Degree or certificate in accounting	Getting accounting certificate in a month
Knowledge of accounting software and related experience	Know Microsoft Office and QuickBooks; have performed basic bookkeeping/ accounting duties
Team environment	Am a team player
Responsible, dependable, hardworking candidates	Possess all these traits

B Think about a job that you would like to apply for, one that is a good match for your experience and personality traits. What would the job requirements be? If you don't know, make them up. Review the job qualifications and character traits you highlighted on your résumé in Exercise 1B. Then use a T-chart like Iris's to brainstorm and organize ideas for a cover letter.

4 WRITE

Use your T-chart to write a three-paragraph cover letter for a specific job. Follow the same letter format as the writing model on page 206.

5 CHECK YOUR WRITING

A STEP 1. **Revise your work.**

1. Does your letter match the job's requirements?
2. Have you presented skills and traits that make you an ideal candidate for the job?
3. Have you used the correct letter format?

B STEP 2. **Edit and proofread.**

1. Have you checked your grammar, spelling, and punctuation?
2. Have you proofread for typing errors?

1 REVIEW

For your grammar review, go to page 227.

2 ACT IT OUT — What do you say?

PAIRS. You are discussing ways to conduct an effective job search and create a good impression during a job interview.

> **Student A:** Review Lessons 1–3. Explain how to prepare for a job search and write an effective résumé.

> **Student B:** Review Lessons 4–7. Describe ways to prepare for a successful job interview, including interview do's and don'ts.

3 READ AND REACT — Problem-solving

STEP 1. Read about José.

José has been searching for a sales job for several months. He answered a job ad for a junior sales position in the inventory department of an electronics store. The human resources manager called him to come in for an interview. José is very excited but also very nervous about how he will act during the job interview. He's afraid that he might forget to follow the correct etiquette. He's also worried about remembering exact details about his previous job experience.

STEP 2. GROUPS. What is José's problem? What can he do?

4 CONNECT

For your Community-building Activity, go to page 213.

Which goals can you check off? Go back to page 25.

Road Trip

Preview

Do you have a car? Do you drive to work or school? Do you take driving vacations?

UNIT GOALS

☐ Identify car parts and related problems

☐ Talk about highway safety do's and don'ts

☐ Decide which insurance is best for you

☐ Identify what to do if the police stop you

☐ Describe traffic problems

☐ Use the Internet to get maps and directions

Life Skills

1 IDENTIFY CAR PARTS

A **GROUPS.** Discuss. What parts of your car should you check before you start driving?

B **PAIRS.** Identify the parts of a car. Write the correct number of the word next to the line pointing to the car part in each picture.

1. accelerator/gas pedal	6. emergency brake	11. ignition	16. taillights
2. battery	7. engine	12. rear-view mirror	17. tire
3. brake	8. headlight	13. seat belt	18. trunk
4. bumper	9. hood	14. side-view mirror	19. windshield
5. dashboard	10. horn	15. steering wheel	20. windshield wipers

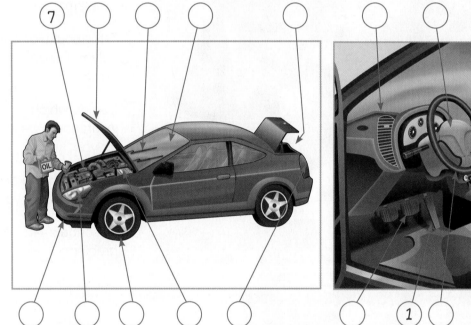

C What are the different fluids used in cars? Match the fluids with their purpose.

_____ 1. wiper fluid   a. powers the engine

_____ 2. oil   b. keeps the engine cool

_____ 3. gas   c. lubricates, or greases, the moving part of an engine

_____ 4. engine coolant   d. washes the windshield

Write the name of the correct car part next to each verb. Some items have more than one correct answer.

1. change a _____tire_____
2. turn on/off the _____
3. honk the _____
4. put the key in the _____

5. step on/let up on the _____
6. open/close the _____
7. lift or raise/lower the _____
8. fasten your _____

CD1 T16

A Listen to each conversation about car problems. Then listen to the questions and possible answers that follow each conversation. Circle the letter of the correct answer.

Conversation 1
1. What is the situation?   a   b   c
2. What does the woman have changed or replaced?   a   b   c

Conversation 2
1. What seems to be the problem?   a   b   c
2. If the car is jump-started, how long should it be driven afterward?   a   b   c

Conversation 3
1. What does the man want the woman to do?   a   b   c
2. What does the woman remember?   a   b   c

CD1 T17

B PAIRS. Listen to the excerpts and try to figure out the meanings of the words. Circle the letter of the correct answer.

1. **top off**
   a. add more fluid until it's at the correct level   b. remove and replace fluid

2. **run**
   a. turn on a machine and keep it going for a while   b. accelerate or increase speed

3. **tune-up**
   a. adjustments made to help a car run well   b. change stereo or audio system

GROUPS. Discuss the questions.

1. Can you do any kind of car maintenance or repairs? If so, what can you do?
2. Which car problems would be hardest for you to fix? Why?

Can you…identify car parts and related problems? ☐

Reading

1 BEFORE YOU READ

CLASS. Discuss the kinds of car trouble you can have on the highway or freeway.

2 READ

CD1 T18

Listen to and read the article about car trouble.

What to Do If Your Car Breaks Down on the Highway

What should you do if your car breaks down on the highway? The National Safety Council has some suggestions.

If you're experiencing a problem with your car—such as the engine not working correctly, a strange noise, or a flat tire—act quickly. At the first sign of car trouble, gently let up on the accelerator. Carefully pull over to the **shoulder** of the road. On an **interstate**, you should try to reach an exit. Signal to drivers behind you, using either your turn signal or your **emergency flashers** (hazard lights). If you have to change lanes, watch your mirrors closely.

Once you are off the road, make sure your car is visible. If you have reflecting triangles, put them behind your vehicle to alert other drivers; keep your emergency flashers on. If it's dark, turn on the car's **interior** light.

If you have a flat tire, be sure that you know how to replace it, that you have the necessary **equipment**, and that you can do it safely.

If you can't get the car running, get **professional** help. Contact the **highway patrol** or roadside assistance. Don't try to **flag down** other vehicles. Raise your hood and hang a white cloth out a window so that the police or **tow truck operators** can find you. If the car is in the roadway, stand away from it and wait for help to arrive.

If your car is safely out of traffic, wait inside with the doors locked. Use your cell phone to call for help. If you don't have a phone, put a sign in your window that reads, "Please call the highway patrol." If someone stops and offers to help, open the window a little and ask him or her to call the police. Watch for a **uniformed** police officer or other emergency **personnel**.

It is not a good idea to walk along the side of an interstate. However, if you have to, be sure to take the key from the ignition. Lock the doors. Walk on the shoulder, facing traffic, and keep as far away from traffic as possible. Safety is your **priority!**

© 1995–2008 National Safety Council. Adapted by publisher.

3 CHECK YOUR UNDERSTANDING

A Write the answers to the questions.

1. What is the first thing you should do if you realize you are having car trouble?

   _____

2. How can you make sure other drivers see your car when it is sitting on the shoulder?

   _____

3. How else can you alert others to your need for help?

   _____

4. If you are inside your car and someone stops to offer assistance, what should you do?

   _____

B Read this paraphrase of one of the paragraphs from the article on page 48. Then skim the article. Identify and circle the original paragraph.

> If you can't fix your car yourself, call the highway patrol or a roadside assistance service, or wait for a highway patrol car to come by. Don't try to stop other cars to ask for help. Lift your hood and tie some white cloth to the car or hang it out the window. Don't stand near your car if your car is still in the road.

C GROUPS. Each student should choose a different paragraph from the article to paraphrase. Share your paraphrased paragraphs.

> **Reading Skill:**
> Paraphrasing
>
> When you read, it's helpful to pause occasionally and try to repeat information in your own words. This will help you recognize places where you have trouble understanding the text. It will also give you an opportunity to practice producing language about the topic and help you to remember information from the text.

4 WORD WORK

GROUPS. Choose three words or phrases in the article that you would like to remember. Discuss the words and their meanings. Then record the words and information about them in your vocabulary log.

5 MAKE IT PERSONAL

GROUPS. Discuss. Have you experienced a car breakdown on the highway? Were you a driver or a passenger? What happened? What did you do?

Grammar

Inseparable Phrasal Verbs

Make sure your car is visible so that other drivers don't **run into** it.

Watch out for traffic if you need to walk to get help.

Separable Phrasal Verbs

Don't try to **flag down** other vehicles.

Don't try to **flag** other vehicles **down**.

Don't try to **flag** them **down**.

Grammar Watch

- **A phrasal verb is made up of a verb + a particle**. Particles are words such as *up, down, on, off, after, by, in, into,* and *out.*
- For **inseparable phrasal verbs**, the verb and the particle must stay together.
- For **separable phrasal verbs**, the verb and the particle can stay together or be separated.
- Many phrasal verbs are **transitive**; this means they can take **objects** (nouns or pronouns). When the object of a separable phrasal verb is a noun, the object can come before or after the particle. When the object is a pronoun, the object must come before the particle.
- Some phrasal verbs are **intransitive**; they **don't take objects** and are **always inseparable**.
- Inseparable phrasal verbs sometimes have two particles, for example, *get along with.*

For lists of separable and inseparable phrasal verbs and their meanings, go to page 224.

1 PRACTICE

There are seven phrasal verbs in the paragraph. Underline six more phrasal verbs. Which ones do you think are separable? Check the lists on page 224 to see if you are right.

You wouldn't believe the problems Sylvia had on her way to work this morning. She'd forgotten that road construction workers were <u>putting in</u> a new lane, and traffic was moving very slowly behind the construction crew. An impatient driver tried to pass Sylvia on the right shoulder, and he ran into the rear of her car and broke her taillight. It took the police over half an hour to arrive. After the police came, Sylvia turned on the ignition and the engine light came on. She was very worried that her car was going to break down. Thankfully, later, after the police officer was finished, her car started again. Everything turned out all right. But Sylvia is definitely going to figure out another route to take to work tomorrow!

A PAIRS. Complete the sentences with the correct form of the phrasal verbs from the box. Compare your answers.

> blow out   break down   come on   cut in   pick up   put in

1. If your car ___breaks down___ on the highway, call for help. Don't accept a ride from a stranger.

2. Never _____ a hitchhiker on the highway. If you see a person walking and you think he or she needs help, call the highway patrol.

3. If traffic is moving slowly, don't try to _____ ahead of other drivers. It can cause an accident.

4. If your engine or oil light _____ while you are on the highway, slowly drive to the nearest exit and call roadside assistance.

5. You should check your tires regularly. When they get old and worn, they can _____ while you are driving, causing a very dangerous situation.

6. Always drive slowly in construction zones when workers are repairing roads or _____ new ones.

B Circle the object in each sentence. Then rewrite the sentences using object pronouns (*it, them, her,* or *him*).

1. If it's dark outside, turn on the interior light.
2. Never try to flag down other vehicles.
3. Hang out a white cloth so that the highway patrol can find you.
4. Put up reflecting triangles so that other drivers can see you.

> *Communication Skill:*
> Taking Part in Discussions
>
> During group discussions, state your ideas clearly and listen carefully to other people's ideas. To enter or participate in a group discussion, you can use phrases such as these:
>
> *First of all, I think that . . .*
> *I agree/disagree with that because . . .*
> *I have a different view of . . .*
> *I'd like to add . . .*

Show what you know! Talk about highway safety do's and don'ts

GROUPS. Discuss. What can drivers do to avoid dangerous situations on the highway? Use phrasal verbs in your discussion.

Can you...talk about highway safety do's and don'ts? ☐

Listening and Speaking

1 BEFORE YOU LISTEN

CLASS. Look at the photo. What has happened? What should the drivers do?

2 LISTEN

CD1 T19

A Listen to a driving instructor talk about what to do if you are in a car accident with another vehicle. Take simple notes by writing the objects of the verbs below.

If you have a car accident . . .
1. stop *your vehicle.*
2. move
3. turn off
4. make
5. mark
6. collect
7. take
8. exchange
9. don't talk about
10. get

B STEP 1. GROUPS. Compare your simple notes.

CD1 T19

STEP 2. Add more details about each item above. Then listen again to check your work.

STEP 3. GROUPS. Discuss. Were any of these instructions new to you? If so, which ones?

Gerunds and Infinitives in General Statements

Speeding *on the highway is very dangerous.*

It's *dangerous to text while you drive.*

It isn't *a good idea to drive when you're very tired.*

Grammar Watch

- A gerund can be the subject of a sentence.

- Sentences with gerunds as subjects are often general statements.

- You can also make general statements using *It is/isn't* + adjective + infinitive, or *It is/isn't* + noun phrase + infinitive.

3 PRACTICE

PAIRS. Take turns reading and explaining these statements.

1. Leaving the scene of an accident is illegal in most states but wrong in any state.
2. It's important to give the location of the accident right away if you call 911.
3. Getting the names and phone numbers of witnesses is important.
4. It's a good idea to take a picture or draw a diagram of the accident.
5. It isn't a good idea to talk about whose fault the accident is.

Example:
A: *Leaving the scene of an accident is illegal.*
B: *Why?*
A: *Because someone could be hurt or there could be damage to the other vehicle. You should stop and make sure no one is hurt, and you should wait for the police to come and write a report.*

4 MAKE IT PERSONAL

GROUPS. Discuss. What new facts about driving laws and customs have you learned in this unit? Compare and contrast these driving laws and customs with those in your home country. How are they similar? How are they different?

Life Skills

1 UNDERSTAND CAR INSURANCE

A CLASS. Car owners in the U.S. are required by law to have car insurance. Why do you think that it's illegal to drive without having insurance? Do you agree with the U.S. law?

B Read about important terms used in car insurance.

Different Types of Auto Insurance Coverage

Bodily Injury: This pays for the treatment of injuries that you cause to other people.

Personal Injury Protection: This pays for treatment of injuries you cause to yourself and your passengers. Sometimes this protection also covers lost wages or funeral costs.

Property Damage Liability: This pays for damage that you cause to another person's car or other property.

Collision: This pays for damage to your car in an accident involving another vehicle. You may have to pay a deductible (the amount of money that you have to pay before the insurance company pays anything).

Comprehensive: This pays for damage to your car caused by something other than a collision with another vehicle, such as vandalism, an accident involving an animal, or fire.

Uninsured and Underinsured Motorist Coverage: This will cover you if you are hit by a hit-and-run driver or by a driver who doesn't have insurance or enough insurance.

C Write the answers to the questions based on the information in the article.

1. Which types of coverage pay for injuries or damage you do to others?
2. Which types of coverage pay for your own injuries or damage to your car?

2 PRACTICE

PAIRS. Read the situations. Discuss. Which coverage would help each car owner?

1. Glen's car was damaged by a car that ran a red light.
2. Sandra damaged the side of another car when she tried to merge onto a highway.
3. Someone broke into Mr. Chen's car last night. The person broke a window.
4. Janet had to go to the hospital after her car crashed into a fallen tree at night.
5. Tony hit a car that stopped suddenly in front of him, injuring the other driver.

3 UNDERSTAND CAR INSURANCE TERMS

PAIRS. Underline the correct word or words to complete the definitions.

1. *Minimum coverage* is the **smallest / largest** amount you have to have.

2. An *occupant* is someone **inside / outside** a place.

3. To *wreck* something is to **dent it a little / destroy it completely**.

4. To *shop around* is to **look at different options / check online** before you buy something.

4 PRACTICE

CD1 T20

A Read the questions. Listen to two friends talking about insurance. Notice the vocabulary they use to talk about car insurance. Then write the answers to the questions.

1. Does Hua-Ling think it's important to have insurance if you own a car? How do you know?

2. How does the state you live in affect your insurance?

3. What two kinds of insurance does California require?

4. What does *15/30* mean in terms of California's insurance requirements?

5. What does $5,000 cover in California?

6. Do all California drivers buy minimum coverage for property damage? Why or why not?

B GROUPS. Discuss the questions.

1. Have you ever had car insurance?

2. If you have, how did you decide what kind of insurance to buy and what company to buy it from?

3. If you have not had car insurance, how would you make those decisions?

Can you...decide which insurance is best for you? ☐

Reading

1 BEFORE YOU READ

A Do you know what to do if the police stop you? Take the quiz. Check (✓) *True* or *False*. (The answers are at the bottom of the quiz.)

If You're Stopped by the Police, . . .

		True	False
1.	You should always pull over to the left.	☐	☑
2.	After you pull over, you should get out of your car.	☐	☐
3.	You should keep your hands on the steering wheel when the officer talks to you.	☐	☐
4.	The officer will probably ask for your driver's license and registration.	☐	☐
5.	You should address the police officer as "Officer."	☐	☐
6.	You shouldn't try to convince the police officer that he or she is wrong.	☐	☐
7.	You need to pay the police officer immediately if you're given a ticket.	☐	☐

Answers: 1. False, 2. False 3. True, 4. True, 5. True, 6. True, 7. False

B PAIRS. Compare answers.

2 READ

CD1 T21

Listen to and read the story on page 57. Notice the sequence in which the events occur. Underline the clue words that help you figure out the order of events.

Reading Skill:
Understanding Sequence

Knowing the sequence, or order, of events in a text will help you understand and remember what you read. Look for clue words such as, *first*, *next*, *before*, *later*, and *finally*. Also look for dates, days of the week, and times of day.

A Close Call

On Thursday morning, Miriam dropped Daniel off at school and continued on her way to work. She was in heavy traffic when her cell phone rang. She knew it was against the law to use a hand-held phone in the car, so she let it ring until it stopped.

But a few moments later, the phone rang again. Miriam took it from her purse and looked at the number on the **display**. It was Daniel's school. Had he been hurt? Was he sick? She decided to answer.

Soon a voice said, "This is Mr. Mitchell, the vice principal," but Miriam didn't hear more. She was **distracted** by lights flashing in her side mirror. A police car!

Without thinking, Miriam pressed *end call,* dropped her phone on the passenger seat, and stopped along the side of the road. The officer **approached**. "Good morning," he said. "May I see your license and—"

The phone started to ring again. "I'm very sorry, Officer," said Miriam, "but this call is from my son's school. Something could be wrong. May I please take it?"

"All right," said the officer.

Miriam spoke with Mr. Mitchell. "I understand," she said. "I'll talk with him when I pick him up after school. Thank you. Good-bye."

Miriam turned back to the police officer. "I'm sorry. Here's my license, my **registration**, and my insurance card."

The officer took the items Miriam handed him and walked to his car. A few minutes later, he came back, and asked, "Do you know why I stopped you?"

"For talking on my cell phone? I'm so sorry. I thought there was an emergency."

"Well, I'm just going to give you a warning," said the officer. "But next time, you'll get a ticket. So get a headset or turn off your phone when you drive."

"Yes, I will, Officer," said Miriam. "Thank you."

Miriam was glad the police officer hadn't asked questions about the call from Daniel's school. Daniel had broken the same school rule for the third time this week—he had answered his cell phone during class.

3 CHECK YOUR UNDERSTANDING

Write the answers to the questions.

1. Why didn't Miriam answer the phone the first time it rang?
2. Why did she answer it the second time?
3. Who was the caller? What did he tell Miriam?
4. Did the police officer give Miriam a ticket or a warning?
5. Do you think Miriam was right to answer the phone? Why or why not?

4 WORD WORK

GROUPS. **Choose three words or phrases in the story that you would like to remember. Discuss the words and their meanings. Then record the words and information about them in your vocabulary log.**

Life Skills

1 CHECK ONLINE DETOUR INFORMATION

A CLASS. Do you ever listen to the radio, watch TV, or look online to check traffic or road conditions? What stations or websites do you check?

B Look at the map. What does it show?

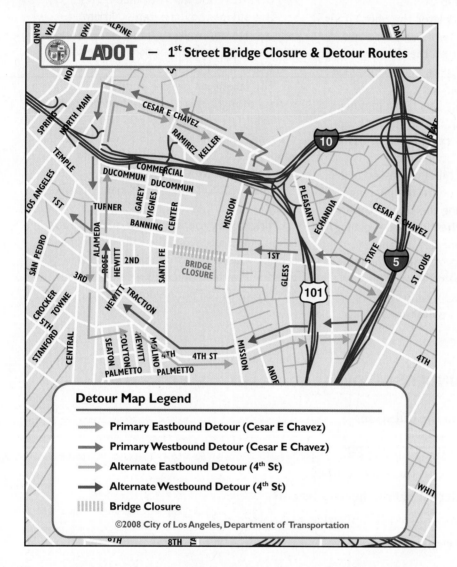

C GROUPS. Discuss the following words from the map. Use the map to explain or show the meaning of each word.

> alternate   closure   detour   legend   primary   route

A Read the notes that the Los Angeles Department of Transportation posted in 2008 about a bridge closure.

> Beginning on Jan. 27, 2008, the 1st St bridge will be closed from Mission Rd to Vignes St on a 24-hour basis for approximately 1 month, weather permitting.

> **Primary Detour Routes:**
> - W/B traffic on 1st St will be detoured N/B on Mission Rd, to W/B Cesar Chavez, to S/B Alameda, and back to 1st St.
> - E/B traffic on 1st St will be detoured N/B on Alameda, to E/B Cesar Chavez Av, to S/B State St, and back to 1st St.
>
> **Details:**
> - No vehicles allowed on the 1st St bridge, except for emergency responders.
> - Crews will be working during daytime, evening and weekend hours.
> - Pedestrian access will be maintained on the south side of the bridge.

B PAIRS. Use the map on page 58 and the notes in Exercise 2A to locate information.

1. Locate the bridge. Locate Mission Rd. and the yellow marks showing the bridge closure.

2. Look at the legend. Use it, along with the map, to figure out what N/B, W/B, S/B, and E/B mean.

3. Locate information in the notes to find out whether fire trucks and ambulances can get across the bridge.

4. Use the notes to find out whether people can walk across the bridge.

C GROUPS. Discuss the questions.

1. What are the biggest reasons for detours or traffic delays where you live?

2. Do you know about any road work or construction going on in your town or city right now that requires drivers to take a detour? Explain.

3. Are there roads you would advise people to avoid because of construction or slow traffic or frequent accidents? If so, what roads could they take instead?

4. Have you ever been late for work or school because of a road- or traffic-related problem? Could you have done anything to avoid it? Explain.

Can you...describe traffic problems? ☐

Use the Internet to get maps and directions

Life Skills

1 INTERPRET INTERNET MAPS AND DIRECTIONS

A PAIRS. How good are you at following directions and reading maps? Have you ever used the Internet to get driving directions? Explain.

B GROUPS. Two students are planning to go to a baseball game at Dodger Stadium in Los Angeles. Using the Internet, they find a map and directions from their school to the ballpark. Read the map and directions on page 61 and answer the questions.

1. What do the letters *A* and *B* in the green bubbles indicate?
2. What do the letters *N, S, E,* and *W* mean?
3. What words do the abbreviations *Blvd., Ave.,* and *Fwy.* stand for?
4. What do the black arrows to the left of the driving directions indicate?
5. What color is used to mark the route from W. Olympic Blvd. to Dodger Stadium?

2 PRACTICE

A PAIRS. Reread the map and directions. Then write the answers to the questions.

1. How many miles is the drive?
2. About how long should the drive take?
3. Which road on the route crosses the Hollywood Freeway?
4. If the students have to pick up a friend at the University of Southern California before they head to the stadium, how would the directions change? Explain.

B PAIRS. Use the map on page 61 to give directions.

STEP 1. Student A, give directions from Wilshire Country Club to Silver Lake Reservoir. Student B, mark the route in a color on the map.

STEP 2. Student B, give directions from Exposition Park to Los Angeles City College. Student A, mark the route in a different color.

STEP 3. Check each other's routes.

Can you...use the Internet to get maps and directions? ☐

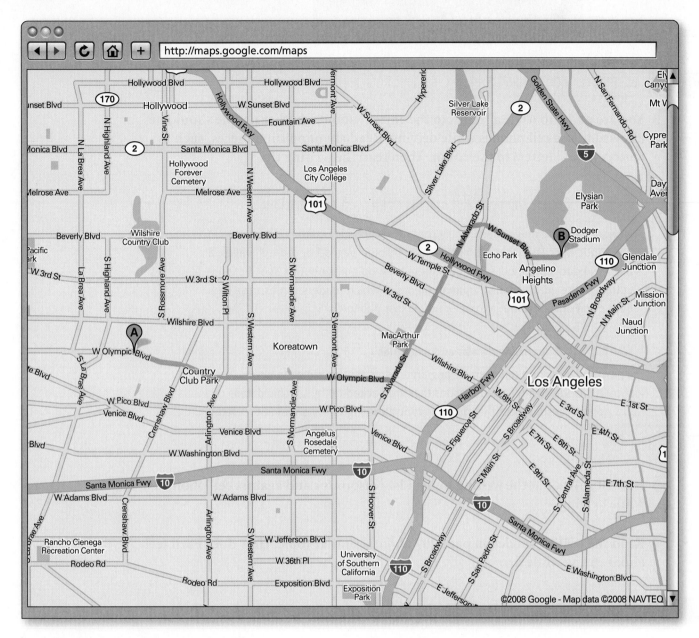

http://maps.google.com/maps

Driving directions to 1000 Elysian Park Ave, Los Angeles, CA 90012
6.4 mi – about 19 mins

Ⓐ **4650 W Olympic Blvd**
Los Angeles, CA 90019

1. Head **east** on **W Olympic Blvd**
   About 8 mins
   go 3.1 mi
   total 3.1 mi

↰ 2. Turn **left** at **S Alvarado St**
   About 7 mins
   go 2.0 mi
   total 5.1 mi

↱ 3. Turn **right** at **W Sunset Blvd**
   About 2 mins
   go 0.9 mi
   total 6.0 mi

↰ 4. Turn **left** at **Elysian Park Ave**
   About 2 mins
   go 0.4 mi
   total 6.4 mi

Ⓑ **1000 Elysian Park Ave**
Los Angeles, CA 90012

These directions are for planning purposes only. You may find that construction projects, traffic, weather, or other events may cause conditions to differ from the map results, and you should plan your route accordingly. You must obey all signs or notices regarding your route.

Map data ©2008 NAVTEQ

State your opinion about cell phone use

Writing

1 BEFORE YOU WRITE

A You are going to write a "letter to the editor" about whether people should be allowed to use cell phones while driving. Read about opinion pieces, such as editorials and letters to the editor. Then read the writing tip.

FYI ABOUT EDITORIALS AND LETTERS TO THE EDITOR

Newspapers and magazines usually contain sections for editorials and letters to the editor. Editorial pages, also known as "opinion pages," or "op-ed" pages, are used by editors and publishers to express their opinions about a specific issue. Letters to the editor are also opinion pieces in which readers can express their own point of view about a topic or article in a publication.

Writing Tip: Supporting details and examples

Opinion pieces should present strong arguments for or against an issue. They should include clearly stated reasons that are backed up by specific details or examples. Any sentences that do not support the argument should be deleted.

B Brainstorm about the writing topic. List reasons for and against cell phone use while driving.

C Read the writing model on page 207 about a similar topic. How does Fazil feel about eating while driving?

2 ANALYZE THE WRITING MODEL

PAIRS. Discuss the questions.

1. What argument does Fazil present in paragraph 1?
2. What are the two reasons he gives in support of his argument?
3. In paragraph 2, what details and examples does Fazil use to support his reason?
4. What does Fazil suggest instead of driving while eating?
5. What do you think is the best reason he gives to support his argument? Explain.

THINK ON PAPER

A Before Fazil wrote his letter to the editor, he used a chart to brainstorm and organize his argument. Do you think he included enough reasons to support his argument? Why?

ARGUMENT: *Eating while driving is dangerous and should be banned.*

Reason 1
Eating while driving means taking hand(s) off wheel.

Reason 2
Spilling or dropping food distracts driver and is dangerous.

Details/Examples
Driving requires coordination; unwrapping burger forces driver to take hand off steering wheel and lose control.

Details/Examples
Sandwich leaks sauce; driver worries about clothes, not driving; roll slips onto brake or gas pedal, causing accident; greasy food gets on steering wheel, causing loss of control.

B Look at the list you wrote about cell phone use while driving in Exercise 1B. Decide whether you will write a letter to the editor for or against cell phone use while driving. Use a chart like the one above to brainstorm and organize your argument.

4 **WRITE**

Use your chart to write your letter to the editor. Be sure to give reasons for your opinions and give details and examples to support them.

5 **CHECK YOUR WRITING**

A STEP 1. Revise your work.

1. Is your argument about the topic clearly stated in your first paragraph?
2. Do you give reasons for your point of view?
3. Do you support your reasons with enough details and examples?

B STEP 2. Edit and proofread.

1. Have you checked your grammar, spelling, and punctuation?
2. Have you proofread for typing errors?

1 REVIEW   For your grammar review, go to page 228.

2 ACT IT OUT   What do you say?

PAIRS. You are discussing car problems, highway do's and don'ts, and car accidents with a friend.

Student A: Review Lessons 1 and 2. Describe some things that can go wrong with a car. Then explain what to do if your car breaks down on the highway.	**Student B:** Review Lessons 3 and 4. Describe what to do in the event of a car accident, for example, if someone hits your car on the highway.

3 READ AND REACT   Problem-solving

STEP 1. **Read about Elena.**

Elena recently moved to Los Angeles from Chile. She works as a receptionist at Shriners Hospital for Children. The hospital is a 45-minute drive from her home in light traffic. Elena usually allows 45 minutes to get to work, but she is often late for various reasons. First of all, her car is ten years old and breaks down frequently. Last week Elena had a flat tire on the freeway and showed up at work two hours late. Second, she is not used to the layout of the city. To avoid getting lost, she always takes the same route to work. But there is a lot of traffic on her route, especially during morning rush hour. Getting stuck in traffic is a major reason why she is late to work. Elena's boss just spoke harshly to her about her frequent tardiness. She said that Elena will be put on warning if she can't get to work on time. Elena can't afford to lose her job.

STEP 2. GROUPS. **What is Elena's problem? What can she do?**

4 CONNECT   For your Study Skills Activity, go to page 214.

Which goals can you check off? Go back to page 45.

Are You Safe?

Preview

What natural disaster is about to happen? What would you do to stay safe?

UNIT GOALS

- [ ] Talk about being safe in natural disasters and emergencies

- [ ] Talk about keeping latchkey kids safe

- [ ] Identify home safety measures

- [ ] Learn about workers' rights to a safe workplace

- [ ] Identify workplace safety measures

Listening and Speaking

1 BEFORE YOU LISTEN

A CLASS. Discuss. What is happening in each picture? Have you or has anyone you know ever experienced one of these events? Describe what happened.

B PAIRS. Discuss the meaning of each word below.

rescuers people who save others from harm or danger

rubble broken stone, bricks, and other objects from a building, wall, or other structure that has been destroyed

survivors people who continue to live after a terrible event, such as a natural disaster, accident, or illness

2 LISTEN

CD1 T22

Listen to one man's story of survival. Write the answers to the questions.

1. How many people were killed in the earthquake?
2. Where did Mr. Liu live?
3. Where was Mr. Liu when the earthquake struck?
4. How long was he trapped under the rubble?
5. Who found him?
6. Who rescued him?

CD1 T22

The story of the earthquake is organized in chronological (time) order. Listen again and answer the questions.

1. What happened first on Monday morning?
2. What happened after that?
3. When was Mr. Liu found?
4. What did his daughter do after he answered her?
5. What happened about 12 hours later?

> To determine the sequence of events in a story, note clue words, such as dates, months of the year, and days of the week. Also note words that signal time order, such as *first*, *after*, and *later*.

4 RETELLING A NEWS STORY

STEP 1. Read the news story about an earthquake in China.

One of China's worst earthquakes in recent times occurred on May 12, 2008. Nearly 70,000 people died in the earthquake, and approximately 5 million people lost their homes. The earthquake affected towns in the eastern part of China's Sichuan province, including the city of Pengzhou. Newspapers reported the amazing story of a retired woman in Pengzhou who had survived by drinking rainwater after being trapped for 195 hours. When the quake first hit, the 60-year-old woman, later identified as Wang Youqun, was knocked unconscious by a steel beam. When Wang became conscious again, she was able to move, but an aftershock later trapped her between two large stones. After more than eight days of being trapped in rubble, Wang Youqun was rescued alive. The rescuers were amazed that after all Wang had been through, she had only a broken hip and bruises on her face.

STEP 2. PAIRS. Close your books, and retell the story. Use words that signal time order. Help each other remember all the details.

5 MAKE IT PERSONAL

GROUPS. Discuss. What personality traits help someone survive a terrible natural disaster like the one described above? How do you think you would do during a natural disaster? Explain your thoughts.

Reading

1 BEFORE YOU READ

CLASS. Discuss. Do tornadoes occur in your native country? Are they common where you live now?

2 READ

CD1 T23

Listen to and read the article about what to do during a tornado warning and a tornado watch.

Tornadoes: What They Are and What to Do

A tornado is a **violently rotating** column of air that extends from a thunderstorm cloud to the ground. Tornadoes can be between a few feet and a mile wide, and they rotate at speeds of up to 300 miles per hour. The most violent tornadoes can rip roofs and walls from houses and other buildings, **uproot** trees, **overturn** trains, and pick up cars and throw them through the air.

Tornadoes can happen at any time and can occur in any part of the United States. But they happen most often in the spring and early summer in "Tornado Alley" or "the Tornado Belt"—an area that extends from Texas to Ohio, from parts of the Rockies to the Appalachian Mountains.

If you live where tornadoes are common, it is extremely important to be ready. Planning is important. Everyone should know what to do and where to go during a **tornado watch** or *warning*. At the first sign of bad weather, tune in to local TV or radio weather news. During a *watch*, the weather conditions are right for tornadoes, but none have been

☐ Tornado Alley

seen. Continue to listen to weather reports, and be ready to move quickly to a safe place. During a *warning*, a tornado has been reported. Take shelter immediately!

Know the safest place in your house. That's the basement if you have one. Another safe place is a **central** room away from windows, such as a closet or bathroom. If you live in a **mobile home** and there is a tornado watch, leave for sturdier shelter. But if there isn't any and there is a warning, run outside. Lie flat in a **ditch** or on low ground in clear, open space, and cover your head with your hands. It's

extremely dangerous to be in or near a **vehicle** in a tornado. If there is a warning, or if you see a tornado, run from the car and lie flat in a ditch.

If you are in a large building, go to a hallway or restroom, away from windows, near the center of the structure. Get down on the floor, and cover your head with your hands.

After a tornado, the danger is not over. Avoid lighting matches, smoking, or using candles. If your home is **damaged**, turn off gas and electrical power. Do not touch **power lines** that are on the ground or anything in contact with them.

CHECK YOUR UNDERSTANDING

Reading Skill:
Summarizing

As you read, stop to summarize parts of a text so that you will remember and understand what you read. Write a few sentences about the main ideas. Leave out unimportant events, ideas, and details. When you finish reading, summarize the entire text.

A **Write the answers to the questions about tornadoes.**

1. What is a tornado?
2. How big are tornadoes?
3. When do tornadoes happen most in the U.S.?

B **Write the answers to the questions about tornado safety tips.**

1. During a tornado warning, what should you do first?
2. If you live in a mobile home, why should you go outside and lie in a ditch?
3. If you are in a large building, why should you go to a hallway or restroom?
4. If you are in a building, why should you get down on the floor and cover your head with your hands?
5. After a tornado, why should you avoid lighting matches, smoking, or using candles?

C **Reread the article. Then write a paragraph that summarizes the main ideas.**

4 **WORD WORK**

📝 **GROUPS. Choose three words or phrases in the article that you would like to remember. Discuss the words and their meanings. Then record the words and information about them in your vocabulary log.**

5 **MAKE IT PERSONAL**

GROUPS. Discuss the questions.

1. If you live where tornadoes typically happen:
   a. Does your family have a tornado plan if a tornado strikes when you're at home? Do you have flashlights and spare batteries? Do you have a first-aid kit?
   b. Does anyone in your family work or study in places that have tornado drills? If not, what should family members do if a tornado strikes at work or at school?

2. If tornadoes don't happen where you live, what other natural disasters might strike your region? How can you and your family prepare?

Listening and Speaking

1   **BEFORE YOU LISTEN**

A   CLASS. **Look at the picture. Discuss. Do you live in an area where a flood like this could happen? Have you or has anyone you know ever experienced a flood?**

B   **Read about Hurricane Katrina. What else do you know about this hurricane and the flooding it caused in New Orleans?**

In 2005, Americans experienced one of the deadliest hurricanes in their history: Katrina. Hurricane Katrina hit parts of Mississippi and Alabama, but the city of New Orleans, Louisiana, was affected the most. The levees around New Orleans burst and 80 percent of the city was flooded.

2   **LISTEN**

CD1 T24

A   **Listen to the first part of a news report about Hurricane Katrina. Write the answers to the questions.**

1. When did Hurricane Katrina hit New Orleans?

2. Were there any plans to evacuate people who were sick or old?

3. What is the Superdome? Who was sent there?

4. What happened to the medical supplies?

5. What were people told to do with their pets when they evacuated?

CD1 T25

B   **Listen to the second part of the news report. What could or should have been done? Complete the sentences.**

1. There should have been plans _____.

2. Public buses could have been _____.

3. There should have been police _____.

4. People should not have been _____.

3 PRACTICE

GROUPS. How much do you know about what to do in an evacuation?
Complete the chart with ideas about what you should do.

To be ready for an evacuation...	If you are asked to evacuate...
have a battery-operated radio.	

4 LISTEN

CD1 T26

A Make another chart in your notebook like the one in Exercise 3.
Use a whole page. Write the headings at the top. Then listen to an expert
give advice about flood safety. Take notes in your chart. Write as much
information as you can.

CD1 T26

B **PAIRS.** Compare and revise your notes. Then listen again to
check your information.

5 MAKE IT PERSONAL

GROUPS. Discuss the questions.

1. Do you have a friend or family member you could stay with if you had to
   evacuate? Explain.

2. Do you know about evacuation routes and plans in your area? If not, do you
   know where to get this information? Explain.

3. Do you know how to turn off utilities at your home? Explain.

4. If you have pets, what is your emergency plan for them?

5. What important items would you want to take with you if you had to evacuate?
   Would they be ready if you had to evacuate your home today?

6. Why should you have spare batteries and a battery-operated radio?

7. Where in your community can you find information about emergency shelter?

8. If you had time to do something before a flood, what might you bring indoors or
   move to the highest levels of your home?

Grammar

Past Modals

Active Voice
The government **should have evacuated** us earlier.
The flood **could have killed** our pets.
We **might have saved** our financial records if we'd had them in a safe.

Passive Voice
We **should have been evacuated** earlier.
Our pets **could have been killed**.
Our financial records **might have been saved** if we'd had them in a safe.

Grammar Watch

- Past modals are formed by modal + *(not) have* and the past participle form of the main verb.
- Use *should have* to express regret.
- Use *may have/might have/could have* to express past possibilities or a past choice.

1 PRACTICE

**Read about the experiences of people who evacuated their homes.
Check (✓) the sentence that best completes each passage.**

1. I didn't leave until we were told to evacuate. I'd prepared an emergency kit, and I knew where I was going, but there were long lines at the gas station when I stopped to get gas. I thought about leaving my car and trying to take a bus. But the buses were crowded, and they didn't go directly to my brother's house, where I was staying.

   ☐ a. I should have filled my car with gas before we were told to evacuate.

   ☐ b. I shouldn't have tried to evacuate by car.

2. I took three pairs of jeans, four shirts, four pairs of socks, and underwear. But I still ended up wearing dirty clothes for several days. I thought there would be laundry services available at the shelter. Ha!

   ☐ a. I should have taken more clothes.

   ☐ b. I shouldn't have taken so many clothes.

3. We didn't leave right away after we were told to evacuate because we were worried about people robbing our home. That wasn't smart. We risked our own lives. The water came into our house. It covered our car. We had to go upstairs. Finally, we had to climb out of the upstairs windows and onto the roof. We were lucky to be rescued.

   ☐ a. We might have been able to leave sooner.

   ☐ b. We should have left sooner.

PAIRS. **Complete these sentences about what people did during emergencies.**

1. **A:** Ron was on the top floor of his building when the earthquake hit. He took the elevator to the basement.

   B: He _should not have taken_ the elevator. He _____
   (should not / take)   (could / be)
   trapped inside.

2. **A:** Susan was driving her car across the bridge when she felt the earthquake. She pulled over to the side, stopped her car, and waited for the shaking to stop.

   B: She _____ the bridge. It _____.
   (should / get off)   (could / collapse)

3. **A:** Are they still looking for survivors of the tornado?

   B: Yes. People _____ trapped under the debris.
   (may / get)

4. **A:** Did you hear the sirens this morning? What were they for?

   B: I didn't hear them. They _____ a test. But next time, turn on your
   (might / be)
   TV and check the weather station or a news station.

5. **A:** What did your neighbor in the mobile home do when he heard the tornado warning?

   B: He stayed inside the trailer. Luckily, he survived, but he _____
   (should / leave for)
   a sturdier shelter.

Show what you know! Talk about mistakes made during emergencies

STEP 1. GROUPS. **Think about emergencies you have heard about in the news or that people you know have experienced. List three mistakes people have made in different emergencies.**

1. _____

2. _____

3. _____

STEP 2. GROUPS. **Discuss the mistakes. What should the people have done?**

Can you... talk about mistakes made during emergencies? ☐

Listening and Speaking

1 BEFORE YOU LISTEN

A CLASS. **Discuss the questions.**

1. In your home country, is it common for children to spend time alone, without their parents or others looking after them?

2. At what age do you think a child can be responsible for taking care of himself or herself? At what age do you think a child can be responsible for taking care of younger siblings? Explain.

3. If you have children, where do they go after school?

B **Read the information about latchkey children.**

"Latchkey children" or "latchkey kids" refers to children who spend time home alone without parents or others to supervise them. Some people believe that the term became widely used during World War II, when many fathers were away fighting the war and many mothers went to work in the factories. Today, there are still many latchkey children, and their numbers are rising. In some cases, children want to go home after school, and they feel they are too old to have a baby-sitter. Older children may pressure parents to allow them to go home after school, even when child care or after-school programs are available. However, many parents of latchkey children do not have a choice: They simply can't afford to pay for child care and have no other options.

C GROUPS. **Latchkey children can get into different kinds of trouble when they are home alone. Look at the categories in the chart. Can you think of examples? Write at least one example for each category.**

Pressure from Friends to Break Rules	Accidents and Emergencies
Strangers	**Emotional and Psychological Issues**

2 LISTEN

CD1 T27

A  Tania is a single mother who doesn't get home until after 6:00. Her 12-year-old son, Greg, is home alone after school. Listen to her talk with her neighbor Nick about the things she is worried about. Write the problems and the solutions her neighbor suggests.

Possible Problems	Possible Solutions
1. What if strangers call?	
2.	
3.	
4.	
5.	

CD1 T27

B Read the information in the Communication Skill box. Then listen again. Write the phrase Nick uses to offer each suggestion.

Suggestion 1: _Why don't you_

Suggestion 2: _____

Suggestion 3: _____

Suggestion 4: _____

Suggestion 5: _____

> **Communication Skill:**
> Making Suggestions
>
> You can begin a suggestion with these phrases:
>
> *Why don't you* (+ verb)?
> *Have you thought about* (+ gerund)?
> *Maybe you could* (+ verb).
> *If I were you, I'd* (+ verb).
> *Could you* (+ verb)?

3 CONVERSATION

ROLE PLAY. PAIRS. Work with a partner who was not in your group in Exercise 1C. Student A is the parent and Student B is the neighbor.

STEP 1. Select a problem to work on from the chart in Exercise 1C.

STEP 2. Create a conversation like the one between Tania and her neighbor. Use expressions from the Communication Skill box. Write the conversation down.

STEP 3. Practice the conversation. Use gestures and appropriate emotion.

STEP 4. Perform the role play in front of the class.

Life Skills

1   DISCUSS CHILD SAFETY PRODUCTS

A CLASS. Everyone wants children to be safe, but children, especially young children, can get injured in accidents at home. Discuss. What kinds of home accidents can children have?

B Read the online catalog page. Where have you seen or purchased any of these items?

http://www.childsafetyproducts.com

Childsafetyproducts.com
Because we care about kids!

check out | contact us | Your Cart ☐ items

Safety Gates

Prevent falls down stairs and keep children out of unsafe areas. Screws to wall for added security. Good for pets, too. $26.00

Door Stops and Door Holders

Prevent little fingers from getting caught, slammed, or pinched in doors.

Door Stop and Door Holder $5.95

Cabinet Latches

Keep children from opening cabinets containing household cleansers, medicines, plant chemicals, and other poisonous substances. Easy to install. $2.95. Pkg. of 4, $10.00

Electrical Outlet Covers

Reduce risk of electric shock with outlet covers. Large enough to pose no choking risk and difficult for children to remove. $2.00

Window Guards

Keep your children safe when windows are open. Easy to install and remove. $15.95

◄ previous | next ►

C PAIRS. Answer the questions about the child safety products above.

1. Susan's daughter had to go to the emergency room because she swallowed ant poison from a cabinet under the sink. What product would have prevented this accident?

2. John's new puppy ran out the front door and bit a neighbor's six-year-old son. What product should John have bought?

3. Roberto and Candy have just moved from a ground floor apartment to a high-rise building. They have a two-year-old daughter. What product should they buy first? Why?

CD1 T28

A Listen to four conversations and complete the chart.

Who are the speakers?	What is the situation?	What is the catalog item?
1. parents	Wife has installed latch on cupboard.	Safety latch
2.		
3.		
4.		

CD1 T28

B Listen again and write the answers to the questions.

Conversation 1. Why do the people need this safety device?

_____

Conversation 2. What dangers are discussed?

_____

Conversation 3. Where was the child protection item purchased?

_____

Conversation 4. What incident was reported in the newspaper last month?

_____

C GROUPS. Discuss. Which of the safety items discussed is the most important for young children? Why? How might some of these products keep certain elderly people safe as well?

Can you...identify home safety measures? ☐

Learn about workers' rights to a safe workplace

Reading

1 BEFORE YOU READ

CLASS. Discuss. Why do workers need protection? What kind of safety information is available for employees at your workplace?

2 READ

CD1 T29

Listen to and read the poster about workers' rights on page 79. Monitor your comprehension as you read.

> **Reading Skill:**
> Monitoring Comprehension
>
> Monitoring your comprehension will help you understand difficult texts, such as government documents. Reread such texts slowly and carefully. List any difficult words. Try to figure out their meanings from clues in the surrounding words and sentences. If you can't figure out a word, look it up in a dictionary. Then try to restate the information in your own words.

3 CHECK YOUR UNDERSTANDING

Read the statements. Write *T* (*true*) or *F* (*false*).

___T___ 1. OSHA is a division of the U.S. Department of Labor.

_____ 2. You can keep your name confidential if you contact OSHA to report unsafe work conditions.

_____ 3. You can ask OSHA representatives to come to your workplace to inspect for safety hazards.

_____ 4. Your boss can fire you or reduce your hours if you call OSHA to report a safety problem.

_____ 5. OSHA can make recommendations, but your employer does not have to follow them if the company or organization cannot afford it.

4 WORD WORK

GROUPS. Choose three words or phrases in the poster that you would like to remember. Discuss the words and their meanings. Then record the words and information about them in your vocabulary log.

5 MAKE IT PERSONAL

GROUPS. Discuss the questions.

1. What are some reasons people might not want to complain about unsafe working conditions? What advice would you give them?

2. Are there any unsafe or unhealthy conditions at your workplace or school? What could you do, or who could you talk to, to correct them?

Job Safety and Health
It's the law!

OSHA
Occupational Safety and Health Administration
U.S. Department of Labor

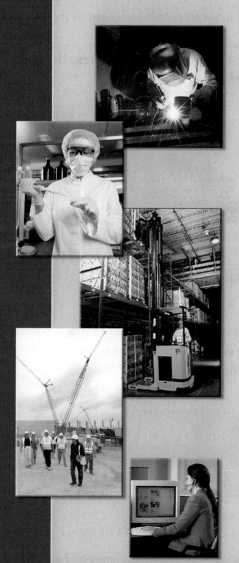

EMPLOYEES:

- You have the right to **notify** your employer or OSHA about workplace **hazards**. You may ask OSHA to keep your name **confidential**.

- You have the right to request an OSHA inspection if you believe that there are unsafe and unhealthful conditions in your workplace. You or your representative may participate in that inspection.

- You can file a complaint with OSHA within 30 days of **retaliation** or **discrimination** by your employer for making safety and health complaints or for **exercising your rights** under the *OSH Act*.

- You have a right to see OSHA **citations** issued to your employer. Your employer must post the citations at or near the place of the **alleged violation**.

- Your employer must correct workplace hazards by the date indicated on the citation and must certify that these hazards have been reduced or eliminated.

- You have the right to copies of your medical records or records of your exposure to **toxic** and harmful **substances** or conditions.

- Your employer must post this notice in your workplace.

- You must **comply** with all occupational safety and health standards issued under the *OSH Act* that apply to your own actions and conduct on the job.

EMPLOYERS:

- You must **furnish** your employees a place of employment free from recognized hazards.

- You must comply with the occupational safety and health standards issued under the *OSH Act*.

This free poster available from OSHA -
The Best Resource for Safety and Health

Free assistance in identifying and correcting hazards or complying with standards is available to employers, without citation or penalty, through OSHA-supported consultation programs in each state.

1-800-321-OSHA
www.osha.gov
OSHA 3165-12-06R

Life Skills

1 | TALK ABOUT WORKPLACE SAFETY

A   **CLASS.** **Discuss the questions.**

1. Why do you think most injuries at work occur?
2. How can employees help to make their workplaces safer?

B   **PAIRS.** **Look at the pictures. How can these products help make a workplace safe?**

Skid-resistant shoes

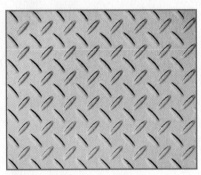

Skid-resistant flooring

Worker safety equipment

C   **PAIRS.** **Read and discuss these safety guidelines. Then decide if they are for the employer, the worker, or both. Write *E* (*Employer*), *W* (*Worker*), or *B* (*Both*) before each guideline.**

AVOID SLIPS, TRIPS, AND FALLS

_____ Establish a floor-cleaning schedule.

_____ Install non-slip flooring, if possible.

_____ Consider non-slip rubber or fabric mats.

_____ Clean up spills as soon as they happen.

_____ Wear closed-toe, skid-resistant shoes and keep shoelaces tied.

_____ Make sure uniform pant legs don't drag on the floor.

_____ See that electric cords don't run across aisles.

_____ Make sure there is enough light.

D   **GROUPS.** **Compare answers with another pair.**

A **GROUPS.** Look at these other safety categories for workers in the food preparation industry. Write at least two safety tips for each category.

SAFETY TIPS

To Avoid Cuts	
Workers	Employers
To Avoid Burns	
Workers	Employers
To Avoid Injury While Lifting	
Workers	Employers

B **STEP 1.** **GROUPS.** Discuss safety tips for your own jobs (or for a job you would like). Think of as many tips as possible. Write a list of workplace safety tips for each member of your group.

STEP 2. **GROUPS.** Discuss each of your lists. Are there safety tips that are not followed at your workplace? For each tip that is not followed, what would be the best advice? Discuss these (or other) options.

1. Follow the safety tip by yourself.
2. Talk to your co-workers about following the safety tip.
3. Ask your boss to provide safety materials, equipment, or procedures.
4. Talk with your co-workers and/or your boss about forming a safety committee.
5. Talk with your Human Resources (HR) department.
6. Notify OSHA.
7. Do nothing.

Can you...identify workplace safety measures? ☐

Write safety instructions

Writing

1 BEFORE YOU WRITE

A You are going to give instructions about how to avoid a common safety hazard. Read about instructions. Then read the writing tip.

FYI ABOUT GIVING INSTRUCTIONS

Often you will have to give instructions or explanations about how to do something. Instructions and explanations, particularly those involving safety, should be clear and easy to follow. Present your instructions in a logical order, for example, from most important to least important or from first to last. Use signal words to help readers follow the instructions, for example, *first, next, then, afterwards, finally,* and *last.*

Writing Tip: Imperatives

When giving instructions, use imperatives: base forms of verbs without the pronoun *you.*

B Select one of the topics. Brainstorm safety tips about it.

1. poisonings inside or outside the home
2. fires in the home
3. common household accidents

C Read the writing model on page 207 about how to prevent falls in the home. How has Eva arranged her instructions?

2 ANALYZE THE WRITING MODEL

A PAIRS. Discuss the questions.

1. What is the purpose of this article?
2. According to Eva, what should you do first to prevent falls in the home?
3. What is the main idea of each paragraph? Use your own words.

B Read the article on page 207 again. Underline signal words the writer uses to connect one paragraph to the next.

3 THINK ON PAPER

A Before Eva wrote her article, she used a chart to brainstorm and organize her instructions about how to prevent falls. Then she wrote her introductory paragraph. Read Eva's chart. Do you think that she put her instructions in a logical order?

First,	evaluate home for hazards and fix them.
Next,	check shoes; wear only sturdy ones.
Then	consider some kind of exercise to improve balance.
Finally,	know the side effects of medications you take.

B Look at the notes you made about safety tips in Exercise 1B. Then use a chart like Eva's to organize your instructions about how to prevent a safety hazard.

C PAIRS. Exchange your charts, and give each other feedback. Make changes if necessary.

4 WRITE

Use your chart to write an article about preventing a safety hazard. Be sure to include an introductory paragraph to let readers know your topic.

5 CHECK YOUR WRITING

A STEP 1. Revise your work.

1. Does your introductory paragraph explain your topic clearly?
2. Did you put your advice and instructions in a logical order?
3. Did you use signal words to connect one paragraph to the next?

B STEP 2. Edit and proofread.

1. Have you checked your spelling, grammar, and punctuation?
2. Have you proofread for typing errors?

1 REVIEW   For your grammar review, go to page 228.

2 ACT IT OUT   What do you say?

PAIRS. You are discussing safety measures with two friends.

> **Student A:** Review Lesson 2. Explain how to stay safe during a tornado.

> **Student B:** Review Lessons 3 and 4. Describe how to stay safe during a flood.

> **Student C:** Review Lessons 7 and 8. Explain some safety measures you can take at work.

3 READ AND REACT   Problem-solving

STEP 1. Read about Jean-Pierre.

Jean-Pierre has been working for a short time in a piano factory. He is learning how to rebuild and refinish pianos. He loves musical instruments and he likes the work, but some of the chemicals the factory uses make him sick. When he arrives at work, he can smell fumes from the paints and refinishing chemicals. By the end of a workday, he usually has a bad headache. Many of his co-workers are also suffering from headaches and stomach problems. Some workers have told Jean-Pierre that the factory needs to install more windows and get fans. If the air circulated better, there would be less fumes. No one has been willing to speak to the manager about the situation. Jean-Pierre is a new employee and he doesn't want to cause trouble, but he is afraid that the chemicals are a serious safety hazard.

STEP 2. GROUPS. What is Jean-Pierre's problem? What can he do?

4 CONNECT   For your Community-building Activity, go to page 215.

> **Which goals can you check off? Go back to page 65.**

Advancing on the Job

Preview

This man is a manager. How do you think he got this job?

UNIT GOALS

- ☐ Identify factors that influence promotion

- ☐ Understand performance reviews

- ☐ Talk about how to respond to constructive criticism

- ☐ Discuss job-training opportunities

- ☐ Use a course catalog

Reading

CLASS. Discuss. How and why do people get promoted at work?

CD2 T2

🔘 **Listen to and read the newsletter. Identify the main idea.**

Reading Skill:
Identifying the Main Idea

Identifying the main idea in a reading helps you understand a writer's key point about the topic. To identify the main idea, look at the title. Ask yourself: "What is the topic of this text?" As you read each paragraph, look for the author's main idea about the topic. Sometimes a writer states the main idea in a sentence. Other times you will have to put the main idea into your own words.

Factors That Influence Promotion

If you come to work on time, do a good job, and stay out of trouble, you will eventually be promoted, right? Not necessarily! Employers expect this of all employees. If you want a **promotion**, you should know the **factors** employers consider when they choose people to promote. Here are a few.

Length of time with the employer

It usually takes months, or even years, to be promoted. There are good reasons for this. First, an employee has to work long enough to **master** the skills required for his or her current job. Second, the employer needs a chance to see how the employee might respond in a variety of situations—especially situations that might come up in the employee's next position.

Relationships with other employees

Some employees have a very strong **work ethic** and are excellent at what they do, but they don't get promoted. Anyone who wants to be a leader or supervisor has to put the success of the team or the company ahead of personal success. It's important to acknowledge co-workers for their work, **share credit** for ideas, and encourage and **mentor** others. Managers want to know that the people they promote are "**team players**."

Flexibility and willingness to learn new things

Employers want to promote people who will **adapt** to new responsibilities easily. They need people who can be **flexible** during times of change and who can help others **adjust** to changes in the workplace. They select people who are eager to learn more about the organization, to improve the skills necessary for their current job, and to develop the skills that may be needed in the future.

Communication skills

Employers value employees who can read and write well. A leader or supervisor needs to be able to choose the right approach and the right words to explain, to offer criticism, to inspire or motivate, and to persuade. Good listening skills are important, too. A supervisor may have to communicate—effectively!—with people from **diverse** backgrounds and in various positions. Whether dealing with customers, co-workers, or bosses, communication skills are important.

Initiative in solving problems

In almost any workplace, you can find people who avoid dealing with problems. They may think, "That's not my job." Or they may be afraid of becoming involved or making a mistake—so they wait for someone else to solve the problem. Employees who **take the initiative** to solve problems stand out. These people are more likely to be considered for promotion than colleagues who don't take action when problems arise.

A Check (✓) the statement that best describes the main idea.

☐ 1. Promotion depends on getting to work on time and staying out of trouble.

☐ 2. Promotion depends largely on five main factors.

☐ 3. Promotion depends on many factors, none more important than the others.

B Write the answers to the questions.

1. Why can it take time to get a promotion? Give two reasons.

2. What does an employee have to put ahead of personal success in order to be a leader?

3. Why is flexibility important to employers?

4. What are two examples of ways leaders or supervisors need to use communication skills?

5. Why do you think employers like employees who take the initiative?

C PAIRS. Compare answers.

4 WORD WORK

GROUPS. **Choose three words or phrases in the newsletter that you would like to remember. Discuss the words and their meanings. Then record the words and information about them in your vocabulary log.**

5 MAKE IT PERSONAL

STEP 1. **Rate yourself for each category (1 = excellent; 5 = poor). If you don't have a job, skip number 1 and give yourself a general rating in the other areas.**

1. Length of time with your employer	1	2	3	4	5
2. Relationships with other employees (or students)	1	2	3	4	5
3. Flexibility and willingness to learn new things	1	2	3	4	5
4. Communication skills	1	2	3	4	5
5. Initiative in solving problems	1	2	3	4	5

STEP 2. GROUPS. **Explain your ratings to one another. What are your strengths? What are your weaknesses?**

Reading

1 BEFORE YOU READ

CLASS. Eva Rivera works at a manufacturing plant. Look at her performance review on page 89. Discuss. Why do you think many employers have performance reviews?

2 READ

Scan the yellow-tinted part of Eva's performance review. What eight categories are reviewed? Underline them.

> **Reading Skill:**
> Scanning
>
> Scanning helps readers find specific information and key words in a text. Scan to answer a specific question or to decide whether a text contains information you need.

3 CHECK YOUR UNDERSTANDING

A PAIRS. Read the yellow-tinted part of the performance review more thoroughly. Discuss. Which category do you think is most important? Why?

B Look at the ratings section on the right side of the performance review. Write the answers to the questions.

1. In which category did Eva get the highest rating from her supervisor?
2. In which category did Eva give herself the lowest rating?
3. Which categories did Eva and her supervisor agree on?

C Read the comments section at the bottom of the performance review. Write the answers to the questions.

1. What does Eva's supervisor say she needs to work on?
2. How will Eva work on this skill?

4 WORD WORK

GROUPS. Choose three words or phrases in the performance review that you would like to remember. Discuss the words and their meanings. Then record the words and information about them in your vocabulary log.

5 MAKE IT PERSONAL

STEP 1. Read the performance review again. If you have a job (or if you had a job in the past), give yourself a rating for each category.

STEP 2. GROUPS. Discuss your self-ratings. If you don't have a job, talk about areas that you think you might be strong or weak in.

PERFORMANCE REVIEW RATINGS

Name: Eva Rivera   Date: May 6, 2010

1—exceeded expectations 2—met expectations 3—improvement needed 4—failed to meet expectations	Employee Rating	Supervisor Rating
Knowledge of work: Understands key job duties; uses appropriate equipment, materials, and procedures.	1	2
Quality of work: Work is complete, accurate, and neat.	2	2
Time management: Prioritizes and plans work; meets deadlines; adjusts to unexpected changes to finish tasks on time; can handle multiple assignments.	2	2
Interpersonal relationships: Has a positive attitude; relates well to customers, co-workers, and supervisors; cooperates when working as part of a team.	2	1
Communication: Listens carefully to others and asks questions to understand; speech is clear, brief, appropriate; contributes ideas in team or group situations; understands telephone language and etiquette; can read, write, and type well enough to perform job duties.	2	3
Initiative and problem solving: Performs duties with minimal supervision; requests extra responsibilities when time allows; suggests improvements; continues to develop own skills and to take advantage of training opportunities; identifies problems and finds ways to solve them.	1	2
Attendance / Punctuality: Dependable; comes to work regularly and on time; returns promptly from breaks; absences are requested, in advance if possible; when sick, calls in to report absence at the beginning of shift.	1	2
Attention to safety: Follows safety procedures; uses safety equipment; reports accidents; attends safety training.	3	2

Employee comments:
Sometimes I have trouble taking telephone messages. And sometimes I can't follow everything or think of the right words fast enough to contribute when I'm talking with my whole team or group. But I do good work and I'm always on time. I take classes at night to improve my English, and I think my communication skills are improving.

Supervisor comments:
Eva is very good at what she does, and she does more work than anyone else on my staff. She has good attendance, is punctual, and follows safety procedures. She uses time well and often asks for additional responsibilities or offers to help co-workers. Everyone loves to work with her. However, Eva still needs to work on her English.

Goals / Objectives / Special Assignments
1. Eva will continue taking English classes at night this term.
2. Eva and a volunteer language tutor will meet once a week for eight weeks to work on Eva's English.

Eva Rivera	5/06/10	Elena White	5/06/10
Employee signature	Date	Supervisor signature	Date

Talk about how to respond to constructive criticism

Listening and Speaking

1 **BEFORE YOU LISTEN**

GROUPS. **Discuss the questions.**

1. What is "constructive criticism"?
2. What are some reasons supervisors offer constructive criticism?

2 **LISTEN**

CD2 T3

A Eva and her supervisor, Elena, are talking about Eva's performance review. **Listen and answer the questions.**

1. Why did Eva get a 3 in communication?
2. Why didn't she get a 1 in initiative?
3. Did Eva get a 1 in attendance/punctuality? How do you know?

CD2 T3

B Listen to the conversation again. **Take notes in the chart.**

Elena's constructive criticism	Eva's response
Writing needs improvement.	
Need to participate more in group discussions.	

C PAIRS. **Discuss. Do you think Eva responded well? Why or why not?**

CD2 T4

A 🎧 PAIRS. Listen to two people responding to criticism from supervisors and co-workers. Discuss. How well did they respond to criticism?

CD2 T4

B 🎧 The sentences and expressions below are useful for responding to constructive criticism. Read through them. Then listen again to the conversations from Exercise A and check (✓) the expressions you hear.

- ☐ 1. What can I do to improve?
- ☐ 2. Thanks for the feedback. I'll work on that.
- ☐ 3. You have a point. It's true I . . .
- ☐ 4. Can you give me some examples?
- ☐ 5. What should I do differently in the future?
- ☐ 6. Do you have any suggestions for improvement?
- ☐ 7. I didn't realize this was a problem. I'll work on it from now on.
- ☐ 8. Thanks. You're right.

4 MAKE IT PERSONAL

ROLE PLAY. PAIRS. Assign roles. Student A is a supervisor. Student B is an employee.

STEP 1. Choose a category in the performance review on page 89.

STEP 2. The supervisor offers constructive criticism about a category in the performance review on page 89. The employee responds to it, using ideas and expressions from Exercise 3B and the Communication Skill box.

STEP 3. Practice your role play and then perform it for the class.

> *Communication Skill:*
> Clarifying
>
> If you need to clarify a supervisor's constructive criticisms, do so tactfully. Use phrases such as these:
>
> *Are you saying that...?*
> *Sorry, but I'm not sure I follow you.*
> *Could you explain what you just said in more detail?*
> *What did you mean when you said...?*

Grammar

Clauses with *Although* and *Unless*

Although **you can do your work**, your writing needs improvement.

I can't give anyone a 2 in communication *unless* **their reports are well written**.

Grammar Watch

- Clauses with *although* and *unless* are dependent clauses. These clauses can come at the beginning or the end of a sentence. When they come at the beginning of a sentence, they are followed by a comma.

- Use *although* to show contrast or an unexpected outcome.

- *Unless* means *if . . . not.*

  | *I'm going to look for another job* *unless* **I get a promotion this year.** | = | *I'm going to look for another job* *if* I do **not** *get a promotion this year.* |

1 PRACTICE

Read the first sentence. Check (✓) the sentence that has the same meaning.

1. He knows he won't get a promotion unless he works on his interpersonal skills.

    ☑ a. If he doesn't work on his interpersonal skills, he won't get a promotion.

    ☐ b. If he gets a promotion, he won't work on his interpersonal skills.

2. I didn't get the promotion although I was qualified for it.

    ☐ a. I didn't get the promotion because I wasn't qualified for it.

    ☐ b. I was qualified for the promotion, but I didn't get it.

3. Although her communication skills improved, she still didn't get a better rating.

    ☐ a. The rating didn't improve, but her communication skills did.

    ☐ b. Because her communications skills improved, she can get a better rating.

4. Unless you ask for a raise or promotion, you probably won't get one.

    ☐ a. You probably won't get a raise or a promotion if you don't ask for one.

    ☐ b. If you ask for a raise or a promotion, you probably won't get one.

5. She hasn't been promoted yet although she has worked here for three years.

    ☐ a. She hasn't been promoted because she hasn't worked here for three years yet.

    ☐ b. She has worked here for three years but hasn't been promoted.

A Complete the sentences. Use *although* or *unless* and an item from the box.

> your writing needs some work   you have good problem-solving skills
> you manage your time better   you can speak clearly
> your attendance this month is good   I'd like a promotion

1. _Unless you can speak clearly_, you won't be able to handle phone calls.

2. Your communication skills are generally good _____.

3. _____, last month you missed three days.

4. You can't be in charge of difficult situations _____.

5. You won't be able to complete all your work _____.

6. _____, my boss doesn't think I'm ready yet.

B Write a sentence that has the same meaning as the sentence provided. Use *although* or *unless*.

1. He's very quiet all the time even though he has great language skills.

   Although he has great language skills, he's very quiet all the time.

2. He seems friendly, but he isn't really a team player.

3. It is very hard to be a leader if you can't accept criticism.

4. He's smart, but he's not very flexible.

5. How can you improve if you don't know your areas of weakness?

Show what you know! Discuss job performance and promotions

STEP 1. **Complete the sentences about yourself.**

1. Unless I _____, I won't be able to _____.

2. Although my _____ skills are not perfect, _____.

3. My plan is to _____ unless _____.

4. Although I'm skilled in _____, _____.

STEP 2. GROUPS. **Discuss your answers.**

Can you...discuss job performance and promotions? ☐

Listening and Speaking

1 BEFORE YOU LISTEN

A CLASS. Have you ever taken a career training course? What was the experience like?
Would you like to take such a course? Which one?

B GROUPS. Read the advertisement. How can you get more information about the courses
at Eastchester Community College? For which jobs can you get career training there?

Thinking about changing jobs?
Looking to improve your skills?

Eastchester Community College
School of Continuing Education
Credit and Non-Credit Courses

Accounting and Bookkeeping	Electronics	Hotel and Tourism
Aircraft Maintenance	General Business	Landscaping and Horticulture
Automotive Technology	Graphics Design	Nursing
Computer Applications	Health Care	Restaurant and Food Service

Check out our course offerings at **www.eastchester.edu**.
Make an appointment with a career counselor. Call **555-5000** for more information.

2 LISTEN

CD2 T5

A André and Claudia are talking about getting job training. Read each statement.
Then listen to their conversation. Write *T* (*True*) or *F* (*False*). Correct the false statements.

__T__ 1. Claudia's supervisor is pleased with her job performance.

_____ 2. Claudia asked her supervisor if she is qualified to work as a sales rep.

_____ 3. Claudia's supervisor thinks she might be qualified to become an administrative assistant.

_____ 4. Claudia's supervisor would like Claudia to develop her skill in speaking English.

_____ 5. Claudia's supervisor suggests that she look into online courses.

B CLASS. What suggestions would you give Claudia? What other places offer job training?

3 LISTEN

CD2 T6

Mei and Marco are discussing their jobs and opportunities for growth in their company. Listen to their conversation. Then answer the questions.

1. What section of the company is Marco currently working in? What kind of work would he like to do? Why?

2. How can Marco prepare for a different position at the company where he currently works?

4 MAKE IT PERSONAL

ROLE PLAY. PAIRS. Look at the information about on-the-job training on a company Intranet site. Role-play a conversation between two employees about getting on-the-job training.

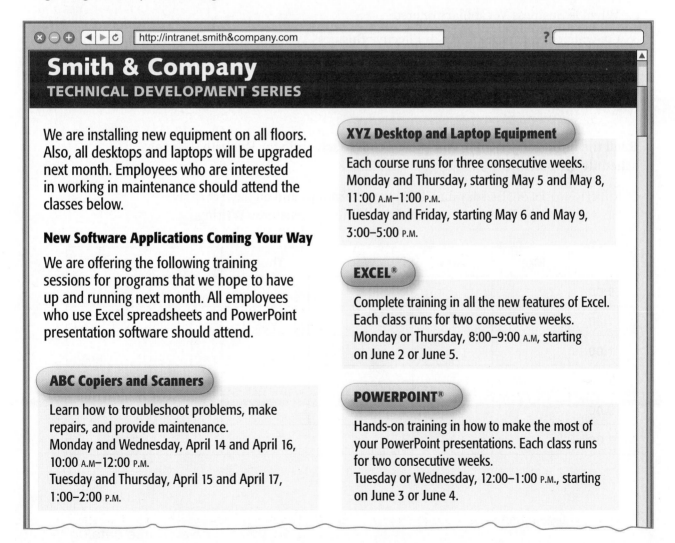

Smith & Company
TECHNICAL DEVELOPMENT SERIES

http://intranet.smith&company.com

We are installing new equipment on all floors. Also, all desktops and laptops will be upgraded next month. Employees who are interested in working in maintenance should attend the classes below.

New Software Applications Coming Your Way

We are offering the following training sessions for programs that we hope to have up and running next month. All employees who use Excel spreadsheets and PowerPoint presentation software should attend.

ABC Copiers and Scanners

Learn how to troubleshoot problems, make repairs, and provide maintenance.
Monday and Wednesday, April 14 and April 16, 10:00 A.M–12:00 P.M.
Tuesday and Thursday, April 15 and April 17, 1:00–2:00 P.M.

XYZ Desktop and Laptop Equipment

Each course runs for three consecutive weeks.
Monday and Thursday, starting May 5 and May 8, 11:00 A.M–1:00 P.M.
Tuesday and Friday, starting May 6 and May 9, 3:00–5:00 P.M.

EXCEL®

Complete training in all the new features of Excel. Each class runs for two consecutive weeks.
Monday or Thursday, 8:00–9:00 A.M, starting on June 2 or June 5.

POWERPOINT®

Hands-on training in how to make the most of your PowerPoint presentations. Each class runs for two consecutive weeks.
Tuesday or Wednesday, 12:00–1:00 P.M., starting on June 3 or June 4.

Life Skills

1 READ COURSE CATALOGS

A Read the course descriptions on page 97. Discuss. Which course or courses should each of these people take?

1. Marta is the administrative assistant in the accounting department. She wants to improve her skill in working with numbers.

2. Linda works in customer support. She receives many phone calls from customers.

3. Carlos wants to improve his writing skills and expand his vocabulary.

B Read the schedule on page 97. Write answers to the questions.

1. What are the abbreviations for Monday–Saturday in the course schedule?

2. When is Business Vocabulary offered?

3. On which days do the classes in Effective Business Writing meet?

4. Which courses can be taken in the evenings? Which ones meet on Saturdays?

2 PRACTICE

Read the information. Then complete a course schedule for Roberto. Use the schedule form below.

Roberto works on Tuesday and Thursday afternoons and all day Saturday. He wants to take Business Vocabulary and Effective Business Writing.

	Mon.	Tues.	Wed.	Thurs.	Fri.	Sat.
9:00						
11:00						
1:00						
3:00						
5:00						
7:00						

Can you...use a course catalog? ☐

52173, 52174. Conversational Business English

Focuses on listening and speaking skills needed in a business setting. Students will develop both language and interpersonal skills that they need to communicate clearly and effectively with supervisors, co-workers, and customers.

52363, 52364. Effective Business Writing

Development of skills needed to write effective business letters and other documents. Review of business vocabulary and rules of grammar, punctuation, and capitalization. Use of office reference materials.

52625, 52626. Business Vocabulary

Strategies for expanding general vocabulary useful in business as well as specific business terms. Emphasis will be on correct usage of vocabulary in written and spoken communication.

52629, 52630. Business Math

Review of basic arithmetic—including fractions, decimals, and percentages—and its application to common situations in business and commerce.

Ref. No.	Course Title	Credits	Meeting Days	Time
52173	Conversational Business English	3	M, W, F	9:00 A.M.–11:00 A.M.
52174	Conversational Business English	3	T, Th, Sa	1:00 P.M.–3:00 P.M.
52363	Effective Business Writing	3	M, W, F	5:00 P.M.–7:00 P.M.
52364	Effective Business Writing	3	T, Th, Sa	11:00 A.M.–1:00 P.M.
52625	Business Vocabulary	2	M, W	3:00 P.M.–5:00 P.M.
52626	Business Vocabulary	2	T, Th	9:00 A.M.–11:00 A.M.
52629	Business Math	2	M, W	7:00 P.M.–9:00 P.M.
52630	Business Math	2	Th, Sa	11:00 A.M.–1:00 P.M.

Reading

1 BEFORE YOU READ

CLASS. Are there people who do things that annoy you at work, at home, or in your neighborhood? If so, do you say anything to them?

2 READ

CD2 T7

Listen to and read the chart of *I* statements and *You* statements. Which kind of statements do you make most often? Which would you rather receive?

I Statements—A Path to Better Communication

I statements simply tell about yourself and your feelings and needs. They are about you rather than the person you are speaking to.

You statements blame the other person. They can make the person feel defensive.

I Statements	*You* Statements
I need to **concentrate** on this right now.	*You*'re bothering me.
I 'm allergic to perfume.	*You* wear too much perfume.
I can't take my **break** when you don't get back from yours on time.	*You* always get back from break late.
When you don't come in on time, *I* have trouble getting things ready by myself.	*You* need to come to work on time.
I could hurt my back if I do this without a safety belt.	*You* need to give me a safety belt.
I need more training to **operate** that equipment.	*You* don't give us any training.
I'd like to know how I'm doing.	*You* never give me any feedback.
I waste time when I have to look for equipment.	*You* never put things away.
I think there's a problem.	*You* made a mistake.

Change these statements to *I* statements.

1. Your jokes are inappropriate.

   I feel uncomfortable when you tell jokes.

2. You don't explain things clearly.

   _____

3. You should get better headphones. Your music is too loud.

   _____

4. You need to do your share of the work or I'll fall behind.

   _____

5. You didn't return my pen.

   _____

6. You talk too much.

   _____

4   WORD WORK

☑ **GROUPS.** **Choose three words or phrases in the chart that you would like to remember. Discuss the words and their meanings. Then record the words and information about them in your vocabulary log.**

Show what you know!   Use *I* statements

STEP 1. **Think of things people do that cause you problems at work or other areas of your life. Complete the chart.**

Who does it?	What do they do?	I Statement

STEP 2. **ROLE PLAY.** **PAIRS.** **Discuss your *I* statements and specific requests. Role-play a conversation for each situation.**

Reading

1   BEFORE YOU READ

A   GROUPS. Look at the pictures. Discuss. Which of these sports have you played? Which of these sports do you watch? Do you know the rules for these sports?

B   CLASS. What do you think the idiom "curveball" means?

> An *idiom* is a group of words that has a special meaning that is very different from the ordinary meaning of the separate words. In English, there are many sports idioms. For example, you can say, *"He really threw me a curveball!,"* which comes from baseball.

2   READ

CD2 T8

Listen to and read the quiz about idioms.

Calling the Shots—
English Sports Idioms

Many English idioms that are used in the workplace come from the world of sports. Take this quiz. Do you know which sports have given us these expressions?

1 call the shots: When you call the shots, you have control and make the decisions. For example, *It's too bad, but we really have nothing to say about the solution to this problem. The manager calls all the shots around here.*

2 carry the ball: When you carry the ball, you are in charge. For example, *Jerry, this is a very important contract. I want you to carry the ball in the negotiations.*

3 have two strikes against you: When you have two strikes against you, you have two or more things that make it very difficult for you to succeed. For example, *Maria isn't likely to get a promotion. After all of the complaints from co-workers and customers, she has two strikes against her.*

4 kick off: When you kick something off, you get it started. For example, *The advertising people just kicked off their new campaign.*

long shot: When something is a long shot, it's very unlikely to happen. For example, *I'd love to get the job, but it's a long shot—300 people applied for it!*

 slam dunk: When something is a slam dunk, it's sure to happen. For example, *Will you pass the course? It's a slam dunk—you've been studying for weeks!*

Answers: 1. billiards, 2. football, 3. baseball, 4. football, 5. horse racing, 6. basketball

3 CHECK YOUR UNDERSTANDING

PAIRS. Read the sentences. Replace the underlined words with the correct form of one of the idioms in the quiz.

1. Harry is on vacation this week and he asked Kate to <u>be in charge</u> while he's away.

2. Are you going to that meeting on Wednesday? I heard they are <u>starting</u> a new project and they want to tell us all about it.

3. I don't think more staff should be hired right now, and I'm the one <u>making the decisions</u>.

4. Ivan wanted to take a couple of days off, but I told him it's <u>not likely to happen</u> since I asked him to finish that big project.

5. I made a big mistake on my report last week, and today I got a speeding ticket in the company car. With <u>two things against me,</u> it's going to be very hard for me to get a promotion.

6. Alicia will be moving to a nicer office. It's <u>sure to happen</u> now that she got that big raise.

4 WORD WORK

GROUPS. Choose three words or phrases in the quiz that you would like to remember. Discuss the words and their meanings. Then record the words and information about them in your vocabulary log.

Show what you know! Talk about common workplace idioms from sports

GROUPS. Discuss the questions.

1. Which of the idioms in this lesson have you heard before? In what contexts?

2. Which of the idioms in this lesson do you already use?

3. Which of the idioms in this lesson are new to you?

4. What other sports idioms have you heard?

Can you...talk about common workplace idioms from sports? ☐

Writing

1 BEFORE YOU WRITE

A CLASS. You are going to write a self-evaluation about your performance at your current job or a job you had in the past. If you have never had a job, you can write a self-evaluation of your performance at school. Read about self-evaluations. Then read the writing tip.

> **FYI**   ABOUT SELF-EVALUATIONS
>
> Many companies ask employees to write self-evaluations, usually during an annual performance review. This allows employees to participate in the review process. In a self-evaluation, you analyze your work performance. You assess your performance and support your judgment with descriptions of your accomplishments, strengths, weaknesses, objectives for the coming year, and long-term career goals. You should present yourself in a positive way. Even weaknesses should be presented as opportunities for growth and learning. A self-evaluation should be organized logically and supported with relevant details, examples, and evidence.
>
> **Writing Tip: Using Good Examples**
>
> When you describe and evaluate your performance, give concrete examples to support your assessment of yourself. Select specific examples that will help your employer picture exactly what you accomplished.

B List your strengths and weaknesses on the job or at school.

C Read the writing model on page 208. Do you think that Pham has done a good job of describing her strengths and weaknesses?

2 ANALYZE THE WRITING MODEL

PAIRS. Discuss the questions.

1. What does Pham feel her greatest strengths are?
2. Why does she give herself a "superior" rating? What examples does she give to support this rating?
3. What weaknesses does Pham mention? How does she present these areas positively?
4. What is she planning to do to improve as a CNA?
5. What is her long-term career goal?

3 THINK ON PAPER

A Before Pham began writing, she used a simple outline to organize her self-evaluation. Compare her outline to her self-evaluation. How are they similar?

> I. Introduction—General Self-Assessment
>   A. Work as a CNA
>   B. Take care of elderly patients
>   C. Strengths: compassion and attention to detail
>
> II. Accomplishments That Show My Strengths
>   A. Named "CNA of the Month" because of praise from patients' relatives
>   B. Praised by lead nurses during three-month review for accuracy
>   C. Never missed a shift
>
> III. Opportunities for Improvement
>   A. Would like to learn more about complicated medical equipment
>   B. Want to learn more about medical problems seniors face
>
> IV. Conclusion—Future Goals and Long-Term Career Goal
>   A. To take a series of workshops about medical equipment
>   B. To take a special nursing course on elder care
>   C. To eventually become a Registered Geriatric Nurse

B Use the notes you made about your strengths and weaknesses in Exercise 1B to create an outline for your self-evaluation.

4 WRITE

Use your outline to write your self-evaluation. You can use Pham's outline as a guide. Be sure to present yourself—even your weaknesses—positively.

5 CHECK YOUR WRITING

A STEP 1. Revise your work.

1. Does your first paragraph give a general evaluation of your performance?
2. Did you describe your strengths, weaknesses, and accomplishments?
3. Did you include concrete examples to support your claims about yourself?

B STEP 2. Edit and proofread.

1. Have you checked your grammar, spelling, and punctuation?
2. Have you proofread for typing errors?

1 REVIEW For your grammar review, go to page 229.

2 ACT IT OUT What do you say?

PAIRS. You are discussing promotions and performance reviews with two co-workers.

Student A: Review Lessons 1 and 4. Explain five factors that influence job promotions.	**Student B:** Review Lessons 2 and 4. Describe the purpose and content of a performance review.

3 READ AND REACT Problem-solving

STEP 1. Read about Diem.

Diem has been working for two years as a receptionist at a fabric design company. She is proud of the work she does, and she thinks that she is good at her job. On her self-evaluation, she included among her strengths her willingness to learn new systems, her helpfulness to co-workers, and her communication skills, particularly with clients. Diem is always on time and rarely takes a sick day. She just received her yearly performance review from her manager, and she is very disappointed by some of the ratings. Her manager wrote on the review that Diem met expectations in five categories: knowledge of work, quality of work, communications skills, punctuality, and attention to safety. But he also noted that Diem needs improvement in time management, initiative, and problem solving. Diem is upset with her manager and feels that he is being overly critical of her. She feels angry and unsure of herself now but she has to meet with him in a week to discuss her review.

STEP 2. GROUPS. What is Diem's problem? What can she do?

4 CONNECT For your Study Skills Activity, go to page 216.

Which goals can you check off? Go back to page 85.

Health

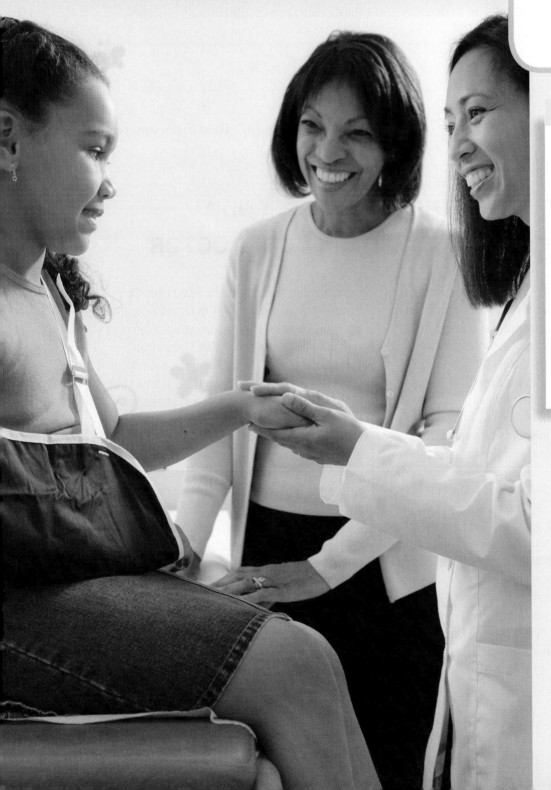

Preview

What is happening to the child? How do you feel about visiting doctors?

UNIT GOALS

- ☐ Describe medical problems
- ☐ Identify how to take medication properly
- ☐ Learn about first aid
- ☐ Ask and answer questions about health
- ☐ Learn about health screenings

Reading

1   BEFORE YOU READ

GROUPS. **Discuss the questions.**

1. Do you prepare before you go to the doctor? What do you do?
2. How do you feel about talking to doctors and other health care professionals? Explain.
3. What kinds of questions do you ask?

2   READ

CD2 T9

 A Skim the article and check (✓) the main idea on page 107. Then listen and read.

MAKE THE MOST OF YOUR APPOINTMENTS WITH YOUR DOCTOR

Before you go to the doctor, prepare. First, ask questions when you make your appointment. If you have **health insurance**, find out if your visit is covered by your insurance company. Find out if you should have other doctors send any **records**. Second, prepare a **medical history**. Include a list of medical problems and **diseases** you have had, a list of medical problems and diseases that run in your family, and a list of any **symptoms** you have. Also list any medications you take, including OTC (over-the-counter) drugs, **prescription medicines**, and **supplements**. Note **allergies** to any medications. Also write a list of symptoms if you are going because of a problem rather than for a checkup. Third, arrange for someone to go with you if you would like to have another person there to help ask questions or remember answers.

During your appointment, ask questions. Clearly state your main concerns. Describe symptoms in detail. Answer all of your doctor's questions, even if they seem personal or embarrassing. Ask questions. Take notes. Don't be afraid to ask your doctor to repeat or write information, or to draw a picture. For example you can ask, "Can I check that I understand your instructions?" or say, "Let me make sure I understand." Then repeat what the doctor said. If you have doubts about the **treatment** your doctor suggests, say so. Ask if there are other possible treatments or if you might get better without treatment. If you need more time than your doctor can provide, ask if you can speak with a nurse or a **physician's assistant**, or if you can call later to speak with someone.

After you get home, continue to be an active patient. If you don't get better or if you have trouble with medicine, call the office. If there is anything you forgot to ask your doctor or if you have new questions, call. If you had tests but do not hear from your doctor, call to ask for the results. If your doctor suggests that you have tests or wants you to see a **specialist**, be sure to make an appointment.

MAIN IDEA

☐ 1. Good communication is the responsibility of the patient as well as the doctor.

☐ 2. You can make your doctor's appointments more successful by preparing lists of information and questions to take with you before you go.

☐ 3. You can make your doctor's appointments more successful by being active and taking responsibility before, during, and after your visits.

B Read the article again more carefully.

3 CHECK YOUR UNDERSTANDING

Write the answers to the questions.

1. In your own words, what is the main idea of:

    a. the first paragraph?   b. the second paragraph?   c. the third paragraph?

2. What four lists should you write and take to your appointment?

3. Why might you want another person to go to your appointment with you?

4. What can you do if you aren't sure you understand the doctor's instructions?

5. What can you do if you need more time than the doctor has for your appointment?

6. What are some reasons you might call your doctor after your appointment?

4 WORD WORK

🖊 **GROUPS. Choose three words or phrases in the article that you would like to remember. Discuss the words and their meanings. Then record the words and information about them in your vocabulary log.**

5 MAKE IT PERSONAL

GROUPS. Discuss the questions.

1. Think about the last time you went to the doctor. How active a patient were you? Did you do any of the things suggested in the article? If so, which ones?

2. Are there things mentioned in the article that you wish you had done? If so, which ones?

3. Choose a suggestion from the article that you think you might like to try on your next visit to the doctor. Explain why.

Listening and Speaking

1 BEFORE YOU LISTEN

PAIRS. Often a general doctor, or general practitioner, will recommend that you see a specialist to help you with a medical problem. Read the chart. Discuss. What other medical specialists do you know of? What conditions do they treat?

Specialists	Conditions They Treat
allergists	allergic reactions and conditions such as rashes, hay fever, and asthma
cardiologists	heart diseases, such as strokes or heart attacks
dermatologists	skin, hair, and nail ailments, such as eczema and nail fungus
neurologists	diseases of the nervous system, such as epilepsy
oncologists	cancer or precancerous conditions
ophthalmologists	conditions and diseases that affect the eyes
orthopedists	bone injuries and diseases, such as fractures, arthritis, and osteoporosis
psychiatrists	mental illnesses, such as depression
surgeons	medical conditions that require operations

2 LISTEN

CD2 T10

Carmen and Bianca are good friends, but they haven't seen each other for a few weeks. Listen to their conversation and discuss the questions.

1. What symptoms has Bianca been having?
2. What did she find?
3. What did she do about it?
4. What kind of specialist does her doctor want her to see? Why?
5. When is her appointment?
6. What does Carmen offer?

3 PRACTICE

A **PAIRS.** Match the symptoms on the left with possible causes on the right. There may be more than one possible cause for a symptom.

	Symptoms	Possible Causes
_d_	1. blurry vision	a. heart disease
___	2. a painful rash	b. cancer
___	3. loss of appetite	c. depression
___	4. a lump	d. farsightedness/nearsightedness
___	5. a sharp chest pain	e. asthma
___	6. shortness of breath	f. eczema

B **GROUPS.** Bianca's doctor recommended that she see an oncologist. Look at the chart on page 108. Discuss. Which specialist would you go to for each of the symptoms in Exercise 3A? You may want to consult more than one specialist.

4 MAKE IT PERSONAL

STEP 1. Think of someone you know well who had to see a specialist.

STEP 2. **PAIRS.** Complete the chart. Compare your information.

Symptom	Specialist seen	Condition	What happened?

STEP 3. **PAIRS.** Think about symptoms you might see a doctor about. Describe the symptoms, and offer each other suggestions about what to do.

Life Skills

1 UNDERSTAND TIPS FOR TAKING MEDICINE

A CLASS. A side effect is an effect that medicine has on your body in addition to the intended effect. Discuss. Have you or has anyone you know ever had a side effect or allergic reaction from taking medicine?

B PAIRS. Read the handout from the U.S. Food and Drug Administration about taking medicine safely. What are some of the risks of taking medicine?

U.S. Food and Drug Administration's TIPS FOR TAKING MEDICINES:

How to Get the Most Benefits with the Fewest Risks

Both prescription and over-the-counter (OTC) medicines can have risks. Medicines may cause side effects or allergic reactions, and they may be affected by interactions with foods, drinks, or other drugs.

For prescription drugs, a patient should ask the doctor questions with each new prescription. For example:

- ◼ What is the medicine's name, and what is it supposed to do?
- ◼ How and when do I take it, and for how long?
- ◼ While I'm taking this medicine, should I avoid:
  - ● Certain foods or supplements?
  - ● Caffeine or alcohol?
  - ● Other medicines, prescription and OTC?

- ◼ Will this new medicine work safely with the prescription and OTC medicines I'm already taking?
- ◼ Are there side effects, and what do I do if they occur?
- ◼ Will the medicine affect my sleep or activity level?
- ◼ What should I do if I miss a dose?
- ◼ Is there written information available about the medicine? (At the very least, ask the doctor or pharmacist to write out complicated directions and medicine names.)

Source: © 1995, 1997, 2001 U.S. Food and Drug Administration

C Read the sentences. Which questions in the handout do they answer? Write the questions.

1. It might cause headaches or drowsiness; this is normal, so continue the medication.
   Are there side effects, and what do I do if they occur?

2. Don't drink alcohol while you're taking this medicine.

3. Take it twice a day on an empty stomach for seven days.

4. You may feel weak and sleepy, so don't drive or operate any machinery.

5. Do not take an additional capsule. Take the next dose at the normal time and in the normal amount.

PAIRS. Practice the conversation.

Patient: Does this medication cause any side effects?

Pharmacist: Sometimes. Some people experience a little nausea or dizziness.

Patient: What should I do if I experience these side effects?

Pharmacist: Any side effects are usually mild, and they're usually nothing to worry about. They'll stop when you quit taking the medication. But call your doctor if they bother you.

Patient: And I should take this medicine twice a day, right?

Pharmacist: That's right. With breakfast and dinner. But be sure not to take it with milk or other dairy products.

Patient: Thank you. You've been very helpful.

A Read and take the medicine safety quiz. Check (✓) *Yes* or *No* to answer each question.

MEDICINE SAFETY QUIZ	Yes	No
1. Do you throw outdated medicine away?		
2. Do you keep all medicines out of children's sight and reach?		
3. Do you finish your prescription unless your doctor says not to?		
4. Do you try to use the same pharmacy to fill all prescriptions?		
5. Do you ask for written information about your medicine?		
6. Do you read the written instructions and the instructions on the label?		
7. Do you use only medicine prescribed for you?		
8. Do you keep medicines in their original, labeled packaging?		
9. Do you make sure there is light to see your medicine when you take it?		
10. Do you store medicine away from dampness or direct sunlight?		

B GROUPS. Score your quizzes: 10 *yes* answers = *very safe*, 8 *yes* answers = *not very safe*, 7 or fewer *yes* answers = *extremely unsafe*. Compare your scores.

Can you...identify how to take medication properly? ☐

Reading

1 BEFORE YOU READ

A CLASS. Why do you think first aid is called "first aid"? What kinds of accidents or emergencies might require first aid?

B GROUPS. Discuss the questions.

1. Have you ever received first aid? If so, for what?
2. Have you ever given first aid? If so, for what?
3. Have you ever had any first aid training? If so, tell about it.

> *Reading Skill:*
> Visualizing
>
> It is helpful to visualize, or form mental pictures, as you read. Use descriptive details in a text to picture the things, actions, or events you are reading about. This will help you to understand and remember information.

2 READ

CD2 T11

Listen to and read the article about first aid. Visualize the actions you should take for each emergency. Imagine yourself going through the correct steps.

First aid is what you do to help someone while you are waiting for **professional** help—it's the first help given in an emergency. And sometimes the first things that are done in an emergency can be the most important things.

BAD BURNS

Before medical help arrives, remove any clothing around the burn, unless the clothing sticks to the burned area. **Immerse** the burn in cool water or run cool water over it for at least ten minutes. A shower is good for this. If it's not possible to run water over the burn, place clean, cool, **moist** towels on the burn—but keep them cool and moist. Don't put anything else on the burn. Don't break blisters. Gently remove items such as rings or belts from the areas around the burn. Later, these areas may swell, and the items may be difficult to remove. It may be necessary to treat a burn **victim** for shock.

SHOCK

A person who has a severe **injury** or emotional **upset** may go into shock. Signs include cold and clammy skin, a colorless or gray face, chills, confusion, weakness, anxiety, **nausea**, fast **pulse**, and weak breathing. The eyes may seem to stare. Until emergency help arrives, have the person lie down with the feet higher than the head, unless this position would cause pain or injury. (Don't move a person who may have a head, neck, or back injury.) Loosen belts and tight clothing, and cover the person with a blanket.

POISON

Call 911 if the person has **collapsed** or stopped breathing. Otherwise, for someone who took the wrong medicine, or too much medicine, call the Poison Control Center (1-800-222-1222 in the U.S.) for instructions. For someone who swallows a household **chemical**, read the poison warning and instructions on the label. Follow the instructions, then call the Center. If a person **inhales** a poison, get the person into fresh air before calling the Poison Control Center. If a person is poisoned through the skin—for example by contact with a chemical—remove any clothing the poison has touched and **rinse** the skin with water for 15–20 minutes, then call the Center. For poison in an eye, rinse the eye with cool water for 15–20 minutes. Adults can stand in the shower to do this. Have a child lie in the bathtub, or support the child over a sink, and pour cool water on the forehead above the eye. If poison has gotten into both eyes, pour the water on the **bridge** of the nose. Don't pour water directly on the open eye. Don't hold the eye open. Call the Poison Control Center.

CHECK YOUR UNDERSTANDING

A **GROUPS.** Reread the article on page 112. Choose one action that you should perform to help a person suffering from burns, shock, or poisoning. Visualize yourself performing the action. Describe the action to the group.

B Write the answers to the questions.

1. What should you do if clothing sticks to a burn?
   Leave it.

2. What is something you *shouldn't* do to a burn?

3. Why should you remove rings and belts from the area of a burn?

4. What can cause shock?

5. What are four possible signs of shock?

6. What's the number for the Poison Control Center in the U.S.?

7. What should you do if a person inhales poison?

8. How long should an eye be rinsed if poison gets into it?

4 WORD WORK

GROUPS. Choose three words or phrases in the article that you would like to remember. Discuss the words and their meanings. Then record the words and information about them in your vocabulary log.

5 MAKE IT PERSONAL

STEP 1. GROUPS. Have you ever been involved in an emergency related to burns, shock, or poison? If so, describe what happened. If not, imagine what you would do in one of these emergencies.

STEP 2. PAIRS. After reading the advice in the article, are you better prepared for an emergency? Explain.

Reading

1 BEFORE YOU READ

CLASS. Do you have native-born American co-workers or neighbors? If so, what greetings do you use with them?

2 READ

CD2 T12

Listen to and read the message board posts. What are the people discussing?

	Message: What does "How are you?" really mean?
↓ Posted - 10/9 11:02 A.M.	
● **Elsa** From Poland Posts: 4	I'm confused. I work in a big hotel, and there are a lot of employees there. Sometimes, one of the other employees I only **know by sight** will say, "Hi! How are you?" when we pass in the hall, but the person doesn't want me to answer. He'll just keep walking. Why does he ask, "How are you?" Can anyone tell me what he expects me to say?
↓ Posted - 10/09 11:15 A.M.	
○ **Kamila** From Czech Republic Posts: 10	Hi, Elsa. I don't know what this guy's problem is, and I'm not sure whether this will help, but that's **normal behavior** for Americans! When people don't know each other well—like co-workers or neighbors—and they greet each other, they often say "Hi! How are you?" but no one expects an answer! You can say, "Fine, thanks. How are you?" Then the other person says, "Fine" and just keeps on going.
↓ Posted - 10/09 11:32 A.M.	
○ **Tuan** From Japan Posts: 24	This **took me by surprise**, too, when I first came to the U.S. One time, someone said, "Hi. How are you?" and I actually answered! I said, "Oh, I don't feel well. I have a bad cold and a sore throat. Thank you for asking." The person looked at me as if I was crazy! I thought the person was angry with me for going out with a cold. I don't know if you know this, but in my country, we wear masks over our nose and mouth when we go out if we have a cold or the flu. The next day, I told the story to my friend, and she told me what I had done wrong. I was really **embarrassed**!
↓ Posted - 10/09 11:59 A.M.	
● **Elsa** From Poland Posts: 5	Could you explain why Americans ask the question if they don't want to know the answer? It seems rude.
↓ Posted - 10/09 12:06 P.M.	
● **Kamila** From Czech Republic Posts: 11	I don't know whether it's rude in your home country, but in the U.S. it's not rude. You just have to get used to it.
↓ Posted - 10/09 12:18 P.M.	
● **Tuan** From Japan Posts: 25	I heard two of my American co-workers joking around once. One of them said, "Hi. How are you?" and the other one said, "Do you have an hour?" They both laughed and kept going. I think Americans just don't have time to listen to a lot of details about how you're feeling if they don't know you well. Next time a co-worker or neighbor asks, "How are you?" just think of it as another way of saying, "Hi."

《 previous page   1 | 2 | 3   next page 》   Reply

CHECK YOUR UNDERSTANDING

Write the answers to the questions.

1. What happened to Elsa? Why was she confused?

2. What did she learn about how Americans greet one another?

3. What does Elsa think about the American style of greeting? Do you agree with her? Why or why not?

4. What difference does Tuan describe between practices in his home country and practices in the U.S.?

4 **WORD WORK**

📝 **GROUPS.** Choose three words or phrases in the message board posts that you would like to remember. Discuss the words and their meanings. Then record the words and information about them in your vocabulary log.

Show what you know! Interpret casual questions about health

GROUPS. How do people respond to the question, "How are you?" in your home country? Is it different from how they respond in the U.S.? If so, explain how.

PAIRS. Complete the chart. Discuss similarities and differences.

Responses in the United States	Responses in Your Home Country
Formal:	Formal:
Informal:	Informal:

Grammar

Embedded *Wh-* Questions

Direct Question	Embedded Question
What does he expect me to say?	Can anyone tell me **what he expects me to say**?
Why do Americans ask the question?	Could you explain **why Americans ask the question**?
What is this guy's problem?	I don't know **what this guy's problem is**.

Embedded *Yes/No* Questions

Direct Question	Embedded Question		
Will this help?	I'm not sure	if	**this will help**.
		whether	
Do you know this?	I don't know	if	**you know this**.
		whether	

Grammar Watch

- An embedded question is a type of question that is included inside another sentence. Use embedded questions to ask for information politely or to express information you don't know.

- Put embedded questions inside questions like *Do you know…?* or *Can you tell me…?* Use a question mark at the end of these sentences.

- Put embedded questions inside statements like *I don't know…* or *I wonder…* Use a period at the end of these sentences.

1   PRACTICE

Change each direct question about health to an embedded question.

1. When did you start having headaches?

   Can you tell me when you started having headaches?

2. What medications do you take every day?

   _____

3. How tall are you, and how much do you weigh?

   _____

4. What can I do to lower my blood pressure?

   _____

5. Will this medication cause side effects?

   _____

A Unscramble the words and phrases to create an embedded question.

1. what is causing / my shortness of breath / I'm not sure

   I'm not sure what is causing my shortness of breath.

2. had the same illness / if anyone / I don't know / in my family

   _____

3. make my appointment / I don't know / on Friday / whether I can

   _____

4. why I need / can you explain / this medication / to take

   _____

5. whether / I wonder / vitamin C / I should take

   _____

B Use the phrases below to form questions and statements about your own health.

1. Do you know if *there is a more effective treatment for my headaches?*

2. I wonder whether _____

3. Can you tell me when _____

4. Can you explain why _____

5. Can you tell me if _____

6. I'm not sure how _____

7. I don't know where _____

Show what you know! Ask and answer questions about health

STEP 1. GROUPS. Discuss. Why is it a good idea to prepare a list of questions before you have a medical exam? What kinds of questions should you ask a doctor when you have a regular checkup? Talk about the kinds of questions you should ask. Compare your experiences.

STEP 2. Prepare a list of general questions that patients might ask their doctors during a routine exam. Share your list with the class.

Can you... ask and answer questions about health? ☐

Reading

1 BEFORE YOU READ

CLASS. Check (✓) the statement that is true for you. Then discuss your answers and the reasons for them.

- ☐ I never go to the doctor.
- ☐ I go to the doctor only when I am very ill.
- ☐ I go to the doctor whenever I think something may be physically wrong with me.
- ☐ I go to the doctor for preventive screenings every year, even if I feel fine.

> **Reading Skill:**
> Recognizing Cause and Effect
>
> To understand explanations in texts, look for causes and effects. An effect is "what happened." A cause is "why it happened." Certain words signal causes and effects, including *so, because, because of, therefore, lead to, result,* and *as a result.*

2 READ

CD2 T13

Skim the article. Then listen to and read it carefully. Identify causes and effects.

PREVENTIVE HEALTH SCREENINGS

Early **detection** of certain illnesses and medical conditions is very important. If left untreated, many problems get worse until they are very serious. Regular **screenings** can catch a problem early enough to **eliminate** it completely or to control it.

■ WHY SCREEN FOR DIABETES?

In the U.S., 20.8 million people have **diabetes**. Almost one-third are unaware that they have the disease. People with diabetes can't produce or properly use **insulin**, a **hormone** needed to change sugar into energy. When this happens, sugar and starches build up in the blood instead of going into **cells**. Untreated, diabetes can lead to blindness, heart disease, kidney failure, and even to conditions requiring **amputations**. The most common form of diabetes, called

"type 2 diabetes," can occur at any time. Symptoms of diabetes in its early stages may be mild and are often not recognized or are mistaken for symptoms of minor conditions and illnesses.

■ WHY SCREEN FOR HIGH BLOOD PRESSURE?

Blood pressure is the force with which blood moves through your body. Almost one in three adults in the U.S. has high blood pressure. But because there are often no symptoms, many people live with high blood pressure for years without knowing it. Uncontrolled high blood pressure can lead to stroke, heart attack, heart failure, or kidney failure. The only way to tell if you have high blood pressure is to have your blood pressure checked.

WHY SCREEN FOR HIGH CHOLESTEROL?

When there is too much **cholesterol** in your blood, it builds up in the walls of your **arteries**. As a result, they become narrow, or clogged, and blood flow to the heart is slowed down or blocked. Blood carries oxygen to the heart, and if not enough blood and oxygen reach your heart, you may suffer chest pain. When the blood supply to a part of the heart is blocked completely, the result is a heart attack. Many people who have high cholesterol are unaware of it; for some, the first symptom is a heart attack.

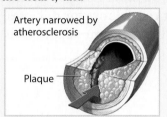

Artery narrowed by atherosclerosis

Plaque

To find out about other preventive screenings, check the websites for the U.S. Department of Health and Human Services, the Centers for Disease Control and Prevention, the American Medical Association, the American Cancer Society, and the American Heart Association. You can also check the Department of Health and Human Services for your state. If you have insurance, call or check the company website to find out about recommended screenings covered by your insurance.

Source: http:www.cdc.gov/cholesterol/index.htm

3 CHECK YOUR UNDERSTANDING

Write the answers to the questions.

1. What is insulin? What happens when the body doesn't produce or use it properly?
2. What are some possible results of leaving diabetes untreated?
3. What effects can uncontrolled high blood pressure have on the body?
4. What happens when there is too much cholesterol in your blood?
5. When the blood supply to a part of the heart is blocked completely, what is the result?
6. Where can you find more information about preventive health screenings?

4 WORD WORK

GROUPS. **Choose three words or phrases in the article that you would like to remember. Discuss the words and their meanings. Then record the words and information about them in your vocabulary log.**

5 MAKE IT PERSONAL

GROUPS. **Discuss the questions.**

1. Do you agree that it's important to have health screenings? Why or why not?
2. Does anyone you know have diabetes, high blood pressure, or high cholesterol? If so, what do they do about it?
3. Some drugstores and discount stores offer free blood pressure checks at certain times. Do you know of any place that does this in your area?
4. Do you know about any free diabetes or cholesterol screenings in your area? If not, whom could you contact to get this information?

Listening and Speaking

1 BEFORE YOU LISTEN

CLASS. Think about the conditions discussed in the article on pages 118–119. Risk factors are things that make you more likely to get an illness or disease. Discuss. What do you know about risk factors for diabetes, high blood pressure, and high cholesterol? What are some suggestions for prevention or improvement of each condition?

2 LISTEN

CD2 T14

A Listen to three students give a presentation about type 2 diabetes. Take notes in the outline.

In the introduction, the speaker presents the topic and explains what will be discussed in the body of the presentation. ("Pierre will talk about risk factors for type 2 diabetes, and Min-Ji will give suggestions for reducing risk and living with the disease.")

I. INTRODUCTION (Marisa)

II. BODY

   A. Risk factors (Pierre)

    1.

    2.

    3.

    4.

   B. Suggestions for reducing risk (Min-Ji)

    1.

    2.

    3.

III. CONCLUSION (Marisa)

For each subtopic in the body of the presentation, the presenter should identify exactly what he or she will discuss. (Pierre: "There are many different risk factors for type 2 diabetes, but I'm going to focus on four of them." Min-Ji: "I'm going to discuss things people can do to reduce the risk of becoming diabetic or to help control diabetes.")

In the conclusion, the speaker should summarize the main ideas and ask if there are any questions.

B 🔊 **Listen to the presentation again. Answer the questions.**

1. What is glucose?

2. What does insulin do with glucose?

3. What two problems can occur if there is too much glucose in the blood?

4. What does family history have to do with diabetes?

5. How can a poor diet lead to diabetes?

6. What can regular exercise and a good diet do for people who have or might get diabetes?

7. Why should people with high blood pressure consume less alcohol and salt?

3 PRACTICE

A CLASS. **Discuss. Are diabetes, high blood pressure, and high cholesterol common in your home country? Are other medical problems more common there? What do you know about risk factors and treatment for the problems?**

B GROUPS. **Diabetes, high blood pressure, and high cholesterol are common in the U.S. In Asia and other parts of the world, these problems have been less common but are now occurring more and more often. Discuss. Why do you think this is true?**

Communication Skill: Giving Advice

To give someone advice orally, use *should* or *ought to* followed by the base form of a verb. Start your sentences with polite words and phrases, such as *I think, Maybe, or Perhaps*.

> ***I think*** you ***should check*** with your doctor before starting an exercise program.
>
> ***Maybe*** you ***ought to go*** to a nutritionist to discuss a balanced diet.

---

4 MAKE IT PERSONAL

GROUPS. **Discuss. Do you know anyone who has diabetes? If so, how is the person being treated? Is he or she being careful about diet and exercise? If not, what advice would you give him or her? Discuss high blood pressure and high cholesterol in the same way.**

Writing

1 BEFORE YOU WRITE

A You are going to write a persuasive essay, or argument, for or against smoking bans in public places. Read about persuasive essays. Then read the writing tip.

> **FYI** ABOUT PERSUASIVE ESSAYS
>
> Like an opinion piece, a persuasive essay tries to get readers to agree with your point of view, or argument. A good persuasive essay begins with a paragraph that introduces the topic. The opening paragraph presents the argument. The rest of the essay supports the argument with solid reasons, details, and examples.
>
> **Writing Tip: Introductory paragraphs**
>
> An introductory paragraph should attract the reader's attention, give general background information on the topic, and present the main idea of the essay. The main idea should narrow the topic to a specific point or argument that will be supported by solid evidence in the rest of the essay.

B Brainstorm about the writing topic.

STEP 1. **Ask yourself these questions.**

1. Should the government be allowed to ban smoking in public places, such as restaurants, bars, hotels, banks, bowling alleys, parks, and beaches?
2. Do people have a right to smoke in some or all of these places?

Write down all of your thoughts about this topic—including arguments for and against smoking bans.

STEP 2. PAIRS. **Discuss your opinions about smoking bans. Add your partner's arguments and your own to your notes.**

C Read the writing model of a persuasive essay on page 208. It is about a related subject. What do you think of Zlatan's argument?

2 ANALYZE THE WRITING MODEL

PAIRS. **Discuss the questions.**

1. What argument does Zlatan present in his opening paragraph?
2. What reasons does he use to support his argument?
3. What statistic does Zlatan provide to back up his argument?

THINK ON PAPER

A Before Zlatan wrote his persuasive essay, he used a chart to brainstorm and organize his argument. Do you think that he organized his argument in a logical way?

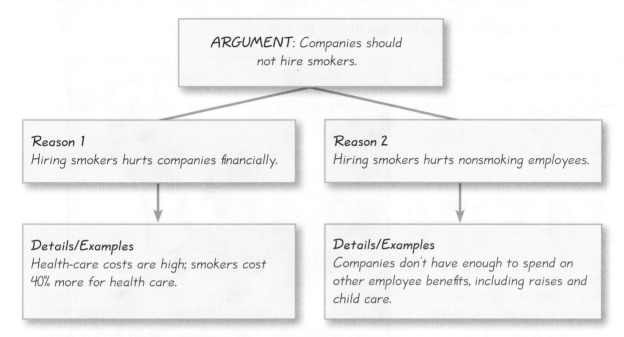

ARGUMENT: Companies should not hire smokers.

Reason 1
Hiring smokers hurts companies financially.

Reason 2
Hiring smokers hurts nonsmoking employees.

Details/Examples
Health-care costs are high; smokers cost 40% more for health care.

Details/Examples
Companies don't have enough to spend on other employee benefits, including raises and child care.

B Look at the notes you made about smoking bans in Exercise 1B. Then use a chart like Zlatan's to organize your argument for or against smoking bans.

4 **WRITE**

Write a persuasive essay about whether the government should or should not have the right to ban smoking in public places. Be sure to use your opening paragraph to state your argument.

5 **CHECK YOUR WRITING**

A STEP 1. **Revise your work.**

1. Have you presented your topic and argument in the introductory paragraph?
2. Does your introduction attract, or "grab," the reader's attention?
3. Do you give solid reasons, details, and examples to back up your argument?

B STEP 2. **Edit and proofread.**

1. Have you checked your spelling, grammar, and punctuation?
2. Have you proofread for typing errors?

1 REVIEW   For your grammar review, go to page 229.

2 ACT IT OUT   What do you say?

GROUPS. You are discussing health with two friends.

Student A: Review Lesson 1. Give your friends advice about how to prepare for a doctor's appointment.

Student B: Review Lesson 3. Give your friends at least five tips for taking medication properly.

Student C: Review Lesson 7. Tell your friends why health screenings for diabetes, high blood pressure, and high cholesterol are important.

3 READ AND REACT   Problem-solving

STEP 1. Read about Zofia.

Zofia is worried about her ten-year-old son, Oskar, because he is overweight for his age and diabetes runs in the family. Oskar enjoys eating fried foods and drinking soda. He is shy and avoids sports. Zofia wants to do all she can to help her son control his diabetes, but it's hard to change his habits.

STEP 2. GROUPS. What is Zofia's problem? What can she do?

4 CONNECT   For your Study Skills Activity, go to page 217.

Which goals can you check off? Go back to page 105.

Citizenship

Preview

What are the people doing? Do ceremonies like this happen in your home country?

UNIT GOALS

- ☐ Discuss the early history of the U.S.

- ☐ Show how the U.S. government works

- ☐ Recognize individual rights in the Constitution

- ☐ Discuss how a bill becomes a law

- ☐ Discuss becoming a U.S. citizen

Reading

1 BEFORE YOU READ

PAIRS. Discuss. What do you already know about these people and events?

> Boston Tea Party   George Washington   Pilgrims   Revolutionary War

2 READ

CD2 T15

Listen to and read the text about the thirteen colonies that became the United States. Were your ideas in Exercise 1 correct?

THE BEGINNINGS OF THE UNITED STATES

In the early 1600s, settlers began arriving in North America from Great Britain. The London Company **founded** the first **permanent** English **colony** at Jamestown, Virginia, in 1607. The colonists at Jamestown grew tobacco to be sold in Europe. The second permanent English colony was founded by the Pilgrims, who left Britain because they were not allowed to practice their religion there. They arrived in 1620 and founded a colony in Plymouth, Massachusetts.

Other colonies were soon **established** along the eastern coast of North America. By 1750, more than 1 million settlers had made the colonies their new homes. There were thirteen colonies, all ruled by the British government: Connecticut, Delaware, Georgia, Maryland, Massachusetts, New Hampshire, New Jersey, New York, North Carolina, Pennsylvania, Rhode Island, South Carolina, and Virginia.

In Britain, voters elected people to **represent** them in the government. But the British government had not given settlers in the thirteen colonies the right to vote. The colonists had to pay taxes to the British government, but since they had no representation, they felt they were being taxed unfairly. In addition, the colonists wanted to trade

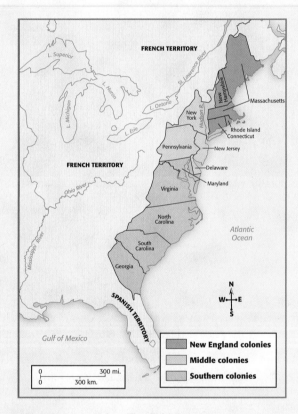

with other countries. The British government allowed them to trade only with Britain.

In 1773, Britain placed a very high tax on tea coming into the colonies. In response, the colonists **protested**. They disguised themselves as Native Americans, boarded a ship that was loaded with tea from Britain—and threw the tea into the water. The event became known as the Boston Tea Party.

At a meeting in Philadelphia in 1774, the colonists decided to stop buying all British **goods**. The British had already lost a lot of money because the colonists refused to buy tea. The colonists also wrote to the king of England to complain about the **unjust** British laws. But the British response was not favorable, and the colonists prepared for war. The Revolutionary War began in 1775, with General George Washington leading the Continental Army.

On July 4, 1776, representatives of the thirteen colonies adopted the Declaration of Independence. The thirteen colonies had become the thirteen American states. The war lasted until 1783, when Great Britain recognized the thirteen colonies as free and independent states. In 1787, representatives from the thirteen states met in Philadelphia and wrote the Constitution, establishing one national government with representation from all states.

3 CHECK YOUR UNDERSTANDING

A GROUPS. **Write the answers to the questions.**

1. How did the reasons for establishing the Plymouth and Jamestown colonies differ?
2. What complaints did the colonists have against the English government?
3. What event was meant to protest a tax on tea?
4. What document was written soon after the Revolutionary War began?
5. What document was written after the war ended? What did it lead to?

B **Complete the timeline with the events from the article.**

1. 1607 *Jamestown colony founded*
2. 1620 _____
3. 1750 _____
4. 1773 _____
5. 1774 _____

6. 1775 _____
7. 1776 _____
8. 1783 _____
9. 1787 _____

4 WORD WORK

GROUPS. **Choose three words or phrases in the text that you would like to remember. Discuss the words and their meanings. Then record the words and information about them in your vocabulary log.**

5 MAKE IT PERSONAL

GROUPS. **Discuss. How is the early history of the U.S. similar to or different from the history of your home country?**

Grammar

The Past Perfect

By 1750, more than 1 million settlers **had made** the colonies their new homes.

The British **had already lost** a lot of money.

The thirteen colonies **had become** the thirteen American states.

By the time the Pilgrims arrived, immigrants to Jamestown **had already established** a successful colony.

When Jamestown was established, the Pilgrims **had not yet come** to North America.

Representatives from the thirteen colonies **had just adopted** the Declaration of Independence **when copies of the document were printed**.

Grammar Watch

Use the past perfect:
- To indicate that something happened before a specific time, event, or action in the past
- With *already, yet,* and *just* to emphasize which event came first
- With *by* + a certain time to indicate the order in which two events happened
- With past time clauses beginning with *by the time, before,* and *when*

1 PRACTICE

Read the sentences. Underline the first event and circle the second event.

1. By the time (the first European settlers arrived on the East Coast,) the Spanish had already explored the area.

2. Because the British had imposed a heavy tax on tea, the colonists threw a shipload of British tea into Boston Harbor.

3. When representatives from the colonies met to write the Constitution, the Declaration of Independence had already been written.

4. Prior to the Revolutionary War, each of the thirteen colonies had had an independent government. In 1787, the Constitution outlined one common federal government but left some power to individual states.

5. Before he became president of the United States, George Washington had commanded the Continental Army.

GROUPS. Read the timeline about Paul Revere, a hero of the American Revolution. Then complete the sentences below. Use the past perfect, with *already, yet,* or *just* if necessary, to show the order of events.

Paul Revere's engraving of the Boston Massacre

1734 born in Boston, Massachusetts

1754 father dies, begins to work in father's silver shop

1760s becomes famous silversmith, supports colonists seeking independence

1770 after British kill five colonists during the Boston Massacre, makes political engraving, or picture, of the scene

1773 plays active role in revolutionary group, the Sons of Liberty

1775 on April 18, rides from Boston to Lexington to warn patriots that the British are marching toward Lexington; next day, first battles of Revolutionary War begin

1788 opens iron and brass foundry in Boston after war ends

1801 opens first copper mill in North America

1818 dies at age of 83, his ride for freedom mostly forgotten

1861 becomes American hero when Henry Wadsworth Longfellow publishes his famous poem "Paul Revere's Ride"

1. It was 1755. Paul Revere _had just begun_ to work as a silversmith in his father's shop.

2. By the end of the 1760s, Revere _____ a famous silversmith and a political activist.

3. Revere _____ an active role in the Sons of Liberty before the British marched toward Lexington in 1775.

4. The Revolutionary War _____ when Revere rode from Boston to Lexington to warn patriots that the British were marching toward Lexington.

5. By 1802, Revere _____ the first copper mill in North America.

6. Most Americans _____ about Revere when Longfellow's famous poem was published in 1861.

Show what you know! Discuss the early history of the U.S.

STEP 1. PAIRS. Reread "The Beginnings of the United States" on pages 126–127 and the timeline about Paul Revere. List three or four important events that occurred before 1775.

STEP 2. GROUPS. Discuss. What events had already happened in the thirteen colonies before Paul Revere made his famous ride?

Can you...discuss the early history of the U.S.? ☐

Reading

1   BEFORE YOU READ

CLASS. The Declaration of Independence says that "all men are created equal" and that all people are entitled to "life, liberty, and the pursuit of happiness." Discuss. What do you think these ideas mean?

2   READ

CD2 T16

Listen to and read the article about the organization of the U.S. government. What does the Constitution describe?

The U.S. Constitution

When the Revolutionary War ended, the new nation needed to establish a government. This became the task of the Founding Fathers—the men who had been responsible for governing the colonies and winning the war. Using the ideas from the Declaration of Independence, in 1787 in Philadelphia they drafted the U.S. Constitution, which formed the basis of the U.S. government.

The Constitution describes the organization of the **federal** government into three **branches**: the legislative, the executive, and the judicial branches:

- The **legislative branch** is the Congress, which is made up of the Senate and the House of Representatives. The legislative branch makes the laws. Each state has two senators. The number of representatives from each state depends on the size of the state's population. The bigger the state's **population**, the more representatives it has.
- The **executive branch** is led by the president. The president applies and enforces the laws. The president is also in charge of the military during wartime and controls the country's **foreign policy**. In addition to the president, the executive branch includes the vice president and the cabinet. The cabinet is made up of advisers to the president, such as the secretary of state, the secretary of the treasury, and the secretary of defense.
- The **judicial branch** is headed by the Supreme Court. The judicial branch interprets the laws and makes sure that all laws that Congress passes follow the **principles** of the Constitution. Other courts—federal, state, and local—are also part of the judicial branch.

The Founding Fathers wanted to ensure that no single branch of government would have too much power, so the U.S. Constitution describes a system of "checks and balances." Each branch "checks," or "balances," the others. This way, no single branch can become too powerful.

3

CHECK YOUR UNDERSTANDING

A Write the missing parts of government in the graphic organizer.

The Three Branches of the U.S. Government

_____
(Congress)

EXECUTIVE

_____

_____

Supreme Court

_____

_____

House of Representatives

Federal courts

_____

Cabinet

_____

Local courts

B Reread the article. Write the answers to the questions.

1. Who were the Founding Fathers?
2. What earlier document did they use when they drafted the U.S. Constitution?
3. What is the job of the legislative branch?
4. What does the executive branch do with the laws?
5. What is the judicial branch's responsibility concerning laws?
6. Why did the Founding Fathers build "checks and balances" into the Constitution?

4 **WORD WORK**

GROUPS. Choose three words or phrases in the article that you would like to remember. Discuss the words and their meanings. Then record the words and information about them in your vocabulary log.

Show what you know! Show how the U.S. government works

STEP 1. PAIRS. Use the graphic organizer to explain how each branch of the government works. Also explain the meaning and importance of the phrase *checks and balances.*

STEP 2. GROUPS. The Founding Fathers wanted to be sure that no single branch of government would have too much power. What problems could occur if one branch had too much power?

Can you...show how the U.S. government works? ☐

Reading

1 BEFORE YOU READ

CLASS. Discuss. What do you know about human rights in the U.S. and your home country? How are they the same? How are they different?

2 READ

CD2 T17

Listen to and read the article on the Bill of Rights. What kinds of protections does this document provide?

Some Protections from the Bill of Rights

The first ten amendments to the Constitution, added in 1791, are called the Bill of Rights. The Bill of Rights guarantees the rights of U.S. citizens, non-citizen residents, and visitors.

The First Amendment guarantees the rights to freedom of religion, freedom of speech, freedom of the press, freedom to peacefully **assemble** (in order to discuss or protest something), and freedom to **petition** the government (to formally ask for a change). The Second Amendment guarantees the right of people to **bear arms**, or carry guns.

The Third and Fourth Amendments limit physical **intrusion** by the government. The Fourth Amendment states that the police must have a **warrant** before they can enter a person's home or take a person's property.

Several amendments protect the rights of people who are accused of a crime. The Fifth Amendment says that a person has the right not to **testify** against him- or herself. He or she can refuse to answer questions. The Sixth Amendment guarantees that in criminal court cases, the accused person has a right to an attorney and a speedy and public trial by an **impartial** jury. The same is true in most civil court cases (non-criminal cases involving business or property); the Seventh Amendment guarantees that the accused person be given a trial by an unbiased jury.

The Eighth Amendment makes sure that a person accused of a crime doesn't have to pay extremely high **bail** or fines, or receive cruel and unusual punishment. The Ninth Amendment says that the people have other rights even if these rights are not stated directly in the Constitution.

Finally, the Tenth Amendment grants the people or the states any power not given to the federal government by the Constitution.

3 CHECK YOUR UNDERSTANDING

A Make a T-chart like the one shown here for the ten amendments. Read the article again. Take notes on each amendment.

Amendment	Notes
First Amendment Second Amendment	

B Write the answers to the questions.

1. Who is protected by the U.S. Constitution and the Bill of Rights?
2. What freedoms does the First Amendment protect?
3. How does the Sixth Amendment protect someone accused of a crime?

4 WORD WORK

☑ GROUPS. Find the boldfaced words in the article. Guess their meaning from context. Then match the words with their definitions. Record the words in your vocabulary log.

_____ 1. assemble

_____ 2. bail

_____ 3. bear arms

_____ 4. impartial

_____ 5. intrusion

_____ 6. petition

_____ 7. testify

_____ 8. warrant

a. not giving special support or attention to one group; unbiased

b. make a formal statement of what is true

c. formally ask someone in authority to do something

d. come together in the same place

e. money exchanged so that someone can be let out of prison while awaiting trial

f. official paper that allows the police to do something

g. carry guns and other weapons for self-defense

h. unwanted person or event that interrupts or annoys you

Show what you know! Recognize individual rights in the Constitution

STEP 1. PAIRS. Compare and contrast your T-charts. Use them to explain the importance of each amendment.

STEP 2. GROUPS. Discuss. Which of the first ten amendments do you think is most important? Why?

Can you... recognize individual rights in the Constitution? ☐

Listening and Speaking

1   BEFORE YOU LISTEN

A   **CLASS.** In recent years, bills regarding immigration, environmental regulations, and health care reform have been proposed in Congress. Discuss. How does an idea become a bill? How does a bill become a law?

B   **GROUPS. Fill in the blanks with words and phrases from the box.**

> abandon   override   speak up   veto   legislation   petition   sponsor

1. The Congress can _____*override*_____ some presidential decisions they disagree with.

2. The senator decided to _____ her proposal when no one supported it.

3. Citizens should _____ and express their opinions without fear.

4. Representatives from both parties will _____ a bill to improve education.

5. The new _____ makes it illegal to travel to certain countries.

6. The president opposed the bill, so he chose to _____ it.

7. Thousands of voters signed a _____ that requested lower fuel taxes.

2   LISTEN

CD2 T18

Listen to a segment of *Americans Rising,* a talk radio show, as Professor Klass explains how a bill becomes a law to host Jim Peters. Then read the sentences below and write *T* (*true*) or *F* (*false*).

__F__   1. A private citizen can sponsor a law.

_____   2. A senator or representative proposes a bill first to his or her own house of Congress.

_____   3. A committee from the house of Congress where a bill is introduced has to approve the bill before the Senate or House votes on it.

_____   4. If a bill passes the first house, it goes to the second house for a vote.

_____   5. After both houses approve a bill, it goes to the Supreme Court.

_____   6. If the president vetoes a bill, Congress must accept the veto.

Passive with *get*

We can sometimes use *get* to replace *be* in passive sentences. This happens more frequently in conversation than in written language. Look at the examples.

*The people **elected** him because of his position on environmental protection.*
*He **was elected** (by the people) because of his position on environmental protection.*
*He **got elected** (by the people) because of his position on environmental protection.*

*I hope Congress and the president **pass** the bill protecting whales.*
*I hope the bill protecting whales **is passed** (by Congress and the president).*
*I hope the bill protecting whales **gets passed** (by Congress and the president).*

3 PRACTICE

Read these statements. Rewrite them in the passive voice. Rewrite them again, changing *be* to *get*.

1. If enough people sign the petition, it goes to a congressperson.

   Passive: _If the petition is signed by enough people,_
   it goes to a congressperson.

   Passive with *get*: _If the petition gets signed by enough people,_
   it goes to a congressperson.

2. Then a senator or representative sponsors the idea.

   Passive: _____

   Passive with *get*: _____

3. The committee votes on the bill.

   Passive: _____

   Passive with *get*: _____

4. If the president vetoes the bill, Congress has three choices.

   Passive: _____

   Passive with *get*: _____

4 MAKE IT PERSONAL

PAIRS. **Explain how a bill becomes a law. Use the vocabulary from Exercise 1B and the information from the listening.**

Reading

1   BEFORE YOU READ

CLASS. Discuss. What are your feelings about becoming a U.S. citizen? What advantages do U.S. citizens have that non-citizen residents do not have?

2   READ

CD2 T19

Listen to and read the pamphlet about citizenship. How do the text structure and formatting help you identify the main points?

Reading Skill:
Using Text Structure and Formatting

To better understand what you read, notice a text's structure and formatting. **Boldface type**, bullets (•), and color can help you find the main points. Bullets can also help you identify items in a series.

What Are the Benefits of U.S. Citizenship?

The Constitution and the laws of the United States give many rights to both citizens and non-citizens living in the U.S. However, some rights are only for citizens, such as:

- Voting. Only U.S. citizens can vote in federal elections. Most states also **restrict** the right to vote, in most elections, to U.S. citizens.
- Bringing family members to the United States. Citizens generally get **priority** when petitioning to bring family members permanently to this country.
- Obtaining citizenship for children born abroad. In most cases, a child born

abroad to a U.S. citizen is **automatically** a U.S. citizen.
- Traveling with a U.S. passport. A U.S. passport allows you to get assistance from the U.S. government when overseas.
- Becoming eligible for federal jobs. Most jobs with government agencies require U.S. citizenship.
- Becoming an elected official. Many elected offices in this country require U.S. citizenship.
- Showing your patriotism. In addition, becoming a U.S. citizen is a way to demonstrate your commitment to your new country.

The above list does not include all the benefits of citizenship, only some of the more important ones.

Source: ©2006, 2008 U.S. Citizenship and Immigration Services

3 CHECK YOUR UNDERSTANDING

A Check (✓) the main idea.

☐ 1. Non-citizens living in the U.S. have rights.

☐ 2. There are certain rights in the U.S. that only U.S. citizens have.

☐ 3. Non-citizens cannot travel abroad.

☐ 4. Some jobs are open only to citizens.

B Check (✓) the most accurate statement.

☐ 1. The main idea of the text is stated in the first paragraph.

☐ 2. The main idea of the text is stated in the last bulleted item.

☐ 3. The main idea is not directly stated in any single paragraph of the text, but you can identify it based on the title and the bulleted text.

C Read the text again. Write the answers to the questions.

1. How is the right to vote different in federal elections and some non-federal elections?

2. What advantage do citizens have when trying to bring family members to the U.S.?

3. What do citizens have to do to get citizenship for their foreign-born children?

4. How does traveling with a passport help citizens?

5. Do you have to be a citizen to get a federal job and become an elected official?

6. What can you demonstrate by becoming a citizen?

D PAIRS. Discuss. Which two benefits of U.S. citizenship do you think are the most valuable? Why?

4 WORD WORK

GROUPS. Choose three words or phrases in the pamphlet that you would like to remember. Discuss the words and their meanings. Then record the words and information about them in your vocabulary log.

Show what you know! Discuss the benefits of citizenship

GROUPS. Discuss. What did the pamphlet explain that you did not already know?

Listening and Speaking

1 BEFORE YOU LISTEN

CLASS. A naturalized citizen is someone who becomes a citizen of a country that he or she was not born in. Discuss. Do you know anyone who has become a naturalized citizen of the U.S.? Do you know anyone who is studying to become a citizen?

ALL OF US WILL LEARN!

2 LISTEN

CD2 T20

A An instructor is giving a lecture to a new group of students in her citizenship class. She is explaining the requirements for naturalization. Listen to her lecture and take simple notes. Look at the example below.

REQUIREMENTS FOR CITIZENSHIP
AGE –
18 + yrs.
RESIDENCY –
legal perm. resident
(has I-551 card) resided continuously past 5 yrs
in country at least 30 mo. past 5 yrs
not gone for more than yr. past 5 yrs

Make headings stand out by underlining, using capital letters, or by separating them from the details (e.g., writing them on the left, and writing the details under them, to the right).

Don't write full sentences. Write only key words, and use abbreviations.

CD2 T20

B **PAIRS.** Listen again and check your notes. Then compare them with a partner's. Did you both include the same information? Could you both pass a test on the lecture by studying your notes? Why or why not?

A Revise your notes. You can keep the same organization as in Exercise 2A, or you can put the information into a T-chart like the one used on page 133. Make sure your heads, or main points, and key words are clear. If you used abbreviations, make sure you can remember what they mean.

B PAIRS. Use your notes to answer the questions.

1. What are some examples of actions that demonstrate lack of good moral character?

   being convicted of a serious crime, being convicted more than once for

   gambling, involvement with smuggling aliens into the country

2. What document does a person need to show an attachment to?

   _____

3. If an elderly person has lived in the U.S. for a long time, what requirements might he or she be excused from?

   _____

4. What are the two parts of the civics test?

   _____

5. What is one thing a person promises when he or she takes the Oath of Allegiance?

   _____

6. Where can you find the complete requirements and documents for U.S. citizenship?

   _____

4 MAKE IT PERSONAL

GROUPS. Discuss the questions.

1. Do you think that all of the requirements are reasonable? Why or why not?

2. Do you know whether it is easy or difficult to become a citizen of your home country? If you know, explain the process to your group.

> **Communication Skill:**
> Exchanging Opinions
>
> To exchange opinions with others, express yourself clearly and politely, and always listen to others' points of view. You can use the following words and phrases:
>
> | | |
> |---|---|
> | *How do you feel about...?* | *What do you think of...?* |
> | *In my opinion,...* | *As I see it,...* |
> | *I agree with you.* | *I think so, too.* |
> | *Yes, but...* | *I see what you mean, but...* |

Life Skills

1 LEARN ABOUT DIFFERENT KINDS OF MAPS

CLASS. Discuss. What kinds of maps have you used? Where and when did you use them? In what ways were they useful to you?

2 INTERPRET A U.S. MAP

A PAIRS. Look at the map of the U.S. Discuss. How can you tell that this is a historical map?

> A *political map* shows how governments have divided land into countries, states, provinces, and cities. A *physical map* shows the earth's features, such as mountains, oceans, and deserts. A *historical map* gives information about a particular time and place in the past; it might present political, economic, or cultural information.

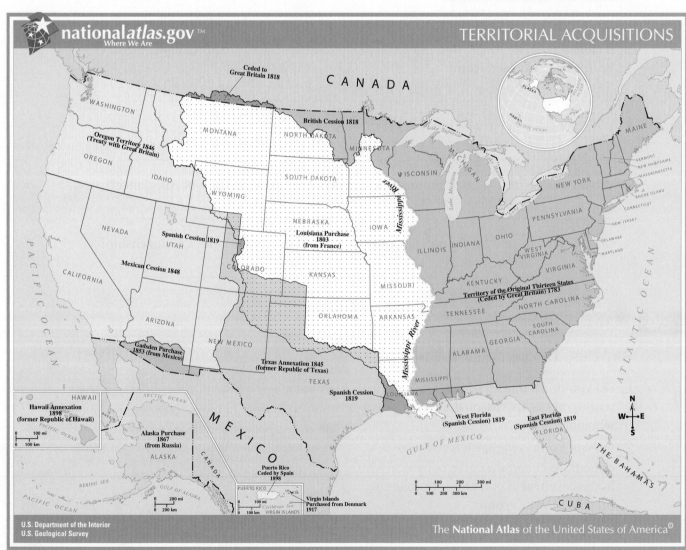

B Use the map to write the answers to the questions.

1. What countries owned parts of the land that later became the U.S?

2. When did the U.S. make the Louisiana Purchase from France?

3. Which country owned Florida before 1819?

4. From which country did the U.S. purchase Alaska?

5. From which country did the U.S. purchase the Virgin Islands?

6. When was Hawaii annexed by the U.S.?

7. Which country once owned parts of North Dakota and Minnesota?

3 DISCUSS MAP FEATURES

A CLASS. Discuss. What are some of the special features of a map? Which special features do the maps on pages 126 and 140 have?

> A *compass rose* shows which way is north, south, east, or west. A *map scale* shows the relationship between the distances on a map and real distances on land. A *map key* is a visual summary of what the colors, patterns, shading, and symbols on a map stand for.

B PAIRS. Use the map on page 140 to discuss the questions.

1. What map feature would you use to figure out the distance from New York to California?

2. What map feature tells you which way is north?

3. If you were creating a map key for this map, what would white with black dots stand for?

4 LISTEN

CD2 T21

A An instructor is giving a lecture on the expansion of the U.S. Listen to the lecture and take simple notes.

B Review your notes. Then write answers to the questions.

1. Who was president when the U.S. made the Louisiana Purchase?

2. When did the U.S. acquire California?

3. Which countries originally claimed the Oregon Territory?

4. Why did the purchase of Alaska become popular with U.S. citizens?

Can you...interpret historical maps of the U.S.? ☐

Writing

1 BEFORE YOU WRITE

A You are going to write a formal e-mail to an elected official about a problem that concerns you. Read about formal e-mails. Then read the writing tip.

> **FYI**   ABOUT FORMAL E-MAILS
>
> In the U.S., sending formal e-mails or letters to elected officials is an important way to participate in the democratic process. Formal e-mails should be set up like business letters. See the example of a cover letter on page 206. Include the full name, title, business, and e-mail address of the person you are writing to. Provide a short, clear subject line. Use a formal greeting and include the person's title or *Ms., Miss,* or *Mr.* Then write a message that is clear and concise. End your e-mail in a polite, diplomatic way, for example, *Thank you for taking the time to read my e-mail. I look forward to hearing from you.* Then use a formal closing, such as *Sincerely* or *Sincerely yours,* followed by your full name.
>
> **Writing Tip: Using a problem/solution structure**
>
> Stating a problem and suggesting a solution is an easy way to structure an essay, business letter, or formal e-mail. First, explain what the problem is and why it is a problem. Then give one or more suggestions about how to solve the problem. Be sure to explain why your solution(s) will work.

B List problems in your community that concern you. Write down as many as you can. Select one problem you can write to your local representative about.

C Read the model of a formal e-mail on page 209. It is to an elected official. What problem does Guillermo present? Is his solution a good one?

2 ANALYZE THE WRITING MODEL

PAIRS. Discuss the questions.

1. Why is Guillermo e-mailing Representative Garcia?

2. Guillermo presents a problem in his first paragraph. Why is it a problem?

3. What solution does Guillermo suggest in his message? Why does he believe that this solution will work?

3 THINK ON PAPER

A Before Guillermo wrote his formal e-mail, he used a T-chart to brainstorm and organize his message. Compare his chart to his final e-mail on page 209. How are they similar?

PROBLEM	SOLUTION
Funding for adult literacy has decreased	Increase city budget for adult literacy
Lack of productivity and satisfaction among workers	Improve basic skills: ability to read, write, speak English well
Workers need to get and keep jobs that pay well, city needs strong economy	Increase literacy rates

B Think about the problem you selected to write about in Exercise 1B. Use a problem/solution chart to plan and organize your formal e-mail.

4 WRITE

Use your T-chart to write a formal e-mail to a local representative. Ask your teacher to help you locate the official's name, street address, and e-mail address. Use Guillermo's e-mail as a guide to the format.

5 CHECK YOUR WRITING

A STEP 1. **Revise your work.**

1. Have you stated the problem clearly in the opening paragraph?
2. Have you presented a solution and explained why it will work?
3. Does your e-mail contain a formal greeting and closing?
4. Is your wording polite and formal?

B STEP 2. **Edit and proofread.**

1. Have you checked your spelling, grammar, and punctuation?
2. Have you proofread for typing errors?

1 REVIEW

For your grammar review, go to page 230.

2 ACT IT OUT — What do you say?

GROUPS. You are taking a citizenship class and are in a study group with two other classmates. You are helping one another review.

Student A: Review what you learned in Lesson 3 about the three branches of government. Then explain what the executive, judicial, and legislative branches do. Describe the importance of the checks and balances of power.

Student B: Review the T-chart you wrote for Lesson 4. Then explain to Students A and B why you value three of the ideas expressed in the Bill of Rights.

Student C: Review the notes you took about the requirements of naturalization in Lesson 7. Explain the seven general requirements for U.S. citizenship.

3 READ AND REACT — Problem-solving

STEP 1. Read about Jeffrey.

Jeffrey Yuan lives in a neighborhood where too many new high-rise buildings are being constructed. There have been three construction-related accidents in his community in the past year. One accident injured people in Jeffrey's apartment building. Jeffrey would like to do something to stop the amount of building that is taking place in his community. He is concerned about the safety of the people who live there.

STEP 2. GROUPS. What is Jeffrey's problem? What can he do?

4 CONNECT

For your Study Skills Activity, go to page 218.

Which goals can you check off? Go back to page 125.

Knowing the Law

Preview

What is happening to this man? Have you ever been involved in a situation like this?

UNIT GOALS

- ☐ Identify the rights of people accused of crimes

- ☐ Learn about the right to vote

- ☐ Recognize sexual harassment in the workplace

- ☐ Learn about traffic court

- ☐ Discuss types of crimes

Listening and Speaking

1 BEFORE YOU LISTEN

A **PAIRS.** Discuss the words and their meanings. If you don't know the meaning of a word, look it up in a dictionary.

> arrest   consult   criminal suspect   custody   interrogate

B **CLASS.** Discuss. What happens when someone is arrested in real life or in the movies? What does the police officer say to the suspect about his or her rights?

2 LISTEN

CD3 T2

A Listen to the first part of the lecture and write *T* (*true*) or *F* (*false*) next to each statement.

___T___ 1. If a suspect answers questions, the suspect's answers can be used as evidence against him or her in court.

_____ 2. A suspect may remain silent if he or she doesn't want to answer police questions.

_____ 3. If a suspect wants an attorney but doesn't have money to pay for one, an attorney will be provided.

_____ 4. If a suspect wants to answer some questions without an attorney present, he or she cannot request an attorney later.

_____ 5. If a suspect refuses to answer questions, the suspect cannot have an attorney.

CD3 T3

B Listen to the second part of the lecture. Take notes.

3 PRACTICE

PAIRS. Compare and revise your notes. Then use them to discuss the questions.

1. What two Constitutional rights does the *Miranda* decision support?

2. What was the only evidence against Ernesto Miranda at his first trial?

3. Can the police arrest someone without asking the person any questions or giving the person the *Miranda* warning?

4. What can the police ask about without giving a person the *Miranda* warning?

MAKE IT PERSONAL

A Read the statements, and check (✓) the statement in each group that best represents your opinion.

1. ☐ a. If a suspect doesn't want to answer questions, he or she may just be nervous or confused. The police should try to persuade the person to talk.

   ☐ b. If a suspect doesn't want to answer questions, it could mean that he or she is guilty. The police should have methods of persuading people to talk.

   ☐ c. If a suspect doesn't want to answer questions without an attorney present, the police should simply leave the person alone until an attorney is available.

2. ☐ a. If a suspect can't understand the police officer's English, the police should be required to provide the *Miranda* warning in the person's native language.

   ☐ b. If a suspect can't understand the police officer's English but tries to explain or answer questions anyway, this is not the police officer's fault, and it's OK if what the suspect says is used against him or her.

   ☐ c. A police officer shouldn't be required to provide the *Miranda* warning in languages other than English. But the information provided by a poor English speaker without an attorney present should not be used against the person.

B GROUPS. Discuss your answers to Exercise A. For each item, which opinion did most people check?

C GROUPS. Discuss the questions.

1. Do you have laws or protections like the *Miranda* warning in your home country? If so, do you think that such laws are a good thing? If you don't have such laws, should your home country adopt something similar to the *Miranda* warning? Why or why not?

2. Why do you think some innocent people might make inaccurate or false confessions?

3. Why might a suspect want to speak to an attorney before answering a police officer's questions?

Grammar

Future Real Conditional

If you **decide** to answer questions without an attorney present, you **will** still **have** the right to stop answering at any time.

You **will** still **have** the right to stop answering at any time **if** you **decide** to answer questions without an attorney present.

If you **cannot afford** an attorney, one **will be appointed** for you.

An attorney **will be appointed** for you **if** you **cannot afford** one.

Grammar Watch

- A conditional sentence has an *if* clause describing a condition and a result clause describing a result of that condition.
- To form the future real conditional, use the simple present in the *if* clause.
- Use *will* or a modal such as *can, could, may,* or *might* + main verb in the result clause.
- The *if* clause can begin or end a sentence. Use a comma after the *if* clause when it begins the sentence.
- Use the future real conditional to talk about situations that:
  - occur regularly
  - are likely or possible in the future

1 PRACTICE

A PAIRS. Find the conditional sentences. Underline the *if* clauses. Circle the result clauses.

If the police stop you for drunk driving, you will be required to take a Blood Alcohol Concentration (BAC) test to determine your blood alcohol level. In most states, if you refuse to take the test, you will be required to pay a fine and you will have your license suspended, in some cases immediately. Also, if you refuse to take the test, you will probably be taken to jail, where you may have to spend the night. If you take the test and your blood alcohol content is over the legal limit, you will probably be taken to jail.

Eventually, you'll go to court. You will probably have to pay a fine if you are found guilty. You may also have to go to jail or go to a driver education program. If it is your first offense, you might just have to do community service. But your insurance payments could go up for even a first offense. If it's not your first offense, your penalties could be severe. Your penalties may also be severe if you are under the legal age to drink alcohol. If you caused injury to another person, your penalties could be extremely severe.

B Rewrite the sentences with the *if* clause at the beginning.

1. Your license might be suspended if you refuse a BAC test.

2. Your insurance rates could go up a lot if you are convicted of driving while drunk.

3. Your penalty could be especially severe if you are under the legal drinking age.

4. You will go to jail if the police catch you driving while you are drunk.

A Use the words and phrases to write conditional sentences with the *if* clause first and the affirmative or negative of *will* in the result clause.

1. the police / stop me / not answer any questions

   If the police stop me, I won't answer any questions.

2. the police / ask for my name and address / give them the information

3. I / can't afford an attorney / court / provide one

4. I / become confused / not continue to answer questions

5. the police / read me my rights / show them a card saying I refuse to talk without my attorney

6. you / say anything / be used against you in court

B Unscramble the words and phrases to make complete sentences.

1. jaywalk / if / you / you / could / receive / fine / a / New York City / $50 / in

2. you / $2000 / Texas / trespass / if / you / in / receive / may / a maximum fine / of

3. might / fine / you / if / litter / California / in / you / receive / a / $1000

4. if / pay / $100 and $500 / between / fishing / caught / you / are / you / without / a license / in Mississippi / could have to

jaywalk: walk across the street in an area that is not marked for crossing
litter: leave things like pieces of paper on the ground in a public place
trespass: go onto someone's land without permission

Show what you know!   Identify the rights of people accused of crimes

GROUPS. Discuss the questions.

1. If the police ever stop you and ask you to take a BAC test, what will you do?

2. If the police ever take you to the police station to question you about a crime, will you talk to them without an attorney present? Why?

3. If you want an attorney but can't afford one, what will you do?

Can you…identify the rights of people accused of crimes? ☐

Reading

1   BEFORE YOU READ

GROUPS. Discuss. How important do you think it is for people to vote?

2   READ

CD3 T4

Listen to and read the article about voting rights in the U.S. Which statements are facts? Which are opinions?

Reading Skill: Distinguishing Fact from Opinion

When you read, look carefully at the information. Is it a fact (something you can prove) or an opinion (a belief or feeling)? Opinions often begin with the words *I think, I believe, I feel, probably, perhaps,* and *maybe.* They may express a judgment about whether something is good or bad, safe or dangerous, fair or unfair.

THE RIGHT TO VOTE

Most Americans probably don't think much about their right to vote. But some of their parents, grandparents, and great-grandparents who lived in the United States were not allowed to vote. In fact, the Constitution had to be **amended** in order to establish or protect the voting rights of certain groups of people.

When the country was founded, only white men who owned land could vote. This meant that poor men didn't have any **official** voice in the government. Later, in the early 1800s, the property requirement was replaced with a poll tax—people had to pay a special **fee** to vote. This also made voting difficult for poor people. Poll taxes were legal until the Twenty-fourth Amendment to the Constitution in 1964.

The Constitution never said that only white people could vote. But it did say that only freemen—people who were not slaves—could vote.

Until after the Civil War, most African-American men were slaves, not freemen. So it was illegal for them to vote. However, after the war, in 1870, the Fifteenth Amendment was added to the Constitution, allowing black men to vote. (No women were allowed to vote yet.) Many states were unhappy with black men having the right to vote. In addition to poll taxes, which most **former** slaves could not pay, these states **imposed** literacy tests. Since many black men coming out of slavery could not read, they were prevented from voting even if they could pay the poll tax. Some southern states added "grandfather clauses" to their **regulations.** These clauses said that if a person's grandfather had voted, the person didn't have to take a literacy test. This helped poor white men, but didn't help black men, whose grandfathers had been slaves. The Voting Rights Act of 1965 removed **restrictions** such as literacy tests.

Women were granted the right to vote by the Nineteenth Amendment to the Constitution in 1920, after many years of struggling to win this right. In 1924, Native Americans were granted the right to vote.

For many years, people had to be 21 years old or older to vote. But during the Vietnam War, many people as young as 18 were **drafted** to fight in Southeast Asia. Many felt that if people were old enough to fight and die for their country, they should be old enough to vote, too. In 1971, the Twenty-sixth Amendment gave people aged 18 and older the right to vote.

There are still people who live permanently in the United States who can't vote. Non-citizens cannot vote, even if they are permanent legal residents. Convicted felons (people who have committed serious crimes) cannot vote in most states.

3 CHECK YOUR UNDERSTANDING

A **PAIRS.** **Read the statements. Write *F* next to the *facts* and *O* next to the *opinions*.**

__O__ 1. Most Americans probably don't think much about their right to vote.

_____ 2. In 1870, no women were allowed to vote yet.

_____ 3. In 1924, Native Americans were granted the right to vote.

_____ 4. The Voting Rights Act of 1965 removed restrictions such as literacy tests.

_____ 5. I believe that convicted felons should not have the right to vote.

B **GROUPS.** **Discuss the questions.**

1. What was the grandfather clause mentioned in the article? Why wasn't it fair to black men?
2. How many years after black men received the right to vote did women receive the same right?
3. Why was the voting age lowered in 1971?

4 WORD WORK

GROUPS. **Choose three words or phrases in the article that you would like to remember. Discuss the words and their meanings. Then record the words and information about them in your vocabulary log.**

5 MAKE IT PERSONAL

GROUPS. **Discuss the questions.**

1. Is 18 a good minimum voting age? Why or why not?
2. What arguments might people have used in favor of literacy tests?
3. Should convicted felons have the right to vote again when they get out of jail? Why or why not?
4. Should permanent residents who are not citizens but who pay taxes and contribute to their communities have the right to vote? Why or why not?

Life Skills

1 UNDERSTAND SEXUAL HARASSMENT

A CLASS. What is sexual harassment? Does your company or school have a sexual harassment policy? If so, describe it. If not, should it have one? Why or why not?

B Read the web page on page 153. Check (✓) the types of conduct that are *not* examples of sexual harassment.

☐ 1. Welcome conduct of a sexual nature

☐ 2. Repeatedly telling sexual jokes

☐ 3. Asking a person out one time

☐ 4. Treating someone badly if he or she refuses to go out on a date

☐ 5. Conduct that has no impact on the workplace

☐ 6. Displaying sexual screensavers

☐ 7. Sending e-mails that contain sexual language

☐ 8. Friendly conversations between professors and students

☐ 9. Telling rumors about a co-worker's personal life

☐ 10. Looking a co-worker up and down in an overly friendly way

2 PRACTICE

A GROUPS. Look again at the key features of the web definition of *sexual harassment*. Discuss. Are they reasonable? Why or why not?

- *unwelcome*
- *conduct of a sexual nature*
- *severe or pervasive*
- *affects working conditions or creates a hostile work environment*

B GROUPS. Discuss. Do any of the examples of sexual harassment in the web page *not* make sense to you? If so, which one(s)? Explain.

*Can you...*recognize sexual harassment in the workplace? ☐

http://www.underthelaw.com

Equal Rights Under the Law

Home   Need Advice?   Legal Assistance

What You Need to Know About Sexual Harassment

Sexual harassment can be defined as "unwelcome verbal, visual, or physical conduct of a sexual nature that is severe or pervasive and affects working conditions or creates a hostile work environment." Let's look at what this means.

- **Unwelcome.** In other words, no behavior is sexual harassment if it is welcome. For this reason, it is important that if someone's behavior is making you uncomfortable, you clearly communicate that the person should stop. You can tell the person to stop and you can communicate your message in writing and by your actions.

- **Conduct of a sexual nature.** Some of the behaviors that can be described as conduct of a sexual nature include comments about a person's body, body language, or clothing; sexual jokes; repeatedly asking a person out; asking a person for sex; or telling rumors about a person's personal or sexual life. Inappropriate touching of a person is conduct of a sexual nature. This includes kissing, hugging—any touching that the person indicates is unwelcome. Looking up and down a person's body or making sexual gestures is an example of conduct of a sexual nature. Following or blocking a person is also an example of conduct of a sexual nature (for example, standing in front of someone who is trying to pass through a doorway). Displaying sexual posters, drawings, pictures, or screensavers is behavior that is sexual in nature. So is sending e-mails with sexual content.

- **Severe or pervasive.** *Severe* means serious, and *pervasive* means the behavior happens repeatedly. A single incident is probably not sexual harassment unless it is severe. For example, a man's asking a woman out on a date, once, and having her refuse is not sexual harassment. Continuing to pressure her after she has clearly said she isn't interested, or treating her badly after she refuses, could well be sexual harassment.

- **Affects working conditions or creates a hostile work environment.** If repeated sexual comments make you so uncomfortable at work that your performance suffers, the sexual comments do affect your working conditions. If you are threatened with being fired, denied a promotion, given a poor performance evaluation, or asked to do less desirable work because you refuse sexual interaction with a supervisor, that is almost certainly sexual harassment: The supervisor's reaction to your refusal clearly creates a hostile work environment.

There are federal and state laws to protect people from sexual harassment. Some of these laws only apply to businesses with fifteen or more employees. Employers are usually required by law to prevent and stop sexual harassment. Sexual harassment laws protect students as well. A professor cannot sexually harass a student. Both men and women can be victims of sexual harassment, and both men and women can be guilty of sexual harassment. Sexual harassment can occur between members of the same sex. For more information, check the laws in your state or contact your Human Resources (HR) Department or your Office of Student Affairs.

Source: Adapted from "Know Your Rights: Sexual Harassment at Work" ©2008 Equal Rights Advocates, Inc.

Reading

1   BEFORE YOU READ

CLASS. **Discuss the questions.**

1. What is the difference between child discipline and child abuse?

2. Are there any cultural differences regarding child abuse? Explain.

3. Do you know how to report suspected child abuse? If so, how?

2   READ

CD3 T5

Listen to and read the article. What kinds of child abuse does it discuss?

Child Abuse

For many of us, it's unbelievable that an adult would ever seriously hurt a child. Unfortunately, every year, many adults are guilty of physical abuse, emotional abuse, or **neglect** of one or more children. Child abuse is a shame, but it's more than that—it's against the law.

Federal law basically says that an act, or failure to act, is child abuse if it results in death, serious physical or emotional harm, or neglect. States determine their own definitions of physical or emotional harm and neglect. But the following are some possible examples:

Physical abuse: When a parent or guardian injures a child (causing any harm from minor **bruises** to death), this is physical abuse. Beating, kicking, shaking, throwing, choking, and hitting a child are all types of physical abuse. Even if the abuser did not intend, or mean, to harm the child, what matters is whether the child has been injured.

Emotional abuse: When a parent or guardian constantly criticizes a child, this is emotional abuse. Other types of emotional abuse include threats, **rejection**, and failure to give love, support, or **guidance**. Emotional abuse is often hard to prove, and officials may not be able to take any action, unless there is real evidence of harm. However, emotional abuse often occurs alongside physical abuse.

Neglect: When a parent or guardian fails to give a child necessary food or shelter, this is neglect. Other kinds of neglect include denying a child medical or mental health treatment, failing to educate a child, and ignoring a child's emotional needs, including permitting a child to use alcohol or drugs. Emotional neglect is hard to prove.

In some states, anyone who suspects child abuse is required to report it. In other states, only people in certain positions are required to report child abuse. These people include doctors and other medical personnel, teachers and other school employees, social workers, day-care workers, and others who are in frequent contact with children. When these people have a reason to **suspect** abuse, they are required by law to report it.

Usually reports are made to CPS (Child Protective Services). CPS decides whether there is reason to investigate. Investigations may result in criminal charges, but sometimes even if abuse is confirmed, the abuser will not go to jail but instead must attend a special program to learn to stop the abuse. If the CPS workers decide that it's necessary for the safety of a child, the child may be temporarily removed from the home. In such cases, children are often placed in **foster care** while one or both parents get help. For more information, contact your state's Child Welfare Program.

Source: ©2008 Child Welfare Information Gateway

CHECK YOUR UNDERSTANDING

Write the answers to the questions.

1. What is an example of physical abuse?

   _____

2. What is an example of neglect?

   _____

3. What are some things that might happen if suspected child abuse is reported?

   _____

4 **WORD WORK**

GROUPS. **Find the boldfaced words in the article. Guess their meanings from context. Then match the words with their definitions. Record the words and information about them in your vocabulary log.**

_____ 1. bruises   a. situation in which a non-relative cares for a child without becoming a legal parent

_____ 2. foster care   b. lack of care and attention

_____ 3. guidance   c. injuries caused by a blow or pressure on the skin

_____ 4. neglect (*n*)   d. helpful advice about work, education, and so on

_____ 5. rejection   e. to think that someone may be guilty of a crime

_____ 6. suspect (*v*)   f. the act of refusing to give love or attention to someone else

5 **MAKE IT PERSONAL**

GROUPS. **Discuss the questions.**

1. Do you believe children should be physically punished? If you do, what do you see as the difference between physical punishment and abuse?

2. How would you feel about having a job that required you to report suspected child abuse?

3. How can child abuse be prevented?

Reading

1 BEFORE YOU READ

A **CLASS.** **Have you ever received a traffic ticket? If so, what happened after you got it?**

B **PAIRS.** **Discuss the words and their meanings.**

issue (*v*)	to officially make a statement or give a warning
penalty	a punishment for not obeying a law, rule, or legal agreement
procedure	a way of doing something, especially the correct way
sentence (*v*)	to legally punish someone who has been found guilty of a crime
suspend	to officially stop someone from working, driving, or going to school for a fixed period, because he or she has broken the rules
violation	an action that breaks a law, rule, or agreement

2 READ

CD3 T6

 Listen to and read the handout about traffic tickets. What are the two kinds of traffic cases? What are some examples of each?

Your Traffic Ticket

So you have received a traffic ticket. What do you do now? In our county, there are very clear **procedures** to follow. Read both sides of your ticket carefully. It will tell you what **violation** you are charged with, how you can respond, whether you have to go to court, and what your rights are. The steps you must follow and the **penalties** you may receive depend on whether your case is a civil or criminal traffic case.

Civil traffic cases include violations such as driving without wearing a seat belt, failure to use a child restraint, or speeding. The penalty for a civil traffic violation is usually a fine and/or required attendance at driving school. You may not have to go to court if you agree that you are guilty and send payment for your fine. If you do not think you are guilty, you may request a trial. You can't be **sentenced** to jail for civil violations. However, in addition to a fine, you may get "points" against your license. If you get several points within a certain period of time, your insurance rates will increase.

Criminal traffic cases are more serious than civil cases. DUI (driving while under the influence of alcohol) and driving while your license is **suspended** are examples of criminal traffic violations. These cases require a court hearing. Although most sentences involve payment of a fine and points against your license, jail or prison time is also possible. In a criminal case, you have the right to request a jury trial.

Failure to appear in court is a serious crime. If your ticket says that you have to appear in court and you don't appear, you are in trouble. Whether your case is a civil case or a criminal case, a "bench warrant" could be **issued** for your arrest. This means that if a police officer stops you and checks your records, you can be arrested and taken to jail. Bench warrants can also be issued for failure to pay fines. So if you receive a traffic ticket, don't try to avoid dealing with it.

CHECK YOUR UNDERSTANDING

A **Reread the handout. Then write the answers to the questions.**

1. What is some information you can find on a traffic ticket?

2. If you do not believe that you are guilty of a civil violation, what can you do?

3. What can happen if you get too many points against your license in a certain period of time?

4. What could happen if you don't appear in court when you are required to?

B **GROUPS. Read the sentences below. Check (✓) the sentence in each item that is an inference based on the reading. Discuss why it is an inference and the other sentence is not.**

1. ☐ a. Different counties may have different procedures for responding to a traffic ticket.

   ☐ b. There is information on both the back and the front of a ticket.

2. ☐ a. In a civil case, you don't have the right to request a jury trial.

   ☐ b. Bench warrants are unfair.

> **Reading Skill:** Making Inferences
>
> When you make an inference, you make a logical guess about something that is not directly stated in the text, based on other information that is provided. In other words, you "fill in" information.

4 **WORD WORK**

📝 **GROUPS. Choose three words or phrases in the handout that you would like to remember. Discuss the words and their meanings. Then record the words and information about them in your vocabulary log.**

5 **MAKE IT PERSONAL**

GROUPS. Read the paragraph. Discuss. Do you think the system for paying fines is fair? If not, what improvements would you suggest?

Sometimes, without the money to pay a fine, poor people fail to go to court when they are required to. Other times, they just don't pay their fine in time. A warrant is issued for their arrest, and, in the end, they go to jail. Keeping people in jail costs taxpayers a lot of money. Some people think this is not a good system. However, other people think it would be unfair to fine different people differently. They believe that the law is the law and that the penalty should be the same for anyone who breaks it.

Listening and Speaking

1 BEFORE YOU LISTEN

A CLASS. The box below contains a list of crimes in the U.S. Discuss the words in the box and their meanings. If you don't know the meaning of a word, look it up in a dictionary.

arson	murder	shoplifting
burglary	rape	trespassing
illegal drug use	robbery	vandalism

B CLASS. In your home country, what happens to people who are guilty of the crimes above?

C GROUPS. Now try to put the words from Exercise A into the correct categories in the chart. You can check your chart when you listen in Exercises 2A and 2B.

Misdemeanors (less serious)	Felonies (more serious)

2 LISTEN

A CD3 T7 Listen to the lecture about types of crimes. Check your answers in Exercise 1C.

B CD3 T7 Listen again. Then write the answers to the questions.

1. What are two examples of infractions?
   traffic violations, littering

2. What is the longest prison sentence that can be given for a misdemeanor?

3. What are some other penalties for misdemeanors?

4. What if someone doesn't have money to pay a fine?

5. How long can a person be sentenced to prison for a felony?

6. What is another sentence that is possible for some types of felonies in some states?

PRACTICE

Complete the paragraph with the words from the box.

crimes	infractions	penalty	sentences
death	misdemeanor	prison	serious

Our state divides ___*crimes*___ into three categories: infractions, misdemeanors,

and felonies. _____ are the least serious crimes. Felonies are the most

_____. The _____ for an infraction is just a fine. No jail or _____

time is involved. For a _____, a jail sentence of up to one year is possible, along

with a fine. For most felonies, people receive prison _____. In this state, we

don't have a _____ penalty. The most severe penalty is life in prison.

4 **CONVERSATION**

GROUPS. Practice the conversation. Notice the boldfaced phrases used to qualify opinions.

A: Do you think a person should go to jail for shoplifting?

B: Not **unless** they've shoplifted before. **If** it's a first offense, I think the penalty should just be a small fine.

C: Well, **it depends**. **If** someone steals something small, maybe a small fine is OK. **If** someone steals something very valuable, I don't think the fine should be small.

B: Well, **it** also **depends on** the reason for shoplifting. I don't think the penalty should be severe **if** a hungry person steals food or **if** someone with mental problems steals something small. But I think the fine could be bigger **if** someone steals something like makeup or a CD or DVD.

A: I agree. And **it** also **depends on whether** the person is a child or an adult. For children or teenagers, I think that community service or counseling would be the best response.

> **Communication Skill:**
> Qualifying Opinions
>
> Sometimes when we give an opinion, we want to leave room for exceptions, or we want to indicate that we would need more information before committing to a strong opinion. We want to make it clear that in some cases our opinion might be different. We can do this by using *unless, if,* or *it depends (on)/(whether)*.

5 **MAKE IT PERSONAL**

GROUPS. Discuss. What do you think would be an appropriate fine or sentence for committing each crime in Exercise 1A? Use the Communication Skill box to help present your opinion.

Reading

1 BEFORE YOU READ

CLASS. Discuss. Have you ever paid a fine for overdue or lost library materials? If so, how much was the fine? What happens if you return the materials but you don't pay the fine when you return them?

2 READ

CD3 T8

Listen to and read the newspaper article. How did Keely Givhan end up in jail for failing to pay a library fine?

Ju$t Fine

Keely Givhan was **pulled over** by a police officer because the lightbulb above her license plate was out. When the officer checked her name in the computer system, he found a warrant for her arrest. She was taken straight to Rock County Jail.

Why was there a warrant out for Givhan, a mother and a student at Blackhawk Technical College? It started with late fines on library books. The Beloit Public Library sends three **overdue notices**: the first when materials are two weeks late, the second when they are four weeks late, and the third when they are six weeks late. After the

third notice, a citation (a notice to appear in court) is sent. And failure to appear in court can lead to a warrant for a person's arrest.

Givhan said that she didn't know there was a warrant out for her arrest and that she never received the overdue notices. "I was moving, so I returned some of the things late," said Givhan. "Because I was moving, I didn't receive the notices. I had a fine and didn't know."

At the time she was taken to jail, Givhan owed $172 in court fees as well as $152 in fines from the library. Unable to pay this amount, Givhan spent six days in the county jail.

One of Givhan's professors, Linda Griesman Christopherson, thought her punishment was a bit **harsh**. "This young woman is working really hard to better her life. She has a little boy, and it'd be nice if he could have a good feeling about the library," she said. "Sure, they send letters, but I think they should make a phone call, too."

But Beloit Police Captain Bill Tyler said a fine is a fine. "If someone has a fine they don't pay—let's say I have a traffic ticket for speeding, and you don't pay that—a warrant can be issued for your arrest."

Library director Dan Zach offered his opinion, too, about not returning library books. "It's no different from walking into a retail store and walking out with the **merchandise**." He said that 75 percent of late **materials** are usually returned after the first notice is sent out and that the second and third notices usually bring back the rest of the materials. "This is a free public library," he said. "All the people have this whole building full of wonderful materials they can check out. They get a card at no cost. It's like a credit card for the library. People can check out thousands of dollars of materials every year. All we ask is that they bring everything back."

Source: http://www.4to40.com/newsat4/index.asp?id=1466

3 CHECK YOUR UNDERSTANDING

Circle the letter of the sentence in each pair that is most accurate.

1. a. The police officer stopped Keely Givhan because there was a warrant for her arrest.

   b. The police officer stopped Keely Givhan for a traffic violation.

2. a. Keely Givhan was arrested because she didn't return library books.

   b. Keely Givhan was arrested because she did not make required appearances in court.

3. a. Keely Givhan said that she didn't receive the notices because she was moving when they were sent.

   b. Keely Givhan said that she received the notices but she didn't have time to pay the fines because she was moving.

4. a. Professor Christopherson and Police Captain Tyler thought the punishment was a bit harsh.

   b. Police Captain Tyler and Library director Dan Zach thought the punishment was justified.

4 WORD WORK

GROUPS. **Choose three words or phrases in the article that you would like to remember. Discuss the words and their meanings. Then record the words and information about them in your vocabulary log.**

5 MAKE IT PERSONAL

GROUPS. **Discuss the questions.**

1. Do you think the library had a responsibility to try to phone Keely?

2. It takes taxpayers' money to question someone at the police station and to hold them in jail for six days—much more money than the cost of the library materials. If you were a taxpayer in this county and city, would you agree that keeping Keely in jail was a good use of your money? Explain.

3. Do you agree with the library director that not returning library books is the same as stealing something from a retail store? Why or why not?

4. Do you think that putting Keely in jail will help prevent people in her community from returning books late or failing to pay fines? Explain.

Compare and contrast two legal systems

Writing

1 BEFORE YOU WRITE

A You are going to compare and contrast the legal systems in your home country and the U.S. Read about essays that compare and contrast. Then read the writing tip.

FYI ABOUT ESSAYS THAT COMPARE AND CONTRAST

You will often be asked to compare and contrast two people, places, or things. When you compare, you show how two items are similar; when you contrast, you show how they are different. To write an essay that compares and contrasts choose two topics that have points of similarity and difference. Structure the essay in a simple and logical way. One easy way is to discuss all the similarities in one paragraph and all of the differences in another paragraph.

Writing Tip: **Showing similarities and differences**

Certain words let readers know that you are comparing or contrasting. Use the words *alike, too, both, also, the same,* and *similarly* to show similarities. Use the words *but, yet, in contrast, on the contrary,* and *however* to show differences.

B Brainstorm about the writing topic. Ask yourself: How are the legal systems in my home country and the U.S. similar? How are they different? Think of specific points of comparison and contrast. Then list them.

C Read the writing model on page 209. What does Anand compare and contrast?

2 ANALYZE THE WRITING MODEL

PAIRS. Discuss the questions.

1. What similarities does Anand identify between the legal systems of his home country and the U.S.?

2. What main difference does he present?

3. Which words does Anand use to show readers that he is making comparisons and contrasts?

THINK ON PAPER

A Before Anand wrote his essay, he used a Venn diagram to organize his points of comparison and contrast. Study the diagram. Where has he placed the similarities?

India's Legal System   **U.S. Legal System**

Judge decides verdict in trials

Common laws

Independent Judiciary

Juries decide verdicts in most trials

B Reread the notes you made about legal systems in your home country and the U.S. in Exercise 1B. Use them to create a Venn diagram like Anand's for your essay.

C **PAIRS.** Share your Venn diagrams and give each other feedback. For a short essay, you may need to narrow your topic. If so, cross out any ideas you decide not to use. Discuss your reasons.

4 **WRITE**

Use your Venn diagram to write an essay that compares and contrasts the legal systems in your home country and the U.S.

5 **CHECK YOUR WRITING**

A STEP 1. Revise your work.

1. Does your essay present points of similarity and difference?
2. Is your essay structured in a logical way?
3. Have you included words that show readers that you are comparing and contrasting?

B STEP 2. Edit and proofread.

1. Have you checked your spelling, grammar, and punctuation?
2. Have you proofread for typing errors?

1 REVIEW For your grammar review, go to page 230.

2 ACT IT OUT What do you say?

GROUPS. You are telling two newcomers from your home country about the rights people have in the U.S.

> **Student A:** Review Lesson 1. Tell the newcomers about the importance of the *Miranda* warning and the rights of people accused of crimes.

> **Student B:** Review Lesson 3. Explain about the history of the right to vote in the U.S., including when and how blacks, Native Americans, and women got the right to vote.

> **Student C:** Review Lesson 4. Tell the newcomers how federal and state laws define sexual harassment in the workplace.

3 READ AND REACT Problem-solving

STEP 1. **Read about Arturo.**

Arturo is afraid that the couple that lives next door may be abusing their two-year-old son physically and emotionally. Arturo often hears the parents screaming at their child, and the boy sometimes has bruises on his arms and legs. Arturo hasn't actually observed the parents hitting the child, but he has noticed how they ignore him much of the time. One day they left the boy alone in the front yard. He ran out into the street, and Arturo had to catch him. The couple joked about what had happened, but they didn't seem very concerned.

STEP 2. GROUPS. **What is Arturo's problem? What can he do?**

4 CONNECT For your Study Skills Activity, go to page 219.

Which goals can you check off? Go back to page 145.

Saving the Planet

Preview

What are the father and daughter doing? Do people do this in your home country?

UNIT GOALS

- ☐ Discuss recycling rules
- ☐ Discuss carpooling
- ☐ Note causes and effects of environmental problems
- ☐ Identify ways to protect the environment

Reading

1 BEFORE YOU READ

CLASS. A *carbon footprint* is the amount of carbon dioxide (CO_2) put into the atmosphere by a country, organization, or individual. Discuss. What do you know about reducing your carbon footprint?

2 READ

CD3 T9

Listen to and read the article about ways to protect the environment—and save money. What is the green route?

Taking the Green Route

In the past, our ancestors lived without having much of an **impact** on the planet. Today, however, we're not only using up our **natural resources**, we're also **polluting** our planet. What can we do to save the world for future **generations**? Can we work to reduce our carbon footprints—and our spending, too? Here are four tips designed to help us live— and save—green!

LOOK AT YOUR LIGHTING!

The best rule in using lights (and any **electrical appliance**) is to turn them off when they're not in use. But there's more: Although **energy-efficient** lightbulbs cost more, they make it up by having a longer life and using less

energy. Besides, these bulbs are tough and they don't **emit** the dangerous heat that the traditional lightbulbs do. All in all, energy-efficient lightbulbs can assist your pocketbook as well as **the environment**!

MIND THE DRIPS!

Make sure you repair dripping **faucets**. Would you believe that a slow, steady drip of water (100 drops per minute) wastes 330 gallons of water in a month? That adds up to wasting nearly 4,000 gallons per year! Keeping an eye on your faucets

will not only help **conserve** nature's precious resource but will also save you money on your water bill. When you do your laundry, make sure you only run the machine when it's full. And though many of us love relaxing baths, they often use much more water—and energy to heat this water—than a shower does. You can also save by not letting the water run while doing dishes or brushing your teeth.

SAVE A TREE!

Another money and environment saver is online bill paying. If you pay your bills online—which is now both convenient and safe—you eliminate the cost of stamps and a lot of paper. Furthermore, with online bill paying, companies tell you when it's time to pay your bills so that you can avoid charges for late payments. More paper can be saved by checking bank and credit card balances online and never printing these out.

TAKE A HIKE—OR YOUR BIKE!

Walking—or biking—is better than driving your car for both you and the environment. In addition to saving big dollars on gasoline, you'll get the exercise you need. If your job is far from home, try to find people to carpool with or use **public transportation**. If you do have to drive your car to work or school, organize your schedule so that you can pick up items you need—like groceries—on the way home, instead of making another trip. Remember that energy-efficient transportation always includes options such as buses and subways.

3 CHECK YOUR UNDERSTANDING

Write the answers to the questions.

1. What can you replace in your home to save money and electricity?

2. How much water can a dripping faucet waste per month? Per year?

3. How can you save money, time, and paper when it comes to paying bills?

4. If your job is far from your home, what are tips for getting there in a way that will save money and protect the environment?

5. How else can you save money on gasoline and help to preserve the environment?

4 WORD WORK

GROUPS. Choose three words or phrases in the article that you would like to remember. Discuss the words and their meanings. Then record the words and information about them in your vocabulary log.

Show what you know! Protect the environment—and save money

STEP 1. PAIRS. Take turns asking and answering the questions.

1. Which of the tips in the reading do you currently practice?

2. Which ones could you easily adopt?

3. Of the tips mentioned, which one is the most difficult for you to do? Explain.

STEP 2. GROUPS. Brainstorm: Add two or three additional suggestions for each category discussed in the article.

Life Skills

1 INTERPRET A RECYCLING CALENDAR

A CLASS. Discuss recycling (reusing certain types of garbage). What, if anything, is recycled in your community? Some communities have calendars with information about what, when, and how to recycle. Do you have a recycling calendar? If so, how easy or hard is it to follow?

B PAIRS. Read the following calendar, key, and list of recyclable items. Discuss. What kinds of information do the calendar and key contain? What does the list of recyclable items explain?

April 2010

Sunday	Monday	Tuesday	Wednesday	Thursday	Friday	Saturday
				1 GN	2 GS	3 Community Computer & Electronics Recycling Event
4 GN	5 GN	6 GS	7 Recycling–**P**	8 GN	9 GS	10 City Household Hazardous Waste Drop-Off
11 GN	12 GN	13 GS	14 Recycling–**C**	15 GN	16 GS	17 Citizen Scrap Tire Drop-Off Day
18 GN	19 GN	20 GS	21 Recycling–**P**	22 GN	23 GS	24
25 GN	26 GN	27 GS	28 Recycling–**C**	29 GN	30 GS	

GN—Garbage and trash, North End Zone	**P**—Paper
GS—Garbage and trash, South End Zone	**C**—Commingled (= mixed)

RECYCLABLE ITEMS

Paper
- Newspaper
- Magazines
- Phone books
- Catalogs
- Junk mail
- Office paper
- Boxes—folded and flattened (one box inside the other or tied)

- Place untied in bin (no larger than 33 gallons) or boxes

Commingled

Metal:
- Drink containers
- Food and soup cans
- Pet food cans

- Food trays and tins
- Clean aluminum foil

Plastic:
- Number 1 or 2 on bottom of container
- Shampoo containers
- Milk and juice containers

- Laundry detergent containers
- Soda, water containers (put caps in trash)

Glass:
- Brown, green, and clean containers (any size)

---

2 PRACTICE

PAIRS. Use the calendar, key, and list of recyclable items to answer the questions.

1. What days should people who live in the North End Zone leave their garbage out for collection? What about people from the South End Zone?

   North End: Sunday, Monday, and Thursday; South End: Tuesday and Friday

2. What are commingled items?

   _____

3. On which dates are commingled items recyclable?

   _____

4. When can residents recycle paper?

   _____

5. How should paper be prepared for recycling?

   _____

6. When can computers and other electronic items be recycled?

   _____

7. On what date can residents recycle scrap tires?

   _____

Can you... discuss recycling rules? ☐

Listening and Speaking

1 BEFORE YOU LISTEN

A CLASS. "Greening" refers to efforts to save resources and protect the environment. Do you know of any efforts to "green" your community? If so, describe them. If not, can you suggest any?

B CLASS. Discuss. Have you ever heard of carpooling? What does it mean?

C PAIRS. Discuss the advantages and disadvantages of carpooling. Use your conversation to complete the chart.

Example:
A: *Carpooling is definitely cheaper.*
B: *Sure, but on the other hand, you might not be able to leave home when you want to!*

Advantages	Disadvantages
It's much cheaper.	You might not be able to leave (home or work) when you want to.

D CLASS. Compare your ideas with the rest of the class.

2 LISTEN

CD3 T10

A Listen to a talk show host interviewing a city council member about a carpooling program. Write the answers to the questions.

1. According to Councilwoman Frank, how many gallons of gas could be saved each day in the U.S. by carpooling?

2. If people used carpools, how much less carbon dioxide would be emitted each day?

B 🎧 **Listen again and take notes. Complete the chart.**

How Councilwoman Frank Is Greening Her City
First step: *educate people about the consequences of not doing certain things.*
An example of her efforts:
How people participate online:
How people participate by phone:
A third option:
Where people can get more information:

3 **PRACTICE**

CLASS. **Imagine that you want to start greening your own community. Read the four tips. Discuss. What suggestions can you add to these tips?**

Tips for Greening Your Community

- **Connect with your community**

To help green your community, you have to be a part of it! Talk to your neighbors, find out what's going on around you, and get involved. Then create a community action plan in order to make some changes.

- **Buy locally**

If you shop locally, you reduce food miles (the food doesn't need to travel so far) and it keeps resources in the community. Plus, it's a great way to get to know your neighbors. When did you last chat with the person who grew your tomatoes?

- **Buy (and sell) used items**

Help save natural resources by taking items and clothes that are no longer needed to a second-hand store. (A second-hand store is a place where people can buy donated items at a cheaper price than if they were to buy them brand new.)

- **Organize a community clean-up day**

Work with your friends and neighbors to clean up an area of your community—like one of the parks, or even a section of your city.

Source: ©2008 Planet Green, www.PlanetGreen.com

4 **MAKE IT PERSONAL**

A PAIRS. **Pick one particular way that you would like to improve your school and/or community. Then talk about what to do in order to tell people about it and make some changes happen.**

B GROUPS. **Meet with another pair and take turns presenting the ideas you came up with and the steps needed to make them happen.**

Reading

1   BEFORE YOU READ

CLASS. Discuss. When have you read or written a blog? What are some topics people write about in their blogs?

2   READ

CD3 T11

Listen to and read the blog entry about recycling. What does Todd learn while in Sweden?

http://www.toddskinner.com

Recycling According to the Swedes

September 15, 2010	by Todd Skinner

Time is flying. It's been two months since I arrived here to visit my relatives, and in some ways it seems as if the time has been short, but in other ways I feel as if it's been years. Clearly, this is not California—I miss my family, my friends, and the sun. However, I am happy and grateful to have this experience because I'm constantly learning.

So much is new and different. It's funny how many things you discover about yourself—and your culture—when you live in a new country. Just yesterday I was talking with my "new" family about recycling. Recycling is something the Swedes are very serious about.

The crazy thing is that I thought we—my family/community and I—took recycling seriously. Now I've learned that when it comes to recycling, the U.S. definitely has a lot to learn from Sweden.

In Sweden, there were so many bins, and rules, and instructions. Actually, I found it overwhelming!

But now, after these past eight weeks, I'm finally beginning to understand what and how to recycle. In the U.S., we mostly recycled cans and bottles, but here in Sweden they do so much more. Most homes have several trash bins for different kinds of trash: batteries, **biodegradables**, wood, colored glass, clear glass, **aluminum**, other metals, newspapers, hard paper (like cardboard) and other paper that doesn't fit these two **categories**, and plastics of all sorts.

Honestly, I wish I had known more about recycling before I came to Sweden. If there's one thing I would like to change when I get home, it's our recycling rules; I think we need to learn from the Swedes, and be more aware of our trash—and our future.

Post your comments

Name: _____   E-mail: _____

Location: _____   Message: _____

CHECK YOUR UNDERSTANDING

Write the answers to the questions.

1. Where is this blogger from? How long has he been way from home?

   _____

2. What is a benefit of living in another country, according to Todd?

   _____

3. How is recycling different in the U.S. than it is in Sweden?

   _____

4. What was hard for Todd to understand at first?

   _____

5. What would Todd like to change about his hometown?

   _____

4 **WORD WORK**

☑ GROUPS. **Choose three words or phrases in the blog entry that you would like to remember. Discuss the words and their meanings. Then record the words and information about them in your vocabulary log.**

5 **MAKE IT PERSONAL**

GROUPS. **Discuss the questions.**

1. What are some of the recycling rules in your home country? Are there any that you follow here? If so, what are they?

2. Do you think that everyone should recycle their trash? Why or why not?

3. Is there anything that would help the environment—like recycling—that you would like to "bring" to your home country?

4. Is there anything that you wish you had known about recycling before coming to the U.S.?

5. If you were going to write a blog about your cross-cultural experiences, what would you would write about?

Reading

1 BEFORE YOU READ

CLASS. Discuss. How is our environment being affected by things we do on a daily basis?

2 READ

CD3 T12

Listen to and read the article. How is our environment changing?

How Daily Life Is Changing Our World

Have you noticed that the weather seems crazy lately? Do you feel as if it's getting warmer every year? Scientists who study these things believe that many of the environmental changes that are happening now have speeded up because of human activities. Here are five aspects of our lives that are causing problems.

ELECTRICITY

Most of the electricity we use comes from **power plants** that run on **fossil fuels** (especially coal) and are responsible for emitting huge amounts of **greenhouse gases** and other pollutants.

WASTE

We produce large quantities of waste, and a lot of this is in the form of plastics that remain in the environment forever. Since 1960, the amount of waste produced in America has nearly tripled. In fact, Americans produce 251.3 million tons of garbage per year, much of which contributes to land and water pollution.

FORESTS AND TREES

We use a huge amount of paper made from wood, which is also used in large quantities for building houses. This means that large areas of forest have to be cut down. Trees that are cut down can no longer **absorb** carbon dioxide (CO_2) from the **atmosphere**, and as they

decay, they add new CO_2 to the air.

TRANSPORTATION

Most types of transportation that are used to move people and goods from one place to another run on fossil fuels, such as oil and gas. This type of fuel is responsible for a great deal of our **current** air pollution.

AGRICULTURE

Because the land that we can use for **agriculture** is limited (and getting smaller because of population growth), new varieties of **crops** are being grown to increase agricultural production. However, these crops require large quantities of **fertilizers**, and more fertilizer means more emissions of nitrous oxide, which is a greenhouse gas that contributes to **global warming**. Also, the fertilizer sometimes gets into our water systems and causes more pollution.

3 CHECK YOUR UNDERSTANDING

A **PAIRS.** Write the answers to the questions. Then compare your answers.

1. What is the main source of power in most urban areas?

2. Why are fossil fuels a problem?

3. How much garbage do Americans produce annually?

4. How are most goods and people moved from one place to another?

5. What is one of the consequences of an increasing population?

B Use the information in the article to complete the chart.

Causes	Effects
use of power (electricity)	greenhouse gases in atmosphere
producing large amounts of waste	
cutting down forests	
using oil and gas	
using large amounts of fertilizer	

C **GROUPS.** Compare your charts. Discuss. Do you think that rules or laws can solve the problems listed in the article? Why or why not? What are some other ways that we can work to preserve our planet?

4 WORD WORK

✐ **GROUPS.** Choose three words or phrases in the article that you would like to remember. Discuss the words and their meanings. Then record the words and information about them in your vocabulary log.

Show what you know! Note causes and effects of environmental problems

GROUPS. Talk about specific environmental problems in your community and changes that could improve them.

Can you... note causes and effects of environmental problems? ☐

Talk about doing your share for the environment

Listening and Speaking

1 BEFORE YOU LISTEN

A **CLASS.** Discuss. Does this picture look familiar to you? Do you or your neighbors have bins like these?

B What do you do in these situations? Write the answers to the questions.

1. You've just finished drinking a can of soda in the park.

   You put it in the recycling bin.

2. You have just received a lot of junk mail (advertisements and useless information).

3. You've finished making a salad and have lots of vegetable peelings.

4. You have children's clothing that no longer fits.

C **GROUPS.** Discuss. Compare your answers. Which answers are best for the environment? Why?

2 LISTEN

CD3 T13

Listen to a conversation between two neighbors talking about recycling and answer the questions.

1. Does Joseph think that it's important to recycle?

2. What's Hector's tip for figuring out which items are recycled on which days?

3. Were the regulations the same for recycling where Joseph used to live?

4. What does Joseph wish about the rules in his former town?

5. What does Hector wish he had done differently?

6. Who is Joseph's big helper? How does he help?

7. Who taught Hector about the three Rs?

8. What does Joseph say about his parents and recycling?

3 PRACTICE

GROUPS. Hector mentions the three Rs (reduce, reuse, and recycle). These are ways that you can help the environment and also save money. What are some examples of each? Write your ideas and share them.

Examples:

Reduce (use less of):   Use lunch boxes (again and again) instead of buying brown bags.

Reuse (use again):   Use heavy boxes from the store for storage instead of buying boxes.

Recycle: Return cans and get cash back.

Reduce

_____

_____

_____

Reuse

_____

_____

_____

Recycle

_____

_____

_____

4 MAKE IT PERSONAL

GROUPS. Do any of the suggestions about how to improve the environment differ from what you heard in your home country? Compare and contrast some ways people deal with environmental issues here and in your home country.

Communication Skill:
Expressing Comparison and Contrast

Here are some expressions you can use to compare and contrast.

Words for comparing: *also, similarly, in the same way, like, still, at the same time*

Words for contrasting: *instead, however, on the other hand, on/to the contrary, yet, but, in contrast*

Grammar

The Past Subjunctive with *Wish*

Actual Situation (the Facts)	Expressing Regret
They didn't start recycling years ago.	I **wish** (that) we **had started** recycling years ago.
When he lived in his old town, they had different recycling rules.	I just **wish** (that) we **had had** these types of recycling rules back in my old town.
They weren't as educated then about waste as they are now.	I **wish** (that) we **had been** more educated about the amount of waste we generated.

The Past Unreal Conditional

Actual Situation	Conditional	
	If Clause	Result Clause
Our parents **weren't aware** of the damage they were doing, so they **didn't do** things differently.	If our parents **had been aware** of the damage they were doing,	they **would have done** things differently.
I **didn't know** that before, so I **had** trouble.	If I **had known** that before,	I **wouldn't have had** trouble.

Grammar Watch

- To form the past subjunctive with *wish*, use *wish* + *had* + past participle.
- Use the past subjunctive with *wish* to talk about a past situation you regret (feel bad or are sad about).
- After *wish*, *that* is optional (and is usually omitted when speaking).

For a list of past participles for irregular verbs, see page 225.

Grammar Watch

- A conditional sentence has an *if* clause describing a condition and a result clause describing a result of that condition.
- To form the past unreal conditional, use the past perfect in the *if* clause and *could*, *might*, or *would* + *have* + past participle in the result clause.
- Use the past unreal conditional:
  - to talk about unreal situations in the past.
  - to describe what you would have done differently or how something could have happened differently.

1 PRACTICE

Read the dialogue. Underline sentences that contain examples of the past subjunctive with *wish*. Double underline sentences that contain examples of the past unreal conditional.

Ilya: Did you hear about the government's plan for getting rid of nuclear waste?

Rosa: Yeah. They're going to bury it under a mountain in Nevada. There are earthquakes in those Nevada mountains! <u>I wish they had thought of a better solution.</u>

Ilya: You know, I wish they had never built those plants in the first place. <u>I'll bet if they had known what we know now, they wouldn't have built them.</u>

Rosa: Maybe you're right, but if they hadn't built nuclear plants, they would have built more plants that use coal, and they're big polluters.

Ilya: What a mess! I wish we didn't need so much electricity!

Rosa: Really? Just try doing without it for a few days!

A Read the sentences about actual situations. Use *wish* + the past subjunctive to explain that the people regret those situations.

1. Lupita threw away a lot of plastic containers.

   Lupita wishes she had recycled the containers instead.

2. Andrei didn't reuse any of the boxes from the supermarket.

   _____

3. Maria didn't return any of the cans.

   _____

4. Nicholas put his batteries in the trash.

   _____

B Complete the sentences using the past unreal conditional.

1. Many families would have used less electricity if they _____
   (know)
   how much pollution power plants caused.

2. They would have been better informed about recycling if someone

   _____ them when they were in school.
   (teach)

3. She would have carpooled to work if there _____ other people
   (be)
   in her neighborhood who worked at her company.

4. If we had known about the causes of climate change 100 years ago, we

   _____ many of the ways we do things.
   (change)

Show what you know!   Identify ways to protect the environment

STEP 1. **Based on what you have learned, make a list of ways to improve the environment.**

STEP 2. **Take notes about how you might have done something differently had you known before what you know now.**

STEP 3. **GROUPS. Use your notes from Step 2 to discuss what you might have done differently.**

Can you…identify ways to protect the environment? ☐

Reading

1 BEFORE YOU READ

CLASS. **Imagine that you are designing and building an entirely "green" community. Discuss. What would the houses and streets look like?**

2 READ

CD3 T14

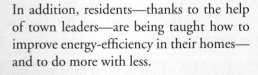

Listen to and read the article. What happened in Greensburg? What is occurring as a result?

> **Reading Skill:**
> Using Visuals
>
> Using visuals—such as photographs and drawings—will help you better understand what you read. Notice what the visual shows. Read any labels or captions carefully. Sometimes a visual will give information that is not in the text.

The Greening of Greensburg, Kansas

Greensburg was not always a green city. In fact, most of the town contained **traditional** houses and public buildings, like many other villages in the central U.S. However, on May 4, 2007, Greensburg was nearly destroyed by a tornado. On that day, a **twister** struck the town of about 1,500, killing nine **residents** and destroying most of Greensburg's homes and businesses.

Today, Greensburg is being rebuilt. Only this time, it will go green. **Civic leaders** and environmentalists are **reconstructing** the town with features that will make it a model environmentally friendly community. Wind **turbines,** tinted windows, and water-saving toilets are just a few of the elements the new buildings will have. The Leadership in Energy and Environmental Design (LEED) Green Building Rating System is a program that sets construction standards for environmentally friendly buildings. The town has decided to follow the very strict LEED **standards** for energy-efficient design, which is expensive but will bring about a 30 to 50 percent savings on energy bills.

Greensburg before

Greensburg after

Here are some of the other changes that are being made as Greensburg is reconstructed:

- Homeowners and businesses are being encouraged to think about energy-saving lights and rainwater-collection systems.
  - Nearly forty families were advised to rebuild with extra **insulation**, double-pane windows, and high-efficiency compact fluorescent lights.
  - Homes will use **solar energy** for heat and light.
  - Builders are being encouraged to use local recycled building materials.
  - Residents are being encouraged to use native plants that don't need so much watering and that give natural shade.

In addition, residents—thanks to the help of town leaders—are being taught how to improve energy-efficiency in their homes—and to do more with less.

Of course, nothing can replace the awful loss caused by such a disaster, but it certainly seems that Greensburg is coming back with great promise for the future.

A Write the answers to the questions.

1. What was the event that so greatly changed Greensburg?
2. What were the consequences of that event?
3. How much can Greensburg save on energy bills because of strict LEED building standards?
4. What are Greensburg's homeowners and businesses being encouraged to do?
5. What materials are the builders being encouraged to use?
6. What kinds of plants are Greensburg's residents being encouraged to grow?
7. What else are the residents being taught?

B PAIRS. Write the answers to the questions. Compare your answers.

1. When did the disaster in Greensburg take place?
2. What was the population of Greensburg before the disaster struck?
3. What kinds of toilets are being included in many of the new buildings?
4. What kind of windows were some families advised to use in rebuilding?

C GROUPS. The people of Greensburg are making the best of a difficult situation and using it as an opportunity to make positive changes. Discuss a similar example of a positive—or good—result that has come out of a negative—or bad—event.

4 WORD WORK

GROUPS. Choose three words or phrases in the article that you would like to remember. Discuss the words and their meanings. Then record the words and information about them in your vocabulary log.

Show what you know! Discuss how to green a community

GROUPS. Discuss what you have learned about greening a community. Which methods do you think are most useful and which are least useful? Why? Are such methods being used in your community? If so, are they working? If not, should they be used?

Write a personal narrative about the environment

Writing

1 BEFORE YOU WRITE

A You are going to write a personal narrative, or story, about how you have tried to help the environment. Read about personal narratives. Then read the writing tip.

FYI ABOUT PERSONAL NARRATIVES

Personal narratives are a type of essay that tells a story. They have a relaxed tone and style, and usually reveal the personality of the writer. You can write a personal narrative about almost any topic, from your experiences in an English class to a visit with a relative. The narrative can be about a person, place, event, or issue. It can include memories, ideas, and details that appeal to the five senses (sight, hearing, taste, touch, and smell).

Writing Tip: Using time order

One way to structure a personal narrative is to use chronological order, or time order. To let readers know the order in which events occurred, you can use these words and phrases: *for a long time, before, a month ago, later, soon, as soon as, afterwards, ever since,* and *since then.*

B Brainstorm about the writing topic. Ask yourself: Have I planted trees, grown my own vegetables, or ridden a bicycle instead of driving a car? Do I follow local recycling rules and reuse plastic containers? Think about ways that you have tried to avoid waste and have had a positive effect on the environment. List them.

C Read the writing model of a personal narrative on page 210. How is Anka's narrative structured?

2 ANALYZE THE WRITING MODEL

PAIRS. Discuss the questions.

1. What is this personal narrative about?

2. What are some of the steps Anka has taken to help the environment?

3. What words has she used to let readers know the sequence in which events occurred? Give three or four examples.

3 THINK ON PAPER

A Before Anka wrote her personal narrative, she used a chart to arrange the events. Notice how Anka puts events in a logical order.

> My kids started learning about the environment. Got me interested, too.

↓

> I began to make changes to reduce my carbon footprint.

↓

> A few months ago, my son suggested that I use cloth bags for groceries.

↓

> Soon, I began to recycle as much as possible.

↓

> Finally, I decided to drive more slowly and use the car air conditioner sparingly so I would save money and gas.

B Use the notes you made in Exercise 1B about how you have helped protect the environment. Use them to make a chart for your personal narrative. You can use a chart like Anka's or some other graphic organizer.

4 WRITE

Use your graphic organizer to write a personal narrative about how you have helped the environment. Be sure to use words to show readers the sequence in which events happened.

5 CHECK YOUR WRITING

A STEP 1. **Revise your work.**

1. Is your narrative in a logical order?
2. Does it have a casual tone and style that expresses your personality?
3. Is the sequence of events clear?

B STEP 2. **Edit and proofread.**

1. Have you checked your spelling, grammar, and punctuation?
2. Have you proofread for typing errors?

1 REVIEW   For your grammar review, go to page 231.

2 ACT IT OUT   What do you say?

GROUPS. You are part of a panel discussion about ways to improve your community's environment. Present information and discuss your opinions about the issue.

Student A: Review Lessons 1 and 5. Tell the rest of the panel about the causes and effects of common environmental problems. Explain what *carbon footprint* means. Describe simple ways that people can reduce their carbon footprint.

Student B: Review Lessons 3 and 6. Add to what Student A has said by explaining some tips for greening a community, including carpooling.

Student C: Review Lessons 2 and 4. Add to the discussion by talking about the importance of recycling. Before you begin, write a comment about Todd Skinner's blog entry. Read it aloud and discuss your ideas with Students A and B.

3 READ AND REACT   Problem-solving

STEP 1. Read about Francesca.

Francesca has just been promoted to office manager at a small newspaper in a suburban town. Most of the employees live close by, but they drive to work. She has been asked to make the office more green and energy-efficient. Although she doesn't have a lot of money to spend on changing the physical office space, she must reduce the money and energy the company uses for lighting, water, paper, and transportation. She also has to improve the company's recycling practices.

STEP 2. GROUPS. What is Francesca's problem? What can she do?

4 CONNECT   For your Study Skills Activity, go to page 220.

Which goals can you check off? Go back to page 165.

Technology

Preview

How has the Internet changed how we connect with one another? What happens when you turn on a computer or send a text message or an e-mail?

UNIT GOALS

- ☐ Understand how to use an instruction manual

- ☐ Discuss the pros and cons of the Internet

- ☐ Discuss virtual training

- ☐ Identify how technology affects our daily lives

Listening and Speaking

1 BEFORE YOU LISTEN

A CLASS. Discuss. Do you use the Internet? If so, what do you use it for? How often do you use it?

B PAIRS. Discuss the meanings of the words in the box. If you don't know the meaning of a word, look it up in a dictionary.

analyze	data	psychologist	vision
calculator	network	store (v)	

2 LISTEN

CD3 T15

A 🔊 An instructor at a community college is giving a lecture on the history of the Internet to the students in her Technology and Society class. As you listen to her lecture, take notes. Use the example notes below as a guide.

> I. Internet grew out of Licklider's unique idea/vision of the future
>
> A. In 1940s, J. C. R. Licklider—experimental psychologist—had different view of computers
>
> B. He collected and analyzed data with computers; thought computers were more than fancy calculators
>
> C. He wanted to use computers as a communications tool, one that would allow computers and humans to work together
>
> D. He envisioned "thinking centers" for storing and finding information; something like libraries, but larger and connected to one another and to individual people in a network
>
> II. Today's Internet is very similar to Licklider's ideas

CD3 T15

B 🔊 PAIRS. Listen again and check your notes. Then compare them with a partner's. Did you both include the same information? Could you both pass a test on the lecture by studying your notes? Why or why not?

3 PRACTICE

A Review your notes and write the answers to the questions.

1. What was the profession of most people working on early computers?

2. What did they see computers as?

3. What was Licklider's profession?

4. What did he want to use computers for?

5. What did Licklider want to find a better way for humans and computers to do?

6. Why did he think that humans and computers could do more working together than either could do alone?

7. What did Licklider call his early version of networks?

Early computers were usually just powerful calculating machines.

B PAIRS. Discuss. What surprised you about the lecture?

4 MAKE IT PERSONAL

GROUPS. Read these quotes taken from some of Licklider's writings. Discuss the questions that follow each quote.

1. *Computing machines can do readily, rapidly, and well many things that are difficult or impossible for man, and men can do readily and well, though not rapidly, many things that are difficult or impossible for computers.*

   What can computers do that are difficult or impossible for people to do? What can people do that are difficult or impossible for computers?

J.C.R. Licklider

2. *In a few years, men will be able to communicate more effectively through a machine than face-to-face.*

   This quote comes from a paper written in 1968. What do you think it means to *communicate through a machine*? Give some examples.

3. *Take any problem… and you find only a few people who can contribute effectively to its solution. Those people must be brought into close intellectual partnership so that their ideas can come into contact with one another. But bring these people together physically in one place to form a team, and you have trouble, for the most creative people are often not the best team players, and there are not enough top positions in a single organization to keep them all happy.*

   This quote gives one of the reasons that in some cases it might be better to communicate online than face to face. Do you agree with this opinion? Explain.

Life Skills

1 USING NEW ELECTRONIC DEVICES

PAIRS. Discuss. When you get a new electronic device, such as a DVD player, how do you usually set it up and learn how to use it? Do you find such tasks easy or hard to do? Why?

Electronic devices such as cell phones and televisions come with instruction manuals. Often the manuals contain diagrams explaining how to use the device. To understand how to set up and use a machine, read the diagram and instructions carefully. Follow the steps in order. Be sure you understand what the terms in the manual mean.

2 READ INSTRUCTIONS AND DIAGRAMS

Read the excerpt from an instruction manual for setting up a remote control for a DVD player. Look at the diagram as you read.

Programming the TV remote control to operate your DVD player

1 Find the three-digit code for your brand of DVD player.

2 Press the FUNCTION button several times until the DVD button lights up.

3 Press SELECT for five seconds or until the DVD button flashes.

4 While the DVD button is flashing, enter the three-digit code (Step 1) on the remote control's number pad.

5 Press ENTER once.

6 Aim the TV's remote control at the DVD player and press SELECT. When the DVD player turns on, you're done.

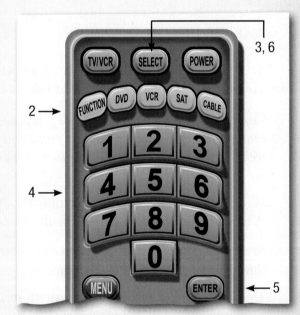

Codes for Different Brands	
DVD Players	
Sovy	571
Parasovic	673
Peer	275

3 PRACTICE

A You need to understand how words are used in instruction manuals in order to follow each step correctly. Complete the sentences based on the way each word is used in the manual on page 188. Circle the letter of the correct answer.

1. A **digit** is _____.
   a. an amount
   b. a single number

2. The **code** for a brand of machine is _____.
   a. a series of numbers and/or letters
   b. a system of laws and regulations

3. When you **aim** something, you _____.
   a. point it carefully at something
   b. try to achieve something

4. When a light **flashes**, it _____.
   a. goes on once and then goes off
   b. goes on and off quickly several times

5. When you **program** a machine, you _____.
   a. arrange instructions in order
   b. set the machine to operate in a certain way

6. The **number pad** on a remote control is for _____.
   a. writing notes
   b. entering numbers

7. A **brand** of DVD player is _____.
   a. the name of the company that makes it
   b. a special mark on the player

B Read the sentences and number the steps in order.

_____ 1. As soon as the DVD button flashes, type the 3-digit code of your brand.

_____ 2. Aim the remote control at the DVD player and press SELECT.

_____ 3. Press the FUNCTION button several times or until the DVD button lights up.

_____ 4. Press SELECT for five seconds or until the DVD button flashes.

_____ 5. Press ENTER once.

_1_ 6. Find the code for your brand of DVD player.

C PAIRS. Check and compare your answers.

Can you...understand how to use an instruction manual? ☐

Listening and Speaking

1 BEFORE YOU LISTEN

CLASS. Discuss the questions.

1. How does the Internet help people communicate?

2. How might the Internet harm communication?

3. Do you know anyone who spends too much time on the Internet? How much time does he or she spend? Are there any negative effects?

2 LISTEN

CD3 T16

A Listen to part of a radio talk show. Psychiatrist Dr. Albert Knowles and host Michelle Allen discuss how the Internet is affecting communication. As you listen, take notes.

Positive Effects	Negative Effects

CD3 T16

B PAIRS. Listen again and compare your notes. Did you miss anything?

C Write the answers to the questions.

1. For which two groups of people has the Internet improved communication?

2. What is one of the most important uses of the Internet today?

3. Does Dr. Knowles believe that the Internet has done more harm or more good?

4. When is using the Internet a problem for young people?

5. What will happen to a naturally shy person who spends too much time online?

6. What part of communication does not exist online?

Communication Skill: Expressing Agreement and Disagreement

When you discuss your opinions, it is important to make clear whether you agree, disagree, or have not yet formed an opinion. It is also important to express your opinions in a polite way. Here are some expressions you can use.

Giving your opinion
From my point of view…
I believe that…
In my opinion…

Agreeing
I couldn't agree more! (= I completely agree with you.)
I agree.
I feel the same way.
That's a really good point.

Disagreeing
I see your point, but…
You've got a good point, but…
That's one way of looking at it, but…
I see things a little differently.

Expressing no opinion
I really haven't thought about it much.
I see both sides.
I'm not sure how I feel about…
On the one hand…on the other hand…

3 CONVERSATION

A GROUPS. Discuss the questions. Use the expressions in the Communication Skill box to express your opinions.

1. Do you agree with Dr. Knowles? Which points do you agree with? Which points do you disagree with? Why?

2. What effects has the Internet or other types of technology had on human relationships and communication? Add at least two positive effects and two negative effects to the chart in Exercise 2A.

B GROUPS. Tell the class what your group added to the chart and why. Express your opinions about other people's views. Use the language in the Communication Skill box.

4 MAKE IT PERSONAL

GROUPS. Discuss the questions.

1. Do people in your home country worry much about the negative effects of using the Internet? If so, what specific problems concern them?

2. Do you think people in the U.S. worry too much about the harmful effects of the Internet and other forms of communication technology? Explain.

3. If a friend or family member was experiencing harmful effects from overuse of the Internet, what would you do?

Reading

1   BEFORE YOU READ

CLASS. Are you familiar with virtual reality (VR) computer games? Have you ever played such games? How might VR be used to train people to perform certain tasks?

Virtual reality (VR) refers to an environment produced by a computer; the environment seems real to the person who experiences it and things happen in real time.

2   READ

CD3 T17

Listen to and read the article about virtual training. How is VR being used to teach driving?

Virtual Driving

Virtual reality, or VR, is an environment that is produced by a computer. However, it looks and seems real to the person who experiences it. VR is used in two main areas: for training and education, and in computer games. VR was first used as a training tool for pilots. Today, with teenage drivers responsible for more fatal car crashes than drivers in any other age group, some communities are investing in VR programs to train drivers. The idea is to give new drivers the practice that they need in front of a **computer screen** rather than on a busy highway.

At about $20,000 each, VR driving **simulators** are not cheap. However, they can also be **leased**. In 2007 there were about 200 simulators leased to driver's education programs in the U.S., and the number is growing. In some cases, the parents of teens who have died in accidents raise money for simulators for the schools in their communities.

One such program, *Virtual Driver Interactive (VDI)*, is made by the same company that makes virtual reality programs to train soldiers. *VDI* takes about five and a half hours to complete. The simulation is very realistic. Students can look in the virtual rear-view or side mirrors and see traffic behind them, just as in real life. If they hit something, they feel and see the results immediately.

During the simulation, drivers are **continuously** evaluated on eighty-five different **criteria**. Mistakes that they make affect their scores. Some violations, such as not wearing a seatbelt or following too closely behind another car, result in a lower final score. More serious violations result in failure.

There are also virtual reality games for **novice** drivers. Chrysler Corporation has developed an online game, which promotes its cars and provides virtual driver training at the same time. The game, *StreetWise*, can be downloaded for free from Chrysler's website. According to the description on the website:

*The game includes five missions which cover the three levels of **learning permits** recognized by the driver education programs of most states. Making the right decisions and mastering basic and advanced driving skills will allow the player to progress through the game. Each level gives the player new liberties and new responsibilities.* *

Will driving simulations be as successful at training drivers as flight simulators have been at training pilots? No one knows. However, with the number of teenagers involved in accidents every year, many agree that it is worth trying.

*Copyright ©2008, Chrysler LLC. All rights reserved.

3 CHECK YOUR UNDERSTANDING

A Write the answers to the questions.

1. What was VR first used for?

2. What are driving simulators? What are they used for?

3. Why do many driver's education programs lease VR simulators?

4. Who raises money to pay for some of the simulators?

5. What is *VDI*? How does it work?

6. What corporation has developed VR games for novice drivers?

B GROUPS. Discuss. What is the author's purpose for writing "Virtual Driving"? Explain.

> **Reading Skill:**
> Identifying an Author's Purpose
>
> Authors write for different reasons. They write to inform, to entertain, or persuade. Sometimes an author has more than one purpose for writing. To figure out why an author wrote a text, ask yourself: Is the text giving me information about a subject? Is it entertaining? Is it trying to persuade me to agree with the author's opinion?

4 WORD WORK

GROUPS. Choose three words or phrases in the article that you would like to remember. Discuss the words and their meanings. Then record the words and information about them in your vocabulary log.

5 MAKE IT PERSONAL

A GROUPS. Discuss the questions.

1. Do you think that the use of VR driving simulators and games will reduce the number of accidents caused by teen drivers? Why or why not?

2. At what age should people be allowed to get a driver's license?

3. Do you think that the government should set an age at which older people should stop driving? Why or why not?

B Look at the chart. Check (✓) the groups you think are the safest drivers. Explain and compare your responses.

Age Group	Male	Female
20–39		
40–54		
55 and up		

Grammar

Adjective Clauses

Main Clause		Adjective Clause	
	Noun/Pronoun	Relative Pronoun	
It seems real to	the person	**who**	**experiences it.**
Virtual reality is	an environment	**that**	**is produced by a computer.**
The game includes	five missions	**which**	**cover the three levels of learning permits.**

Grammar Watch

Adjective clauses:

• are dependent clauses that modify nouns.

• identify, define, or give further information about nouns.

• begin with a relative pronoun. Use *who* or *that* for people and *that* or *which* for things.

1 PRACTICE

A Look at the article on page 192. Underline the adjective clauses.

B Complete the sentences with *that*, *which*, or *who*. More than one answer is possible for each item.

1. Rescue personnel <u>that/who</u> respond to terrorist attacks can train using VR.

2. The simulated program _____ is used is called *BioSimMER*.

3. A company in Santa Clara, California, has developed simulators _____ teach people to use electric shovels and other machines in mines.

4. Truck drivers _____ must learn to handle icy roads and other hazards can use VR for training.

5. In the field of sports, there is a golf simulator _____ promises to improve your game.

6. Cadets at the U.S. military academy _____ may become tank commanders train with a tank simulation game called *Steel Beasts*.

PRACTICE

A Complete the sentences. Write the letter of correct clause. Be careful. There are three extra clauses.

1. Medical students and nurses practice opening veins to draw blood with a VR program __e__.

2. A classroom VR program teaches groups of rail employees _____.

3. Even medical students _____ can learn using VR.

4. Experienced surgeons _____ also use VR.

5. Drivers of police cars, fire trucks, and ambulances can use simulators _____.

6. Some psychiatrists are using virtual reality to learn more about the strange worlds _____.

a. which help them to learn how to travel safely at high speeds

b. that exist inside their patients' minds

c. that hope to become surgeons

d. that teach them how to write speeding tickets

e. ~~that allows them to train without touching living patients~~

f. which they may find when traveling abroad

g. who learn how to evacuate underground stations

h. who want to get easy grades

i. who want to learn and to practice complex techniques for operating on the heart and the brain

B Combine the two sentences using adjective clauses. Write the sentences.

1. Virtual reality is a training tool. It is being used more and more often.

   Virtual reality is a training tool that/which is being used more and more often.

2. A novice driver is a person. He or she hasn't been driving for very long.

3. Driving simulators are virtual reality programs. They are used by novice drivers to learn how to drive.

4. *Virtual Driving Interactive (VDI)* is a driving simulator. It is being used in some communities.

5. *VDI* is a realistic simulation. It takes about five and a half hours to complete.

Show what you know! Discuss virtual training

GROUPS. Suggest new fields for VR training. Use adjective clauses.

Why not use simulators to train people who want to become ships' captains?

Can you... discuss virtual training? ☐

Listening and Speaking

1 BEFORE YOU LISTEN

CLASS. Can you read the message? What does it say?
Do you use text messaging or e-mail? If so, do you use any
abbreviations or shorthand? If you do, which abbreviations
or shorthand do you use? What do they mean?

2 LISTEN

CD3 T18

A A radio commentator is talking to his daughter about
the language of text messaging. Listen and complete the notes
with either the shorthand or the meaning of the shorthand.

SHORTHAND	MEANING
ASAP	As Soon As Possible
FYI	
	Not much. How about you?
	Alive and smiling
BFF	
	Way to go!
	Parent alert
H&K	
	OK
	sleepy
DNBL8	
gratz	
	excellent
	All done, bye bye!

CD3 T18

B PAIRS. Listen again and check your notes. Make sure that you
have the same answers.

3 PRACTICE

A **PAIRS.** Study your notes from Exercises 2A and 2B. Then take turns quizzing each other. Cover the left column of the chart in Exercise 2A and give the shorthand. Then cover the right column and give the meaning.

B **GROUPS.** Play this game. Talk in your group about what each of the following abbreviations means. (These are often used in e-mails, as well as in text messages.) Complete the chart. The group with the greatest number of correct answers is the winner.

Shorthand Phrase	Meaning
2moro	tomorrow
AAMF	
B/C	
CM	
EZ	
GTG	
JAM	
NRN	
OTP	
TBH	
TC	

4 MAKE IT PERSONAL

GROUPS. Discuss the questions.

1. What is your opinion of text messaging as a way of communicating? What are the advantages and disadvantages of writing this way?

2. Some people worry that the shorthand young people use for text messaging is having a negative effect on their writing skills. Do you agree? Why or why not?

3. An emoticon is a symbol that people use in e-mail or text messages to show their feelings. For example, :-) is an emoticon that means *I'm happy* or *I'm smiling*. What other emoticons do you know? Draw them and discuss their meanings.

Reading

1 BEFORE YOU READ

CLASS. Discuss. What do you know about the history of the Internet? When did it appear? What events led to its existence?

2 READ

CD3 T19

Listen to and read the web page carefully. As you read, circle the important dates and events.

http://www.evolutionofinternet.com

History of the Internet

Question: Who invented the Internet?
Answer: The Internet was not invented; it **evolved**. The evolution involved many inventions and **innovations** as well as a large number of people. Many of the people involved in the early days were graduate students at universities. Some of them are big names in technology today. (For a list, click here).
Question: How did the Internet evolve?
Answer: The story begins after World War II, in the 1950s. At that time, the U.S. and the **former** Soviet Union (U.S.S.R.) were in what was called the Cold War. It was not an actual war, because there was no fighting. However, both governments were very worried that the other side would attack their country. When the U.S.S.R. sent the world's first artificial satellite, Sputnik I, into space in 1957, the Americans became convinced that the Soviet Union had gained a dangerous advantage over them. For that reason, in 1957 the U.S. government created the Advanced Research Projects Agency, or ARPA. The agency's goal was to regain a military advantage over the Soviet Union.

To achieve that goal, ARPA needed the best scientists and **engineers** to work closely together. They needed to share ideas, large amounts of **data**, and the computer programs and power to analyze all that data, and they needed to do it fast. However, there was a problem. Computers at that time were not advanced enough for such work. So in 1962, ARPA created the Information Process Techniques Office (IPTO). Its job was to improve computer technology as quickly as possible.

Just seven years later, in 1969, computers at four universities were connected to create the world's first wide area computer network, ARPANET.

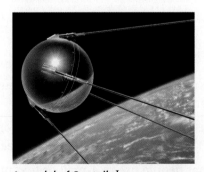

A model of Sputnik I

Question: When did the **general public** start to use the Internet?
Answer: Many improvements were made to ARPANET in the 1970s and 1980s, but most of the users still worked for **research institutions** or the government. In 1983, a common language was established as the official language of what was now called the Internet. At that point, networks all over the world could communicate with each other. In 1981, another important year, the first **personal computers** (PCs) became available. However, it wasn't until 1989 that those first PC owners really discovered the Internet. That was when businesses introduced the first **commercial** e-mail systems. It was also when the first commercial dial-up Internet service provider became available to the public. Suddenly, anyone with a computer and the money to pay the connection fee could go online. In 1991, the U.S. government removed all limitations on commercial use of the Internet. Since then, the number of users has grown at an amazing rate. Today, there are more than 1 billion Internet users worldwide.

3 CHECK YOUR UNDERSTANDING

A Write the answers to the questions.

1. Who invented the Internet?
2. What role did the Cold War play in its development?
3. What was ARPA's goal?
4. When did ordinary people begin to use the Internet?
5. How many people use the Internet today?

Reading Skill:
Using a Timeline

When you are reading about a historical event, it is often helpful to use a timeline. Timelines are usually divided into specific time periods, such as decades (10-year periods) or centuries. Events from long ago are placed on the left; more recent events go on the right. Use your timelines to review what you have read.

B Use the information in the web page to complete the timeline.

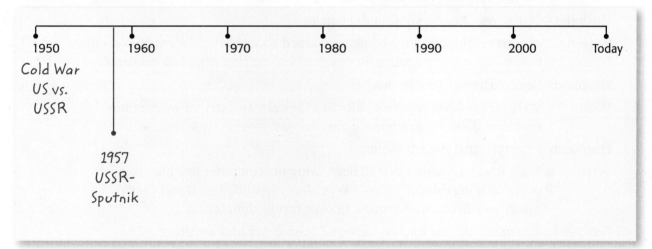

| 1950 | 1960 | 1970 | 1980 | 1990 | 2000 | Today |

Cold War
US vs.
USSR

1957
USSR-
Sputnik

4 WORD WORK

GROUPS. Choose three words or phrases in the web page that you would like to remember. Discuss the words and their meanings. Then record the words and information about them in your vocabulary log.

Show what you know! Identify key events in the history of the Internet

GROUPS. Look at your timelines and describe the evolution of the Internet. One student says a few sentences. Then another student continues, and so on until you finish. Do not look back at the web page.

Reading

1 BEFORE YOU READ

CLASS. Discuss. Do you know how to use a computer? If so, how did you learn?

2 READ

CD3 T20

Listen to and read the dialogue about computer training.

Husband: Hey, honey, how was your day? How did the computer training go?

Wife: It was really exhausting, but exciting too. The best part is that when I finish the course, I'll be able to apply for that job in the accounting department.

Husband: That's great, honey. So what did you learn?

Wife: All sorts of things…First of all, we learned about file management—about how to set up and organize files so that you can find what you need easily.

Husband: Really? How do you do that?

Wife Well, for example, you name files in a logical way…so that your naming system make sense to someone else, not just you.

Husband: Hmmm…that sounds useful.

Wife: Yeah, it was. I realized that I'd been using my computer just like a big personal filing cabinet, where I kept all of my stuff. And it was pretty messy, too. Even I have trouble finding things sometimes!

Husband: You mean like our kitchen cabinets? I can never find anything in there.

Wife: Exactly! Anyway, they helped us reorganize all of our computer files. Then they had us **switch** computers and see how long it took us to find a document we might need if that person was out sick, for example.

Husband: And did it work?

Wife: It was amazing! Everything was so organized and easy to understand. It only took me a few seconds to find what I was looking for. I can already see how this is going to save all of us a lot of time.

Husband: That's great, honey. So what's tomorrow's topic?

Wife: Hakim from Accounting is going to teach us how to use a **spreadsheet**. You know, where you enter lots of numbers or other information in columns, and then you tell the computer what **calculations** to do?

Husband: Fantastic! Well, I know what we're doing this weekend.

Wife: Really? What's that?

Husband: You're going to be teaching me everything you've learned!

3 CHECK YOUR UNDERSTANDING

A **Read the dialogue again. What is the woman learning how to do? Check (✓) the topics.**

☐ 1. apply for a job online   ☐ 3. use a spreadsheet
☐ 2. manage computer files   ☐ 4. prepare her taxes

B **Mark the statements *T* (*true*) or *F* (*false*).**

__T__ 1. The woman wants to change jobs.

_____ 2. She is studying computer science at a university.

_____ 3. She is taking a computer course at work.

_____ 4. The woman doesn't know how to use a computer.

_____ 5. In today's class, she learned about spreadsheets.

_____ 6. Her husband knows less about computers than she does.

_____ 7. Her husband thinks she should study on the weekend.

_____ 8. The woman is going to go to class this weekend.

4 WORD WORK

A GROUPS. **Choose three words or phrases in the dialogue that you would like to remember. Discuss the words and their meanings. Then record the words and information about them in your vocabulary log.**

B CLASS. **Discuss. What does each of the computer terms in the box stand for? Share what you know.**

| browser | document | file | keyboard | monitor | PowerPoint® |
| desktop | Excel® | folder | mouse | Outlook® | spreadsheet |

5 MAKE IT PERSONAL

GROUPS. **Discuss the questions.**

1. What do you know how to do on a computer?

2. Talk about the things you are interested or not interested in learning how to do on a computer. Explain your reasons.

3. If you want to get computer training, what can you do? Talk about any community resources you know of that offer computer training courses.

Writing

1 BEFORE YOU WRITE

A You are going to write an autobiographical essay about a challenge you faced. Read about autobiographies. Then read the writing tip.

> **FYI**   ABOUT AUTOBIOGRAPHIES
>
> Current technology has made it possible for many people who are not professional writers to publish autobiographical essays online. In an autobiographical essay, you describe important people, events, and places in your life. Every person has a life history that's worth telling. You look back and recall, in words, those experiences that have made you who you are.
>
> **Writing Tip:** Using concrete examples and sensory details
>
> Vivid examples and concrete details are what make your life story come alive. When you describe an important moment or person, try to create a picture in the reader's mind. Use sensory details that will help readers see, hear, and touch what you are describing. Be specific about when and where an event occurred. Avoid general phrases such as "a good time" or "a nice person." Show *why* the time was good or *what* the person did that was nice.

B Begin thinking about your life story. Ask yourself: What difficult situations have I faced in my life? What were some key moments during these periods? How did I overcome the challenges? Who helped me? Take notes.

C Free-write about your topic for ten minutes. Write down everything you remember. Get all of your memories and thoughts down on paper.

D Read the writing model on page 211. What is Alexandra's essay about?

2 ANALYZE THE WRITING MODEL

PAIRS. Discuss the questions.

1. What challenge did Alexandra face when she came to the U.S.?

2. What steps did she take to overcome her difficulties?

3. What people and events helped her succeed?

3 THINK ON PAPER

A Before Alexandra wrote her essay, she used a problem/solution/outcome chart to structure her memories. Compare the chart to her essay on page 211. How are they similar? How are they different? For example, what details does the essay provide that are missing from the chart?

> PROBLEM: Came to Los Angeles without enough English or education to get a good job

⬇

> SOLUTIONS: Took English class at the high school; had a great teacher (Mr. Stevens) who helped me learn; studied hard and used all kinds of methods

⬇

> OUTCOME: English improved; got a better job; learned more English on the job—even slang; moved up within the company; got GED; went on to college

B Look at the notes you made of challenges you faced in Exercises 1B and 1C. Select a topic. Use your notes to create a problem/solution/outcome chart for an autobiographical essay.

4 WRITE

Use your problem/solution/outcome chart and your notes to write an autobiographical essay about how you overcame a challenge. You may want to include your future goals the way Alexandra did.

5 CHECK YOUR WRITING

A STEP 1. Revise your work.

1. Does your essay describe a challenge you faced?
2. Have you used concrete examples and sensory details to help readers picture this period in your life?
3. Is your essay structured in a logical way that readers can follow?

B STEP 2. Edit and proofread.

1. Have you checked your spelling, grammar, and punctuation?
2. Have you proofread for typing errors?

1 REVIEW   For your grammar review, go to page 231.

2 ACT IT OUT   What do you say?

PAIRS. You are debating the pros and cons of the Internet in our daily lives.
Review Lessons 1, 3, 6, 7, and 8.

Student A: Argue in favor of the Internet. Tell Student B how the Internet has improved our lives at home and at work. Include some information about the history of the Internet.

Student B: Take a stand against the Internet. Tell Student A how the Internet and e-mail have had negative effects on our lives at home and at work. Include some information about texting.

3 READ AND REACT   Problem-solving

STEP 1. **Read about Edwin.**

Edwin has just started a new office job. It is a step up for him, but he is having trouble learning the technology used at the new company. He's had problems with his computer. He can't figure out how to change his computer password, and his mouse isn't working properly. In addition, he never had to prepare Excel® spreadsheets or PowerPoint® presentations before. His new boss expects him to learn these skills quickly. Edwin is feeling very nervous about his skills. He's even having trouble with some of the abbreviations his boss uses in e-mails.

STEP 2. GROUPS. **What is Edwin's problem? What can he do?**

4 CONNECT   For your Goal-Setting Activity, go to page 221.

Which goals can you check off? Go back to page 185.

Writing Models

Unit 1   Descriptive Essay

My Interests, Skills, and Goals

I have a wide variety of interests, but my main interests are science and nature. Even as a child, I always loved spending time outdoors. I enjoy gardening, and I'm interested in organic gardening methods. I grow vegetables, herbs, and flowers in the community garden in my neighborhood.

I have many skills. I'm good at math, and working with computers has always been easy for me. I keep up with new computer programs, and I do a lot of things online. I think my interpersonal skills are good, too. I'm outgoing and patient. I often help my friends with their computer problems.

I want to work at something that combines my interests and skills. My career goal is to work as a landscape architect for the City Parks and Recreation Department. Right now I'm taking ESL classes at the community college. After I finish my ESL classes, I want to enroll as a credit student and study landscape architecture. While I'm taking classes, I hope to work as a tree climber and pruner in the city parks.

Andrea Fernández

Unit 2   Job Ad

Megametro Media

Growing media firm seeks an entry-level accountant. The qualified candidate will have a degree or certificate in accounting and will have knowledge of Microsoft Office®, QuickBooks®, and other accounting software. Related experience a plus. Team environment. Excellent problem-solving and communication skills required. Only honest, dependable, hardworking candidates need apply.

Unit 2   Cover Letter for a Résumé

Iris Martinez
115 Hammond Avenue ← applicant's name and address
Largo, Florida 33773

April 25, 2010 ← date

Mr. Harvey Samson
Megametro Media ← employer's name and address
12 Communications Drive, 8F
Largo, Florida 33773

Dear Mr. Samson: ← greeting

    I am writing in response to your ad for an entry-level accountant in the *Largo Gazette*. My education and qualifications are a great match for this position.

    As you can see in my attached résumé, I am completing a program in accounting at Hillsborough Community College. I will have my AA degree in one month. I can use all Microsoft Office programs, as well as QuickBooks. In addition to attending classes, I have been working as an Assistant Manager at Robertson's Supermarket, and this job has given me an opportunity to perform some basic bookkeeping and accounting duties.

    Megametro Media is a well-known and respected company. I believe that it is the kind of company where I will be able to make valuable contributions as I grow and learn. I'm dependable, hardworking, and responsible. I'm a team player. And I have excellent problem-solving and communication skills.

    Thank you for considering my application. I look forward to meeting you and discussing the opportunity to work for Megametro Media. ← thank you and indication of eagerness for further contact

Sincerely, ← closing

Iris Martinez ← signature above typed first and last name
Iris Martinez

Unit 3   Letter to the Editor

Letters to the Editor
November 24, 2010
Re: Eating While Driving

Eating while driving is dangerous, and it definitely should be banned. People should eat before they get into the car so that they can focus on the very important job of driving. This would be safer for drivers, passengers, and everyone around them.

One of the reasons eating while driving is so dangerous is because it forces the driver to take a hand off the steering wheel. Even though eating doesn't require brainpower, it does require coordination. Unwrapping a burger or picking out a French fry involves taking a hand—or sometimes two—from the steering wheel. If something suddenly happens, which is always a possibility while driving, without having both hands on the wheel, the driver will not have complete control.

Another reason eating while driving is dangerous is that the food can spill or drop on the driver or critical parts of the car. For example, if someone is driving to work and eating a breakfast sandwich that starts to leak sauce, the driver is going to be more worried about ruining clothing than watching the road. Or imagine that part of the sandwich slips out and onto the brake or gas pedal. A simple attempt to brush it away with a foot could cause an accident. If the food a driver is eating is greasy, it could get onto the steering wheel and cause loss of control. If it is hot, the driver could get burned, causing him or her to make a sudden move and be distracted from the most important task: driving.

Though our lives are all very busy, we should be able to find the time to have a bite before getting behind the wheel. Eating is one of the most distracting and dangerous activities to do while driving. Taking an extra ten minutes to eat something at home could save lives.

Fazil Shankar
San Francisco, California

Unit 4   Safety Instructions

How to Prevent Falls at Home

Falling at home is a serious problem. The good news is that one-third of all falls in the home could be prevented if people followed a few simple steps.

To prevent falls in your home, first, identify potential hazards. Be sure that all areas of your house are well lit. If not, put in brighter light bulbs where needed, and install night-lights in areas you walk through at night. Remove loose objects from the floor and stairs, and keep electrical cords away from walkways. Make sure that handrails and steps are secure and in good condition. Tape down or eliminate area rugs that could cause someone to trip, slip, or fall. Close cabinet doors and drawers—including doors to the dishwasher and clothes dryer. Use rubber mats to prevent slipping in the bathtub.

Next, look at the kind of shoes you typically wear. Wear sturdy shoes, even at home. Walking around in socks or slippers can cause a fall, especially when going up and down stairs. Always be sure that your shoelaces are tied, and avoid high heels or unstable sandals.

Then consider some form of exercise to improve your balance, flexibility, and coordination. Studies show that certain types of exercise, such as yoga and tai chi, can improve balance and prevent falls among people of all ages. The better shape you are in, the less likely you are to fall.

Finally, investigate the side effects of any medications you take. Some drugs can cause fatigue, lack of coordination, or dizziness. If you are taking such a medication, take extra care because you have a higher risk of falling.

Eva Tran

Unit 5 Self-evaluation

Self-evaluation

Since last year, I have been working as a Certified Nurse's Assistant (CNA), taking care of elderly patients. My strengths as a CNA are my compassion and my attention to detail.

I have had a number of successes that show my strengths. For example, I was named "CNA of the Month" in October because of the many positive reports from patients' relatives about the care I gave their loved ones. In addition, I was praised by the lead nurses during my three-month review for the accuracy of my patient records. These achievements, along with my record of never missing a shift, are why I choose to give myself a "superior" rating.

Even though I believe the "superior" rating is well deserved, I know there are still areas in which I could improve. First, I would like to learn more about some of the medical equipment used in our workplace. At times, I have had to depend on more experienced CNAs to help with complicated types of medical equipment. In the future, I would like to be the CNA that others come to for help. Second, I would like to learn more about the unique medical problems that affect our elderly patient population. I get a lot of satisfaction out of helping older people stay healthy. For this reason, I would like to receive more training in elder care.

This year has been a challenging and productive one for me, and I'm looking forward to next year. My future goals are to take a series of workshops to learn more about medical equipment, as well as a special nursing course to learn more about typical medical problems the elderly face. I know these courses will make me a better CNA and will help my long-term career goal of becoming a Registered Geriatric Nurse. Finally, I plan to make next year as successful as this one.

Pham Tuyen, Certified Nurse's Assistant

Unit 6 Persuasive Essay

Why Companies Should Not Hire Smokers

Today, more and more companies who pay employee health care costs prefer not to hire smokers. I think that this policy is a good one because hiring smokers hurts a company as well as its nonsmoking employees.

Hiring smokers hurts a company financially. Smoking causes serious health problems. It increases a person's chances of getting heart disease, emphysema, lung cancer, and many other serious diseases. All of these illnesses require expensive long-term medical care. In fact, according to *The New England Journal of Medicine*, health care costs for smokers can be as much as forty percent higher than those for nonsmokers.

If companies hire smokers, they are also hurting nonsmoking employees. When companies pay too much for health care, they have less money in the budget for other employee benefits. For example, they can't hire additional staff, provide child care, or give raises. Companies and nonsmoking employees should not have to pay the price for people who continue to smoke. This is why I believe that companies should not hire smokers.

Zlatan Ramic

Unit 7 Formal E-mail

From: Camacho, Guillermo <gcamacho@coldmail.com>
Date: 10/9/2010 10:52:47
To: Edwin.Garcia@assembly.state.fl.us
Subject: Funding for Adult Literacy

Representative Edwin Garcia
55 Colonial Drive
Orlando, Florida 32804

Dear Representative Garcia,

I am very worried about what is happening to the adult literacy programs in our community. In the past five years, city funding for these programs has decreased. As a result, local residents are not getting the help they need in order to be productive and happy members of the community. This is a serious problem, one that we need to work to solve.

To solve this problem, I urge you to increase the city budget for adult literacy. Making adult literacy a top concern in our city will help our residents and our economy. In order to be successful in the workplace, our residents must possess good basic skills. Employers want to hire workers who can communicate well in English. Workers need to know how to read, write, and speak English well. We need to increase literacy rates so that our workers can get and keep jobs that pay well. This would improve the economy and well-being of our community.

Funding adult literacy is an investment in the financial success of our residents and our city. The more literate our city is, the stronger our workforce and economy will be. If you work to increase the city budget for adult literacy, you will help all of our residents, our local workforce, and our economy.

Thank you for your attention to this problem. I look forward to hearing from you.

Sincerely,
Guillermo Camacho

Unit 8 Essay That Compares and Contrasts

Legal Systems in India vs. the United States

To many people, my home country of India seems very different from the United States. However, when you look at the legal systems of the two countries, you will find some surprising similarities as well as differences.

Both India and the United States are former colonies of England, which is why their legal systems have similarities. Both countries have *common laws*—laws created by the courts, not the government. Both nations also have what is called an *independent judiciary*. This means that the legal system is separate from other branches of government, such as the executive branch and Congress.

The main difference between the legal systems of the two nations is the way in which trials are conducted. In India, a judge determines the verdict in almost all trials. A single person determines a defendant's guilt or innocence. In contrast, the legal system in the United States puts legal power in the hands of a group of ordinary citizens. Anyone accused of commiting a serious crime has a right to a trial by a jury of his or her peers. The jury is usually made up of twelve citizens. They hear all the evidence in the case and decide whether the person is guilty or innocent.

Anand Ramesh

Reducing My Carbon Footprint

Ever since my kids started learning about the environment at school, they've been trying to convince me to change my ways. Well, if you're a parent, you understand that sometimes things get so hectic it's hard to focus on anything—especially, the environment. However, despite my busy schedule, my kids have convinced me to make a few changes to reduce my carbon footprint.

A few months ago, my seven-year-old son suggested that I use cloth bags instead of plastic ones to carry groceries and other products. At first, it was difficult because I kept forgetting to bring the bags with me. After awhile, though, it became a habit. As soon as I use the bags, I return them to the car. This way I always have them with me. So far, this is working out very well.

Soon, I found myself paying more attention to recycling, too. I decided to buy rechargeable batteries and recycle all my newspapers, magazines, paper bags, and cardboard boxes. My daughter bought me a reusable coffee cup for my birthday. I take it almost everywhere I go. My garbage has been reduced by fifty percent. I can't believe how much stuff I was throwing away before!

Although I'm still driving my big old car, I'm trying to maintain it better. I only use the air conditioning on extremely hot days. I also drive more slowly in order to save gas. These were the tips my kids gave me, and I have to say that they were right. I may not get somewhere as fast as I used to, but I'm saving some gas and money. It amazes me that a little effort can have a big effect on helping the environment.

Anka Sawicki

Unit 10 Autobiographical Essay

Home Delivery.com

HOME | DELIVERIES | EMPLOYEE BLOG | ABOUT US

Search

Home Delivery: Employee Success Stories

November 25, 2010 | Posted by: Alexandra Zambrano

Nothing Can Stop Me Now

I remember when my husband and I first came to the United States to work. I was twenty-two years old. We had borrowed several thousand dollars, and had come to California to start a new life. I didn't know much English—in Ecuador, I had had to quit school in the sixth grade to help raise my brothers and sisters. Now that we were living in Los Angeles, I needed to get a job right away to pay the rent. I didn't have much work experience, but I knew how to care for children, so I spent my first six months babysitting for a neighbor for very little money.

Without enough English to communicate well, I couldn't find a better paying job. So I signed up for an English class at the local high school. The class met three evenings a week. The teacher, Mr. Stevens, was a tall, thin man in his fifties. He had spent years helping students like me learn—and actually love—English. He was a wonderful teacher, who gave me puzzles, games, and exercises to expand my vocabulary. He encouraged me to work on my English all the time. He told me to listen to the radio, read newspapers, and watch TV and movies in English. He even suggested that I get an English pen pal online. Mr. Stevens told jokes in class and made learning English fun.

As my English got better, I decided to apply for a cooking job at a nonprofit organization called *Home Delivery*. This organization prepares and delivers meals to the elderly. I thought, "Great! My English doesn't have to be perfect to cook!" But, as it turned out, I did need English to communicate with my co-workers. Soon I was speaking English in the kitchen and learning a lot of American slang. When supervisors at *Home Delivery* recognized how much better my English was, they offered me a job in the food inventory department. Mr. Stevens was proud of my success and encouraged me to take a GED class. After studying hard, I took and passed the GED exam. Soon I was promoted at work to office assistant. Three years later, I was managing the office.

After five years at *Home Delivery*, I realized that I had a solid nonprofit résumé, so I decided to get a college degree in nonprofit management. I found a local college that offered classes at night. When I think of how I felt when I came to Los Angeles seven years ago, I'm amazed at how my life has changed. Today, I am in college and have a full-time job at a nonprofit organization. I plan to finish my degree in four or five years and start my own organization some day. My goal is to start a nonprofit organization to help new immigrants. I still have a long way to go, but I have come so far. Nothing can stop me now.

Alexandra Zambrano

Sign in to comment on this post | 3 Comments

Unit 1   Exploring Your Expectations

Expectations are the things that you think will occur or will happen in a new situation, based on the information and experiences you have had in the past. For example, when you start a new English class, you may have expectations about how the teacher will behave, the kind of work that you will do, or what you will learn.

A Think about the expectations you had when you started this English class. Look at the situations in column 1. Write your response to each expectation in column 2. If you had additional expectations, write them at the bottom of column 2.

Situation	Your Expectation
Amount of work/homework for the class	
Attendance	
English-speaking ability of other students	
Tests	
Amount of reading and writing	
Amount of listening and speaking	
Teacher	
Other:	

B PAIRS. Talk about your expectations. Where did your expectations come from? Have your expectations been met in the class so far? What could be changed in class to meet your expectations? If they have not been met in certain areas, make suggestions.

C GROUPS. Discuss your expectations with another pair. Discuss: For any expectations that have not been met, how could the class be changed to help you learn English better?

Unit 2   Speaking English Well

We all want to become better English speakers. Sometimes, when you are learning something, it helps to think of and imitate role models—people who do that thing well. Who do you know who speaks English well?

A GROUPS. **Think about people you know who speak English well. They can be people you know personally or people you have seen on TV or heard on the radio. Discuss the questions.**

1. In what ways do these people speak English well? Give examples.

2. Do they have a large vocabulary?

3. Do they speak quickly or slowly?

4. Do they have a formal or informal style of speaking?

5. Do they use body language?

6. Do they use a lot of idioms or slang?

7. Do they use *um* and *ah* often when they are speaking?

B **Use the word web below to list the most important characteristics of a good English speaker.**

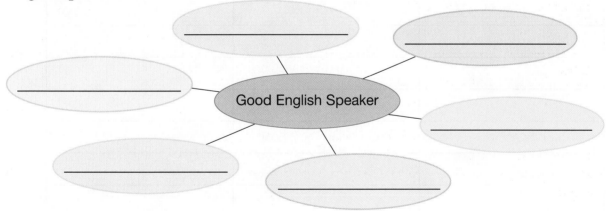

C CLASS. **Share your group's list with the class. Discuss your individual lists and create a class list of the main characteristics of a good English speaker.**

D CLASS. **Look at the class list of characteristics of a good English speaker. Which characteristics do you already have? Which ones do you want to develop? Choose at least one characteristic that you want to work on throughout this class.**

Unit 3   The Importance of Reading

Reading is an important language skill. When you read, you are exposed to many new words, grammar structures, and idioms. You see models of good English, both formal and informal. You use strategies to comprehend what you read, and you use the information you learn for many purposes. So it is important to read regularly and to read different types of texts: novels, magazine articles, labels, forms, street signs, textbooks, notes, work manuals, the newspaper, and so on. Each type of text challenges you to learn more and improve your English skills in different ways.

A **Think about a typical week in your life. What do you read? Complete the chart. If you need more space, draw the chart on a piece of paper and make it bigger.**

What I read	How often I read it	Why I read it

B **PAIRS. Talk about the information in your charts. What do you read in your daily life? How does it help you improve your English? Can you recommend a reading material that your partner might benefit from? Why do you think your partner would learn something from reading it?**

C **Make a list of at least three types of texts that you don't read now but would like to read in the future. Check back in a month and make a chart like the one above. Are you reading any new types of texts? If so, how are they helping you?**

Unit 4   Sharing Strengths and Challenges

We all have different strengths and challenges when learning a language such as English. It is good to share our strengths with others and help them with their challenges. It is also helpful to know people who can help us practice and improve our skills.

A **Think about what you do well in English. Use the categories in the chart to help you brainstorm. If some of your ideas don't fit the categories on the chart, add your own categories.**

In English:	What I do well
Reading	
Writing	
Listening	
Speaking	
Grammar	
Culture	
Other:	

B **PAIRS.** **Share your charts. Talk about what you can do well in English and what you can help others practice and learn. Find out who might need your help. Find out who can help you.**

Unit 5   Building Your Vocabulary All the Time

It is important to continue building your vocabulary in English.

A **Think about how you learn English vocabulary. What are your vocabulary learning strategies?**

B GROUPS. **Discuss. Which of the strategies listed below do you and your classmates use? Are there other strategies that you use? What advice can you give about the strategies you use? Make notes on the chart.**

Vocabulary learning strategy	Person who uses this strategy	Advice/Notes
Visualize (make a picture of the word in your mind)		
Say or write new words ___ number of times		
Translate words into your native language		
Keep a vocabulary log or notebook		
Make and use vocabulary cards		
Consult a dictionary or thesaurus		
Use the keyword method		
Other:		

C PAIRS. **Discuss the questions.**

1. What vocabulary do you have difficulty learning? Individual words? Idioms? Slang or colloquial expressions?

2. Why do you think it is hard for you to learn these types of words?

3. Do you think any of the strategies above might help you learn and remember these words more easily? Which strategies?

> *colloquial expression:* an informal expression used in everyday conversation but not usually used in written communication, for example, *keep your shirt on,* which means *be patient.*

Unit 6   Studying in the U.S.

A Think about what it is like to study in your home country and what it is like to study in the U.S. Then complete the chart.

	In your home country	In the U.S.
What you study		
Where you study		
When you study		
How you study		
Relationship between teacher and student		

B GROUPS. Talk about the information in your charts. Discuss the questions.

1. How is studying in the U.S. similar to studying in your home countries?

2. How is it different?

3. What surprised you about education in the U.S.? What changes did you have to adapt to?

C GROUPS. Make a group list of the things that are different about studying in the U.S.

D Write a short letter to a student who is coming from a foreign country to study in the U.S. What advice do you have for the student? How should the student prepare? What will that student need to do to be a successful student in a U.S. classroom?

Unit 7　Writing Strategies

Writing can be challenging for anyone, but it is especially challenging when you are writing in a foreign language such as English. It is a good idea to have a collection of strategies and skills that you know work for you: a "toolbox" that you can use to work on any writing task.

A **Review the writing lessons in this book and the tools they provide.**

1. Before starting each writing assignment, an FYI box helps you understand the genre, or type of writing you are being asked to do.

2. Then a Writing Tip helps you develop, structure, or format your writing.

3. Throughout the lesson, brainstorming activities, models, questions, graphic organizers, and editing and proofreading checklists help you succeed in every part of the writing process—before writing, while you are writing, and after you have written.

B **PAIRS.** **Look back at the writing you did. Discuss the questions.**

1. Which writing tools helped you the most? Why?

2. Were particular tools helpful for specific kinds of writing? Which ones?

3. Which writing tools have you used in other writing tasks outside of class?

C **Complete the chart.**

My Writing Toolbox		
	Purpose	**Writing tips or strategies that worked for me**
Before writing	To help you plan and generate ideas	
During writing	To help you develop and organize information	
After writing	To help you revise, edit, and proofread your writing	

D **PAIRS.** **Share and discuss your Writing Toolboxes. Explain why certain tools are helpful when you are writing in English, both in and outside of class. Consider using some of your partner's tools. Do you think they would help you? Do you want to add them to your toolbox?**

Unit 8   Reading Skills/Strategies

Most of the readings in this textbook are accompanied by a Reading Skills box. For example, on page 13, a Reading Skills box explains the importance of highlighting or underlining key information as you read. All twenty reading skills in this textbook help you use and develop skills to improve your reading comprehension.

A There are two Reading Skills boxes in each unit of this textbook. Review them all. In the chart below, list the reading skills that helped you the most. You can also add any other reading skills and strategies that you use on your own.

My Reading Skills/Strategies	
Reading skills/strategies I use	**Other resources and materials I use**

B What other resources help you when you read? Do you use a dictionary, thesaurus, or grammar reference book? Write these down too. All of these skills, strategies, and resources are tools that can help you read and comprehend different kinds of texts.

C PAIRS. Share your reading skills/strategies. Explain how they help you when you are reading in English. Does your partner use different skills, strategies, and resources? Do you think they would help you? Add them to your chart and give them a try!

Unit 9   Becoming a Lifelong Learner

Lifelong learning means focusing on what you need and want to learn throughout your life. You might need to learn a new computer software application to help you in your job. You might want to learn yoga in order to stay fit, improve your balance, or relax and focus your thoughts. In both cases, learning is important to you and to your life.

A Think about the subjects and skills that you have learned in the past. What did you need to learn in order to do your job, raise a family, or contribute to your community? What did you want to learn to make you feel happy or fulfilled? What steps did you take to learn all these things? Complete the chart.

What I learned	Why I learned it	Steps I took

B Think about your life right now. What do you need to learn in order to improve your situation or to be more fulfilled? What steps will you take to learn more in these areas? Complete the chart.

What I will learn	Why I will learn it	Steps I will take

C PAIRS. Compare your charts. Discuss. What are the challenges of being a lifelong learner? What are the benefits of always learning new things? How do you find time to learn and grow? What steps can you take to keep on learning? How do you balance what you need to learn with what you want to learn for self-fulfillment?

Unit 10 Moving Forward

In the first unit of this textbook, you talked a lot about your goals and dreams for the future: what you want to be, what you want to have, and what you want to do. You also wrote at least one long-term SMART goal and a flowchart to illustrate your move toward that goal.

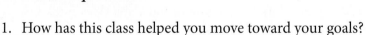

A Review what you wrote in Unit 1, particularly your SMART goal and your flowchart. Then think about this class, the activities you did, and the skills and information you learned. Use the graphic organizer on the right. Write some of the ways this class has helped you move toward your SMART goal.

B PAIRS. Share your organizers and talk about your SMART goal and flowchart from Unit 1. Discuss the questions.

1. How has this class helped you move toward your goals?

2. Can your partner think of any other things that you did or learned in class that might help you? Add them to your flowchart.

C Ask yourself the questions below. Then add them to your flowchart. Make an action plan for yourself for the next week or two so that you can continue working toward your goals after this class ends!

1. What plans do you need to make now that this class is finished?

2. Do you need to take another English class or a different kind of English class? (For example, you might need to take one that focuses on pronunciation.)

3. Do you need to find a class that teaches skills for the job you want?

4. Are there any steps you need to add to your flowchart or other goals you want to pursue?

Nina Sanchez

235 Balboa Street
Markleeville, CA 96120
nina.sanchez@fastmail.com
(915) 555-7686

Objective: To use my practical experience with animal care in a position as a veterinary assistant.

Summary

- Strong career interest in veterinary medicine and care.
- Educational background in science: biology major, with courses in chemistry and physics.
- Extensive experience caring for pets: grooming, feeding, walking, training, showing affection.
- Excellent people skills; good at dealing with customers over the phone and in person.

Professional Achievements

Animal Care

- Provided expert care to dogs and cats of many sizes, ages, breeds, and temperaments.
- Exhibited exceptional ability to work with troubled—fearful or aggressive—pets.
- Learned about grooming and health issues associated with specific breeds.

Customer Relations

- Greeted pet owners.
- Handled phone calls and e-mail correspondence with customers.
- Helped store owners display pet products and services in store windows.

Work History

2006–present:	Assistant and Receptionist, Jill's Pet Grooming and Care, Woodfords, CA
2005–2006:	Independent Dog Walker, Markleeville, CA
2003–2005:	Waitress, Flannigan's Restaurant, Markleeville, CA
2000–2002:	Cashier, Dog-gone Discounts Pet Supply Store, San Francisco, CA

Education

2003–present:	Western Nevada College, Carson City, NV
	BS in Biology Expected 2010
1999–2003:	Lowell High School, San Francisco, CA
	High School Diploma Received

Community Service

2006–2009:	Volunteer, Dogs for Seniors—a group that brings dogs to nursing homes, Gardnerville, NV
2005–2006:	Volunteer, Pet Rescue, Gardnerville, NV

References/Transcripts Provided on request.

Grammar Reference

UNIT 1, Lesson 2, page 8

Verbs Followed by the Gerund (Base Form of Verb + *-ing*)

acknowledge	enjoy	prevent
admit	escape	prohibit
advise	feel like	quit
appreciate	finish	recall
avoid	forgive	recommend
can't help	give up (*stop*)	regret
can't stand	imagine	report
celebrate	justify	resent
consider	keep (*continue*)	resist
delay	mention	risk
deny	mind (*object to*)	suggest
discontinue	miss	support
discuss	postpone	tolerate
dislike	practice	understand
endure		

Verbs Followed by the Infinitive (*to* + Base Form of Verb)

agree	help	prepare
appear	hesitate	pretend
arrange	hope	promise
ask	hurry	refuse
attempt	intend	request
can't afford	learn	rush
can't wait	manage	seem
choose	mean (*intend*)	volunteer
consent	need	wait
decide	neglect	want
deserve	offer	wish
expect	pay	would like
fail	plan	

Verbs Followed by the Gerund or the Infinitive

attempt	hate	regret
begin	like	remember
can't stand	love	start
continue	prefer	stop
forget	propose	try

Phrasal Verbs

Separable Phrasal Verbs sb = somebody sth = something		Inseparable Phrasal Verbs	
Phrasal verb	**Meaning**	**Phrasal verb**	**Meaning**
add sth **up**	calculate the total	**break down**	stop working properly
call sb **back**	return a phone call	**break into**	enter something illegally
call sb **up**	telephone a person	**call on**	ask someone to speak
clean sth **out**	(1) get rid of dirt;	**come across**	unexpectedly find something
	(2) remove contents or occupants	**come in**	enter
clean sth **up**	clean or wash something completely	**come on**	turn on (for example, *My engine light*
close sth **down**	stop operating		***came on.***)
do sth **over**	do something again	**count on**	depend on someone
drop sth **off**	leave or deliver someone or something	**do without**	manage without having something
	somewhere	**drop in**	visit by surprise
figure sth **out**	think about until you understand or find	**drop out of**	quit, especially school
	the answer	**get ahead**	(1) make progress;
fill sth **out**	complete a form with information		(2) succeed
fix sth **up**	make a place look attractive by doing small	**get into**	(1) be allowed in;
	repairs or by decorating		(2) be interested in something
flag sth **down**	make the driver of a vehicle stop by waving	**get together**	meet
give sth **back**	return	**get off**	leave a bus, train, boat, etc.
hold sth/sb **up**	delay something or someone	**get out of**	(1) leave;
leave sth **out**	omit		(2) avoid doing something
look sth/sb **up**	(1) try to find information;	**get through**	finish
	(2) visit someone you know	**look after**	take care of
make sth **up**	invent	**look into**	try to find out the truth
start sth **over**	start again	**pull over**	drive to the side of the road and stop the car
take sth **off**	remove clothing	**run into**	(1) meet someone by chance;
think sth **over**	think about something carefully		(2) accidentally hit a part of your body on
try sth **on**	put clothing on to see how it fits or looks		something
turn sth **down**	(1) refuse;	**run out of**	not have enough
	(2) lower the heat or volume	**sign up**	register
turn sth **off**	stop a machine or light	**slow down**	make someone or something slower
turn sth **on**	start a machine or light	**take off**	depart (a plane)
turn sth **up**	make louder (a TV/radio)	**watch out**	be careful
work sth **out**	find a solution		

Irregular verbs

Base form	Simple past	Past participle	Base form	Simple past	Past participle
awake	awoke	awoken	keep	kept	kept
be	was/were	been	know	knew	known
beat	beat	beaten	lead	led	led
become	became	become	leave	left	left
begin	began	begun	lend	lent	lent
bite	bit	bitten	let	let	let
blow	blew	blown	lose	lost	lost
break	broke	broken	make	made	made
build	built	built	mean	meant	meant
buy	bought	bought	meet	met	met
catch	caught	caught	pay	paid	paid
choose	chose	chosen	put	put	put
come	came	come	quit	quit	quit
cost	cost	cost	read	read	read
cut	cut	cut	ride	rode	ridden
dig	dug	dug	ring	rang	rung
do	did	done	run	ran	run
draw	drew	drawn	say	said	said
drink	drank	drunk	see	saw	seen
drive	drove	driven	sell	sold	sold
eat	ate	eaten	send	sent	sent
fall	fell	fallen	shake	shook	shaken
feed	fed	fed	sing	sang	sung
feel	felt	felt	sit	sat	sat
fight	fought	fought	sleep	slept	slept
find	found	found	speak	spoke	spoken
fly	flew	flown	spend	spent	spent
forget	forgot	forgotten	stand	stood	stood
forgive	forgave	forgiven	steal	stole	stolen
get	got	gotten	swim	swam	swum
give	gave	given	take	took	taken
go	went	gone	teach	taught	taught
grow	grew	grown	think	thought	thought
hang	hung	hung	throw	threw	thrown
have	had	had	understand	understood	understood
hear	heard	heard	upset	upset	upset
hide	hid	hidden	wake	woke	woken
hit	hit	hit	wear	wore	worn
hold	held	held	win	won	won
hurt	hurt	hurt	write	wrote	written

Grammar Review

UNIT 1

A Unscramble the words and phrases to make sentences. Use the simple present with gerunds and infinitives.

1. avoid / Zofia / with computers / work

   _____

2. enjoy / Mr. Jung / blueprints / read

   _____

3. take / Dennis and Mark / plan / a computer course

   _____

4. not mind / Angelique / do / the budget

   _____

5. need / improve / his communication skills / Rodrigo

   _____

6. Guo / be / a manager / not want

   _____

7. hope / Larry and Rita / the problem / solve

   _____

B Match the items in Column A with those in Column B to create six logical sentences.

Column A	Column B
____ 1. Choi is good	a. by talking to a career counselor.
____ 2. He is interested	b. of taking more English classes.
____ 3. He will begin	c. at solving math problems.
____ 4. Choi will ask the counselor	d. for helping him get a great job.
____ 5. He is also thinking	e. about writing résumés and cover letters.
____ 6. He will soon thank her	f. in finding a job as a computer programmer.

UNIT 2

A Complete the conversation with the present perfect form of the verbs in parentheses.

Martina: Hi, Serio. When is your interview?

Serio: It's tomorrow. I'm really nervous. I _____ well since Saturday!
(1. not sleep)

Martina: _____ you _____ for it?
(2. prepare)

Serio: Yes. I _____ already _____ my résumé, and
(3. write)

my mom _____ me by doing a practice interview with me.
(4. help)

Martina: That's good. _____ you _____ the company?
(5. research)

Serio: No, I _____ an opportunity to go online. But I will tonight.
(6. not have)

Martina: _____ you _____ all the requirements for
(7. finish)

your degree?

Serio: Yeah. I _____ all the basic business courses.
(8. complete)

I _____ many computer courses, but I _____
(9. not take)   (10. use)

a computer since I was a kid.

Martina: I'm sure you'll do well. Good luck!

B Complete the sentences. Circle the correct form of the verb.

1. Over the past year, I **have learned / have been learning** many new skills that I could apply to this job.

2. Omar **has been driving / has driven** a taxi since 2001. He enjoys his job and makes a good salary.

3. Hanh **has been making / has made** desserts since 2003. She plans to open her own bakery.

4. Francisco and Luz **have been finishing / have finished** their résumés. Now they need to start their job search.

5. Jonathan **has been working / has worked** the night shift since June. Now he works days.

6. Aisha **has been applying / has applied** to colleges for several weeks. She has three more applications to complete.

7. Naomi and Tamara **have been studying / have studied** together for four years. Now Naomi plans to return to her home country.

8. We **have been doing / have done** a lot of research for this project. How much more do we have to do?

UNIT 3

Unscramble the words and phrases to make sentences. There may be more than one answer.

1. Maria / up / pick / don't forget to

   _____

2. broke / car / down / Sofia's / in front of her house

   _____

3. turns / Mr. Suarez / on / his headlights / always / at night

   _____

4. down / flag / anyone / did you / for help

   _____

5. when you drive / pedestrians / watch / for / out / please

   _____

UNIT 4

Complete the sentences using past modals. Write the first sentence in the active voice and the second one in the passive voice.

1. **should / warn**   ACTIVE: The police _____ us about the storm.

   PASSIVE: We _____ about the storm.

2. **might / evacuate**   ACTIVE: The rescue workers _____ the building.

   PASSIVE: Our neighbors _____ from the building.

3. **could / prepare**   ACTIVE: Chia-Ling _____ for the disaster but didn't.

   PASSIVE: An exit plan _____ but it wasn't.

4. **shouldn't / risk**   ACTIVE: You _____ your life for your belongings.

   PASSIVE: Their lives _____ when it wasn't necessary.

5. **couldn't / protect**   ACTIVE: Elsa _____ her car from the tornado.

   PASSIVE: Elsa's car _____ from the tornado.

UNIT 5

Complete the conversations with *although* or *unless* and clauses from the box.

1. **A:** Are you going to stay at your job?

   B: Well, I'm not going to stay _____.

2. **A:** Did you hear about Alex?

   B: No, what happened?

   A: His boss told him he wasn't getting a promotion _____.

3. **A:** I didn't get that job _____.

   B: That's too bad.

4. **A:** _____, she doesn't always speak clearly.

   B: Really? I don't have any problem understanding her.

5. **A:** I have so much to do!

   B: You won't be able to finish _____.

> I was qualified for it
>
> I get a promotion
>
> I help you
>
> Janice's interpersonal skills are good
>
> he had great ratings on his performance review

UNIT 6

Rewrite the direct questions as embedded questions. Use the prompts in parentheses.

1. Why isn't Patricio feeling well? (Could you tell me)

   _____

2. Does he have a doctor's appointment on Tuesday? (Do you know)

   _____

3. When is his doctor's appointment? (I don't know)

   _____

4. Will he take medicine for his cold? (I wonder if)

   _____

5. What are his symptoms? (Can anyone tell me)

   _____

UNIT 7

Complete the sentences about early U.S. history and William Penn. Use the past perfect form of the verbs in parentheses.

1. The British _____ already _____ a tax on tea before the (put)

   colonists held the Boston Tea Party.

2. By 1733, people in North America _____ thirteen colonies. (establish)

3. William Penn _____ to England yet when he founded Pennsylvania. (not return)

4. The colony Pennsylvania _____ already _____ freedom (grant)

   of speech before the Constitution was written.

5. Penn _____ just _____ to sell Pennsylvania back to (try)

   England when he became sick.

6. By the time he died, Penn _____ all of his money. (lose)

UNIT 8

Rewrite the sentences using the correct form of each verb.

1. If you **trespass / might trespass**, you **might trespass / might have** to pay a fine.

   _____

2. If Abder **gets / got** another ticket, his license **was / will** be suspended.

   _____

3. Yong-Jin's penalties **are / might be** reduced, if he **admits / might admit** he's guilty.

   _____

4. You **go / could go** to jail if you **refuse / will refuse** to take a BAC test.

   _____

5. If Pauline **is / may be** arrested, her parents **hire / will hire** a good attorney.

   _____

UNIT 9

Complete the conversation using the past subjunctive or the past unreal conditional.

Eva: Did you look at that environmental website Sun Mi told us about?

Thomas: Yes, I did. But I wish I _____ it.
(1. not see)

Eva: Why? If I _____ it, I _____ all those tips on how
(2. not read)   (3. not learn)
to protect the environment.

Thomas: I guess you're right. But if I _____ them, I _____
(4. ignore)   (5. not feel)
so bad about throwing out all that paper last week.

Eva: You can make simple changes and still help the environment. For

example, I'm recycling my son's baby food jars now. It's easy, and I wish I

_____ sooner.
(6. start)

Thomas: You're right. My parents _____ more to help the environment if
(7. do)
they _____ about these problems. I'll start by doing something
(8. know)
simple, like turning off unnecessary lights!

UNIT 10

Complete the sentences with *who*, *that*, or *which* and the correct phrases from the box. There may be more than one correct answer.

are in Mr. Costa's class	created a website	don't use the website
improve every day	students do online	

Mr. Costa is the teacher _____ to help students with their

English. The website includes games and interactive exercises _____.

The students _____ love the website. Their test results are higher

than those of students _____. Mr. Costa thinks the scores,

_____, will help prove how important it is to motivate students.

Audio Script

Page 10, Listen, Exercises B and C

Counselor: Hello, Ruben. Come on in and have a seat.
Ruben: Thank you.
Counselor: So, you want to explore some career options—is that right?
Ruben: Yes. I haven't decided on a career yet. I've been thinking about going to school to become a chef.
Counselor: So, you enjoy cooking.
Ruben: No, not really. But right now I work in a hotel restaurant as a waiter. I'm friends with the chef. I found out that he makes a lot more money than I do, and that chefs at top restaurants make a lot of money. And I thought learning to cook might be easy.
Counselor: But you're not good at cooking now. . .
Ruben: My sandwiches are OK. But no, not really.
Counselor: Well, what *are* you good at?
Ruben: I guess I'm good at math. I'm good at working with all kinds of co-workers, and I'm good at dealing with customers. I think I have good interpersonal skills. . .

Page 11, Practice, Exercise B

Counselor: Well, I think there might be jobs that are a better match for you than a job as a chef. Tell me more about yourself.
Ruben: Well, I'm a student, Colombian, single. . .
Counselor: OK. But what are some of your personality traits? What are some *adjectives* you'd use to describe yourself?
Ruben: Oh. Well, I'm honest. For example, sometimes customers leave things in the restaurant—like purses or wallets or cell phones. I always try to find the owner. And I'm cooperative. If another waiter is busy and I'm not, I pour water and coffee for his customers.
Counselor: Your bosses and colleagues must like you.
Ruben: I hope so. . . I like to have good relationships at work. I'm always friendly with new staff; I try to teach them everything they need to know. And I make people laugh—I tell jokes when things get too serious.
Counselor: Um-hmm. So you're extroverted.
Ruben: Yes, I guess you could say that.
Counselor: You said earlier that you have good interpersonal skills . . . What other things do people like about you?
Ruben: I'm optimistic. I don't know what career I want, but I believe it's waiting for me. And I believe I'll find it. I guess I believe in luck. I'm intuitive. When I find the job that's right for me, I'll just *know*. I trust my feelings when I make decisions.
Counselor: Well, you'll make some decisions soon enough. Let's schedule some tests for next week. Talk to Linda, my secretary. She'll set up the times.
Ruben: OK. Thank you.

Page 18, Listen, Exercise A

Counselor: Hi, Ruben. How has everything been going?
Ruben: Great. Thanks.
Counselor: So tell me what you've done since I saw you last.

Ruben: Well, first I looked online for descriptions of jobs in the hotel industry. Second, I met with my manager to talk about careers with our hotel. Then I had an informational interview with the catering manager in my hotel. It was really helpful. Hotel catering didn't really sound that interesting or challenging—and I don't think hotel—catered food is so good. During the informational interview, I asked our catering manager if he'd ever thought about starting his own business. He said no, but he offered to contact someone with a catering business in another city to see if she might talk with me. Oh—and I also went to the library and got the names of places to contact about starting a small business.
Counselor: That's incredible, Ruben. . . . It sounds like you have an idea for a new career.
Ruben: Yes, I think I've made a decision. I want to own a successful catering business someday.

Page 18, Listen Exercise B

Counselor: Well, Ruben, I don't want to discourage you, but starting and running a business could be very difficult. You'll have to spend some time preparing.
Ruben: I know. It may take several years.
Counselor: It's important for you to plan a very clear career path—steps that will move you toward your long-term goal.
Ruben: Well, first I need to pass my last ESL class.
Counselor: What's step two?
Ruben: I'm not sure. I'll probably keep working at the hotel and save money.
Counselor: Well, do you want to stay in your current job at the hotel?
Ruben: No. Maybe, I should switch to the catering department, and change to full-time. I could save more money and take culinary arts classes at night.
Counselor: Well, you would learn cooking techniques in culinary arts classes, so that makes sense. So your second step has two parts: You're going to take a class and you're going to continue working at your hotel, but full-time, and in the catering department.
Ruben: Yes.
Counselor: Well, running a business requires management and accounting skills.
Ruben: I know. Maybe I could get a promotion to supervisor in the catering department. I could learn a lot that way.
Counselor: I suggest talking with the catering manager to find out if that might be possible. Becoming a supervisor might be a good third step.
Ruben: And my fourth step could be to become a manager—either at my hotel or at another hotel. And at the same time, I could collect more information about starting a small business. After getting enough training and saving enough money or getting a loan, my fifth step would be to open my catering business near the campus.
Counselor: Well, plans can change, but this sounds like a good start.
Ruben: Yes. And I'll finish with a successful business here in this city!

UNIT 2

Page 32, Listen, Exercise A

Hello. I'm Dr. Williams from Career Courage—an employment counseling agency. I'm here to talk about do's and don'ts for job interviews.

Answers to interview questions are important, but so are other things. First impressions are very important. So dress appropriately for the job you want. For example, you can wear jeans for a construction job interview, but wear business clothes for an office job. If you're not sure what to wear, be conservative. Always be clean and well-groomed. Don't wear heavy perfume or cologne. Ladies, don't wear too much jewelry.

Body language is important. It should indicate that you are interested, but relaxed. Sit and stand up straight. Use a firm handshake, and smile when you meet your interviewer. Look at your interviewer, make eye contact when he or she speaks, and smile and nod to show that you are listening. Don't make nervous movements, such as tapping your fingers or your feet.

Your voice is important. Speak clearly so that the interviewer can understand you—don't mumble! Your voice should indicate interest. Relax so that you don't sound nervous, and don't speak too quickly or too slowly. Don't use too many sounds like "uh" or "um."

The way you address an interviewer is very important. Always use "Mr." and "Ms.," unless the interviewer indicates another preference. Say "please" and "thank you" if the interviewer offers to do something for you. Show respect by saying "Yes, ma'am," or "Yes, sir" when your interviewer asks questions like "May I call your references?"

So appearance, body language, voice, and the way you address and respond to your interviewer are all important. Just a few other do's and don'ts: Don't bring anything except materials you need for your interview. And always turn off your cell phone before you walk into the building where you will be interviewed. Any questions . . . ?

Page 33, Listen, Exercise D

1. Beatriz

Interviewer: Have a seat, Beatriz.
Beatriz: Thank you.
Interviewer: I see in your résumé that you're getting a certificate in computer repair.
Beatriz: Yes. I'll get my certificate in six weeks.
Interviewer: I'm sorry. I didn't hear that.
Beatriz: I'm sorry. I'm getting my computer repair certificate in six weeks.
Interviewer: I see. And I see that you've been working at Computer Universe.
Beatriz: Yes. I work at the computer service counter three nights a week and on Saturdays.
Interviewer: You know it's a little hard to hear you with that air conditioner on. Did you say you work at the checkout counter?

2. Said

Interviewer: Hello. You must be Said. I'm Dave Mathews.
Said: Hi, Dave! Nice to meet you.
Interviewer: Please have a seat.
Said: Thank you.

3. Bruno

Interviewer: Tell me a little about yourself.
Bruno: Well, um . . . I'm studying to be a medical technician. . . Uh. . . I work part-time at a home improvement store, . . . and, uh . . . I'm dependable and I have good interpersonal skills.

4. Shin-Hae

Interviewer: Please sit down.
Shin-Hae: OK.
Interviewer: I'd like to start by asking you a few questions. I've arranged to show you around the office when we've finished.
Shin-Hae: Cool!

Page 38, Listen, Exercise A

Harvey: Hello. You must be Iris Martinez. I'm Harvey Samson.
Iris: Hello, Mr. Samson. It's nice to meet you.
Harvey: Please come in and have a seat.
Iris: Thank you.
Harvey: Would you like some coffee or tea?
Iris: No, thank you.
Harvey: Tell me a little about yourself.
Iris: Sure. I've been taking courses at Hillsborough Community College, and I'll receive a certificate in accounting next month.
Harvey: And will you be available to start full-time work then?
Iris: Yes. I've been working evenings and weekends as an assistant manager at a supermarket. I'd like to give my supervisor two weeks' notice.
Harvey: How long do you plan to stay here if you're hired?
Iris: I've done a lot of research, and I am very interested in working here. I hope to continue in the job and grow with the company.
Harvey: What do you think is your greatest strength?
Iris: I think my greatest strength is my attention to detail. I keep sight of the big picture, but I focus on every task or problem I encounter, even very small ones. I make sure I don't miss anything. I double- and triple-check my math.
Harvey: And what would you say is your greatest weakness?
Iris: Well, sometimes I become so focused on my work that I might seem shy or unfriendly. But for the last few months, I've been making an effort to greet everyone at the beginning of my shift. And I've been taking a few minutes to help other staff members clean up before I do my bookkeeping and close the store at night.
Harvey: I see. Great. Do you have any questions?
Iris: When will a hiring decision be made?
Harvey: We'll contact you within two weeks. Thank you for coming in.
Iris: Thank you.

Page 38, Listen, Exercise C

Harvey: Hello. You must be Liam. I'm Harvey Samson.

Liam: Hi, Harvey!

Harvey: I'm glad you took a seat. I was caught in a meeting. I'm sorry I'm late.

Liam: No problem.

Harvey: Would you like some coffee or tea?

Liam: Do you have decaf?

Harvey: Certainly. I'll be right back. . . . Here you are. I brought you some sugar and some creamer in case you want it.

Liam: Thank you.

Harvey I see on your résumé that you've been working for Quality Exterior Home Repair for three years. Why do you want to leave your current position?

Liam: Really, I like my position. But I can't stand my new boss. He doesn't know anything about the business, and he's really an obstacle. He has no interpersonal skills whatsoever.

Harvey: It must be hard for you to work there. How do you handle the stress?

Liam: Well, my co-workers and I joke about him a lot. That helps.

Harvey: I see. So obviously, we can't call your supervisor for a reference. Do you have other references we can call if we get to the stage where we'd want to contact someone?

Liam: Uh, . . . a reference? . . . Um . . . I think one of my co-workers would do it. Would that be OK?

Harvey: We accept references from applicants' co-workers. But we only call references after we've made a decision about who we want to hire. I'll be talking with several more applicants, and we won't decide anything for a couple more weeks. If you'd like, you can e-mail or call Human Resources to provide the name of your reference. If you want to come with me, I'll get you the director's card on your way out. Do you have any questions?

Liam: No. Not right now. Maybe later. Do you have any information about the company?

Harvey: I'll get that for you on your way out, too. This way, please.

Page 40, Practice

1. I've been working on my résumé.
2. I've been attending night classes.
3. My friend has proofread my résumé.
4. I've been applying for full-time jobs.
5. Miriam has taken classes in landscape design.
6. Sheena has finished all of her classes for her degree.
7. We've been studying all day for our math exam.
8. She's finally completed her applications for college.

UNIT 3

Page 47, Listen, Exercise A

Conversation 1

A: Person with the Honda Civic?

B: Yes, that's me.

A: Everything looks good. We changed your oil and we checked your other fluids. Your windshield wiper fluid was a little low, so we added a few ounces—just to top it off. We added air to your tires, and we checked your headlights. Your right headlight is out. Would you like us to replace that for you today?

B: How much will it cost?

A: Twenty-two dollars.

B: OK.

A: How are your windshield wipers working?

B: Fine.

A: OK. Well, we'll put that new headlight in. It should just take a few minutes.

Question 1: What is the situation?

a. The woman had a problem with her car and brought it to a mechanic for repairs.

b. The woman brought her car to a shop that does express oil changes and other car maintenance work.

c. The woman is shopping at an auto parts store.

Question 2: What does the woman have changed or replaced?

a. her oil and her headlight

b. her oil and her windshield wipers

c. her headlight and her windshield wipers

Conversation 2

A: Excuse me. Could I borrow your cell phone to make a call? I left mine at home, and my car won't start.

B: Sure. Do you have any idea what the problem is?

A: Well, it might be my battery. It could be dead. Last winter it died when the weather got cold.

B: Do you want me to try to jump-start it for you? I have the equipment in my car.

A: Oh, I do, too, in the trunk. But I don't know how to use it. Do you?

B: Yeah. I had to call a roadside assistance service a couple of times to jump-start my own car. I learned how to do it by watching them.

A: Well, OK. Thanks. I really appreciate it. Do you need me to do anything?

B: Just raise the hood for me, and then turn the key in the ignition when I tell you to. Don't pump the accelerator, though—just step on it once or twice. And if we get the car started, we'll run it for a few minutes. Then you should drive it for at least 20 minutes—out on the highway, if possible. And be sure to get your battery checked as soon as you can.

A: Thanks so much.

Question 1: What seems to be the problem?

a. A woman's car won't start and her cell phone doesn't work.

b. A woman's car has been dead since last winter.

c. A woman's car battery could be dead, but she doesn't know how to jump-start it.

Question 2: If the car is jump-started, how long should it be driven afterward?

a. for a few minutes

b. for at least 20 minutes

c. for as long as possible

Conversation 3

A: I want to take our car in to the garage next week. Can you find a ride to work?

B: Sandra could probably take me. Is something wrong with the car?

A: I'm not sure. I hear a strange noise when it starts sometimes. Haven't you heard it?

B: No.

A: Well, I hope nothing's wrong. But I want to take it in anyway.

B: We shouldn't spend money on that car unless it's necessary. Remember, we want to get a new car next year.

A: I know, but if we keep it in good condition, we'll probably get more money for it when we trade it in. We're overdue for a tune-up, and besides, we're driving to visit your sister at the end of the month.

B: That reminds me. I also want to get a car adaptor for my MP3 player so we can listen to it on the way.

Question 1: What does the man want the woman to do?
a. give him a ride to work
b. find someone to take her to work
c. listen to see if she hears a strange noise when the car starts

Question 2: What does the woman remember?
a. She did hear a noise.
b. There's something wrong with the stereo system.
c. She wants to buy something.

Page 47, Listen, Exercise B

Excerpt 1
Your windshield wiper fluid was a little low, so we added a few ounces—just to top it off.

Excerpt 2
And if we get the car started, we'll run it for a few minutes.

Excerpt 3
. . . if we keep it in good condition, we'll probably get more money for it when we trade it in. We're overdue for a tune-up, and besides, we're driving to visit your sister at the end of the month.

Page 52, Listen, Exercise A and Exercise B (Step 2)

Good morning, everyone. Today I'm going to talk about what to do if you have an accident involving your car and another vehicle. I hope you never have this experience, but you need to be prepared. Basically, there are 10 steps you should follow. Take notes on these steps, because you will be tested on them.

Step number 1. What's the first thing you do if you hit another car or another car hits you? If it's safe and legal, stop your vehicle! Many people don't. But it's illegal to leave the scene of an accident. Stop immediately.

Number 2. Move your vehicle out of traffic. If you can, drive it to the side of the road. But this advice is only for our state. If you are driving in another state, you need to know the laws of that state. In some states, moving your car from the place where it stopped is illegal.

Step number 3. Turn off your ignition. Don't leave your car running. Make sure your car is turned off before you get out. And it's a good idea to take your keys with you.

Step 4. Make necessary phone calls. Check to see if anyone is badly hurt and if they are, call 911. Moving an injured person can be dangerous. Wait for an ambulance, trained personnel, and the police to arrive. If no one is hurt, call the police.

OK. The fifth step is to mark the scene of the accident with reflecting triangles. Do you all know what I'm talking about? Triangles with bright yellow or orange lines on them? Stand these on the road in front and in back of the area of the accident. This will help other drivers see the accident as they approach.

Step number 6 is to collect the names of all the people in the cars and all the people who witnessed the accident. Getting the names and phone numbers of witnesses is important.

Number 7 is a step that many people forget to take. Take notes. Include the date, time, and weather conditions. It's also a good idea to take a picture or draw a diagram of the accident.

Step number 8. Exchange licenses and insurance cards with the other driver. Write down the other driver's name, license number, insurance company, and policy number.

Number 9. This isn't really a step because it's not something you should do. It's something you should NOT do. Don't talk about who caused the accident. It isn't a good idea to talk about whose fault the accident is.

OK. This is the last step. And it's one you do a few days after the accident. A police officer will write a report about the accident. You should get a copy of the report. Call your local police department, and find out if they can send it to you or where you can go to get it.

Page 55, Practice, Exercise A

Rosario: Hi, Hua-Ling. Can I ask you a question?

Hua-Ling: Sure. What's up?

Rosario: You have a car, right?

Hua-Ling: Yes. I share it with my brother. We just bought our car last year.

Rosario: Well, *I'm* going to buy a car . . .

Hua-Ling: That's great!

Rosario: Yes, but now I need to think about car insurance.

Hua-Ling: You sure do! It can be expensive. You know, it depends on the state you're in.

Rosario: Really? What about here in California?

Hua-Ling: Well, here the law requires you to have liability insurance for bodily injury and property damage.

Rosario: Oh, yeah. How much?

Hua-Ling: The minimum coverage you have to have in California is 15/30. That means that for each occupant in a vehicle who gets injured, the insurance will pay up to $15,000 to cover the person's medical expenses. If more than one person is injured, it'll cover up to 30,000 in expenses, total.

Rosario: Is that enough? Medical expenses are so high!

Hua-Ling: I know. I work in a hospital, and the cost of medical care is ridiculous. That's why some drivers get more than the minimum. You may be personally responsible if the insurance doesn't cover everything.

Rosario: Are you serious? That's terrible.

Hua-Ling: I know. But the state only requires 15/30 for bodily injury. So it's up to you to decide if you want more.

Rosario: I see. And what about property damage? What's the minimum coverage for property damage?

Hua-Ling: That's only $5,000.

Rosario: That's so little! So, if you wreck someone else's car, the insurance company pays them only $5,000? Even if it costs them more than that to fix, or even if they can never drive it again?

Hua-Ling: Yup. That's why some drivers buy more than the minimum. You should definitely shop around. Check at least three insurance companies. And go to the California Department of Insurance website. Let me get the website for you . . . oh, here it is . . . it's www.insurance.ca.gov. It has a lot of information.

UNIT 4

Page 66, Listen, and Page 67, Practice

A: I just read this amazing story in the paper.

B: Really?

A: Yeah. You know about the earthquake that happened last week in China?

B: Of course. I heard that about 50,000 people died. It's awful.

A: I know. It was horrible. Well, this story is about one of the survivors. This man, Mr. Liu, was a factory worker in a small town. Apparently, the earthquake struck on a Monday morning after people had gone to work or school.

B: Right. That's what I heard, too.

A: Well, anyway, this man, Mr. Liu, was trapped under the rubble of the factory after the earthquake on Monday, and no one knew if he was alive. But his 23-year-old daughter, Yuan, wouldn't give up hope. On Thursday night, she and some other people in their family were searching the rubble when they heard a muffled cry. She called out to him and he answered back and said he was thirsty.

B: Oh, wow. Thursday? That was the third day after the earthquake! So, did they get him out right away?

A: Well, no. The daughter first had to go for help, and it took the rescuers twelve hours to free him. He was under the rubble for a hundred hours! And the rescue was very dangerous because of the soldiers.

B: The soldiers?

A: Yes, the rescuers were soldiers. So if the soldiers took a wrong step or if they disturbed any piece of rubble in the wrong way, the whole building could have collapsed.

B: It all sounds terrible. I can't imagine what it must have been like.

A: They said that the reason he was rescued was because his daughter wouldn't give up hope. Let that be a lesson for all of us!

Page 70, Listen, Exercise A

On August 29th, 2005, Hurricane Katrina hit New Orleans. Eighty percent of New Orleans was flooded when the levees failed. The government was criticized for its lack of preparation and its failure to respond quickly or effectively. There were no plans to evacuate people without cars, the elderly, or the sick. There were no arrangements for public buses to be used to get people out of the city. And there were no arrangements for bus or taxi drivers to stay and help in an emergency.

Many people without transportation were directed or taken to the Superdome, a football stadium in downtown New Orleans, but there wasn't enough water, food, medical care, or security there. After the hurricane, food, water, and medical supplies were available, but they were not distributed. People were told to leave pets at home. But there were no plans for their rescue after people were evacuated.

Page 70, Listen, Exercise B

More than 1,800 people died, and there was more than $81 billion in damages. What went wrong? Katrina might not have been such a disaster if there had been better planning. For example, there should have been plans to evacuate hospitals and nursing homes. Public buses could have been used to evacuate people without cars. And what about all of those poor people in the Superdome? There should have been police there to keep them safe. And people should not have been told to leave pets at home.

Since Katrina, better preparation, evacuation, and communication systems have been developed in order to provide better responses to events like Hurricane Katrina in the future.

Page 71, Listen, Exercises A and B

Before you are told to evacuate, it's important to be ready. Know where you can stay. It's best to stay with friends or family members outside of the emergency area, or know which hotel or shelter you'll go to.

If you have a family, decide in advance on a safe meeting place. It could be dangerous to come back to your house from work or school. If you have children, contact the school to learn its emergency plans. Learn different routes from your home and workplace to your safe place.

Plan for your pets. Arrange for them to stay with friends or relatives outside the emergency area, if possible. If that's not possible, call your local animal shelter to find out about pet evacuation plans in your area.

Make sure everyone in your family has the name, phone number, and e-mail address of a contact outside your state. You might not be able to make local calls in an emergency, because so many people are trying to call each other. But you can often reach a person in another state.

Prepare an emergency kit, especially if you plan to go to a shelter. FEMA, the Federal Emergency Management Agency, has a website where you can find out what to include in your kit. Basics include a battery-powered radio, a flashlight and batteries, food and medicine, disinfectant wipes to clean yourself, blankets, water, and baby and pet supplies.

If you have a car, try to keep half a tank of gas in it at all times. When your area is under a flood watch, fill your tank. During an evacuation, gas stations will be very crowded.

If you live in a house, protect your property. Bring in any outdoor items. Open your basement windows to let the water come in so that your basement walls don't collapse. Check government websites for more detailed information.

If you are ordered to evacuate, go immediately. Take your emergency kit and important documents, such as your passport and birth certificate, if you have them ready. Unplug electronic equipment and appliances, except your refrigerator and freezer. Shut off your utilities, such as gas and water. Lock your doors. If you have time, leave a note on your property or in your mailbox saying when you left and where you are going. Check TV or radio for the roads you should use to evacuate. Don't take shortcuts. Shortcuts could lead to blocked or flooded areas where you may not be able to get through. Don't drive through water. If your car breaks down in water, get out immediately, and move to higher ground.

For more information, check your federal, state, and local government websites.

Next week, I'll discuss what to do if you are not ordered to evacuate. It's also necessary to be ready to "shelter in place"—to be ready to live for three or four days without help and without leaving your home.

Page 75, Listen, Exercises A and B

Tania: Hi. Nick. How are you doing?

Nick: Oh, I'm fine. What's new with you? I don't see you much anymore.

Tania: Oh, I've been busy. I'm still working at the airport, but my hours changed.

Nick: I hope you don't have to work the night shift.

Tania: No. I work 10 to 6. It's hard, because I don't have mornings, afternoons, or evenings completely free. And I can't be here when Greg gets home from school.

Nick: You mean he's home alone?

Tania: Just for a couple hours. And he's 12 and he's a responsible kid. But I still worry. I mean, what if strangers call? I don't want strangers to know he's here alone.

Nick: Why don't you tell him to say that you're busy? He should say, "I'm sorry. My mom can't come to the phone right now. If you want to leave your number, she'll call you back as soon as she can."

Tania: What if someone comes to the door?

Nick: You already have a peephole and a strong chain lock, right?

Tania: Yeah. I've told him to use the peephole before he opens the door.

Nick: Right. Well, if I were you, I'd tell him not to answer the door unless the person is a neighbor or friend he knows *really* well.

Tania: Sometimes it's friends that I worry about! What if his friends come over? They could get into all kinds of trouble without an adult around.

Nick: Could you make a rule that no friends can come over when you or another adult isn't home?

Tania: Maybe. He's pretty good about following rules.

Nick: He can always call me or come over to my house, you know, if he has any kind of trouble.

Tania: Thanks. Actually, I'd like him to call me if anything happens. But sometimes I can't answer the phone while I'm working. I'd like him to call me when he gets home every day, but sometimes I'm in meetings then.

Nick: Maybe you could have him send you a text message.

Tania: That's a good idea. And for emergencies, I'll give him your number. I worry about kitchen fires if he tries to cook.

Nick: Have you thought about writing a fire safety plan with him?

Tania: Hmmm. We could talk about when and how to get out of the house, the smoke alarm, the fire extinguisher. I could make sure he knows how to call 911.

Nick: That's important. Tell him to give his location first, then his name, then the problem.

Tania: These are all great ideas. You know, I think I'll sit down with Greg and make a list of rules. I'll write contact numbers, and I'll include yours. We'll role-play different situations involving strangers and different emergency phone calls.

Nick: And talk to him about how he feels. He may not tell you if he's afraid or worried or bored or lonely, unless you ask.

Tania: Thanks, Nick. I'll do that. See you later.

Nick: Good talking to you.

Page 77, Listen, Exercises A and B

Conversation 1

A: Did you finish installing it?

B: Yes, I finally got it on. Here . . . try to open it.

A: I can't do it! How does this thing work?

B: You could try reading the instructions.

A: Come on . . . just *show* me! I need some cleanser to clean up that mess.

Conversation 2

A: Are you finding everything you need?

B: I'm not really sure what I'm looking for. My sister and her family are going to visit. They have a son who's one and a half. I'm worried because some of our rooms aren't safe for him. And he could fall down the stairs . . .

A: Well, one thing I would definitely recommend is a safety gate. We have several models.

B: Do they work?

A: Yes! I used them when my own kids were young. Pressure gates aren't as secure as the type that you screw into the wall, but they won't leave holes in the wood of your door frame when you remove them. And you can move them from room to room. We have both kinds.

B: I'm not worried about the wood of my door frame. The safety of my nephew is more important. And I can buy more than one gate. I'd like to see the most secure gates you have.

Conversation 3

A: Here. I brought you something. You told me that Jane hurt her fingers in a door last week. I was out shopping, and I saw these: doorstops and door holders.

B: What a good idea! I never thought of these.

A: I was in the drugstore, and I saw them.

B: How much were they? I'll pay you for them.

A: Oh, don't be silly. They just cost a few dollars.

B: Well, thanks. That was really thoughtful of you.

Conversation 4

A: As you can see, we're very child-friendly and child-safe.

B: Yes, I can see that you take the safety of the children very seriously.

A: We do. You know, there was an article in the paper just last month about a child who almost fell from a window. That simply couldn't happen here. We watch all the children at all times. Also, if you look right here, . . . we have these on all the windows of our building. See?

B: Well, hopefully Pamela will enjoy it here.

A: I'm sure she'll love it.

UNIT 5

Page 90, Listen, Exercises A and B

Elena: Do you have any questions about your ratings?

Eva: Just a few. I don't really understand why I got a 3 in communication. I talk with everyone, and I understand everything you ask me to do. I know my English isn't perfect, but I can do my work.

Elena: Well, although you can do your work, your writing needs improvement. Your reports aren't very clear or thorough. You're a great employee, and you perform most of your duties really well. But I can't give anyone a 2 in communication unless their reports are well written.

Eva: Thanks. I understand. I need to continue to work on my English. Do you have any suggestions for what I can do to improve?

Elena: Actually, yes. I had to give a lot of 3s in communication. So I've decided to start a new "conversation partners" program. Some of the native English speakers on staff will meet once a week with co-workers who are still learning English. I hope you'll participate in this program.

Eva: I will. It sounds great. And I'm going to continue taking English class at night.

Elena: Terrific.

Eva: Was there a reason you didn't give me a 1 in initiative and problem solving?

Elena: Yes. I know that you recognize and solve some kinds of problems on your own. But I've noticed that when groups discuss problems, or team members have to reach an agreement, you're usually quiet. Unless you can offer suggestions in group discussions, I can't say you meet expectations in initiative and problem solving.

Eva: I see. Thanks. I'll work on that.

Elena: And I don't give anyone a 1 in attendance / punctuality. Everyone's expected to be here and on time. There's really no way to exceed that expectation.

Page 91, Practice, Exercises A and B

Conversation 1

A: Joe, your work is good, and I can always count on you to finish on time. But although you're a hard worker, you don't follow safety procedures, and that's a serious issue.

B: Can you give me some examples?

A: Well, for one thing, you run electrical cords across the floor and aisles. The other day, I saw that you had joined three cords together, and you left them on the floor at the end of your shift. Someone could trip on the cords—and joining three together is against our fire code. That's one example. Another is how you handle chemicals. I've seen you carry the cleaning chemicals without tops on the containers, and I've noticed that you don't always wear gloves when you use them.

B: Thanks. You're right. I hadn't thought about the electrical cords. They could cause an accident. I won't leave them out across the floor or aisles again, but what should I do when I don't have a long enough cord?

A: Just ask me for one—we can send someone out to buy one, or I can order it.

Conversation 2

A: You have many strengths, but I can't keep you in the department unless you learn to communicate better on the phone. Customer calls are very important.

B: I didn't realize this was a problem. I'll work on it from now on. What should I do differently in the future?

A: Well, first of all, you need to be clear and professional.

B: Can you give me some examples?

A: Yes. Start with "Hello. Electronic Solutions. How may I assist you today?" instead of "Hi, I need to verify some information." There are scripts for our phone calls in the Procedures file.

B: I see. I didn't realize there were scripts in our files. Of course I should use them, and I will.

A: You went over this in your training during the first weeks you were here.

B: I missed a couple of days of training. But you're right. It was my responsibility to find out what I'd missed. I'm sorry I didn't do that. I'll be sure to do it now.

Page 94, Listen, Exercise A

André: Hi, Claudia. How are you doing?

Claudia: Well, I just had my performance review.

André: Oh! How'd it go?

Claudia: Really well. My supervisor had some great suggestions. . .

André: Who's your supervisor, again?

Claudia: Max.

André: Oh, right. He's a good guy.

Claudia: So we talked a little about promotions.

André: Great! What did he say?

Claudia: I asked him if he thought I was qualified for the administrative assistant position.

André: Good for you!

Claudia: He was very encouraging. He said that I was well organized but that I needed to develop some of my skills. For example, he said that I should try to improve my oral communication skills because the assistants talk with customers and sales reps a lot.

André: So did he give you any ideas about how to do this?

Claudia: Yep. He said I should look into taking a career training course at the community college. Apparently, they have non-credit courses in the evenings and they aren't very expensive.

Page 95, Listen

Mei: Hi, Marco, I was just thinking about you. How are things going?

Marco: Really well. This is a great company to work for. Thanks for helping me get this job.

Mei: You work in Manufacturing, right?

Marco: Yes.

Mei: So you like the job?

Marco: Oh, yes. But I've been thinking. I've always had this knack for fixing things, like office equipment, and I'd really like to develop that skill and use it on the job.

Mei: That's a great idea. This company encourages people to grow and move around. What kinds of equipment would you want to work on?

Marco: Well, maybe copying machines and computer equipment.

Mei: You'd need some training on our equipment.

Marco: How would I get that?

Mei: I think the company offers some on-the-job training for computer repair and maintenance. There may be some training sessions soon. Have you looked in the kitchen on the bulletin board?

Marco: Thanks, I'll do that right away.

Mei: You should also check out the company Intranet site. They're always updating lists of job openings and job-training programs.

Marco: Thanks so much, Mei. Those are great suggestions!

Mei: No problem. I'd really like to know how things go. Keep me posted.

UNIT 6

Page 108, Listen

Carmen: Hi, Bianca. I haven't heard from you lately. How are you?

Bianca: Oh, hi, Carmen. Actually, I've been having some strange symptoms, and I went to the doctor yesterday.

Carmen: Nothing serious, I hope. . .

Bianca: It's probably nothing. I found a lump under my arm, and my doctor wants me to see an oncologist, just to rule out the possibility of cancer.

Carmen: When is your appointment?

Bianca: Thursday at 4:00.

Carmen: Do you have a ride? Is there anything I can do? . . .

Pages 120–121, Listen, Exercises A and B

Marisa: Type 2 diabetes is the most common form of diabetes. In type 2 diabetes, either the body does not produce enough insulin or the cells are unable to use the insulin. What is insulin? Insulin is a hormone. When you eat food, your body changes all of the sugars into glucose, which gives energy to the cells in your body. Insulin takes the glucose from the blood into the cells. When glucose builds up in the blood instead of going into cells, it can cause two problems: First, your cells may not get enough energy. Over time, high blood glucose levels may hurt your eyes, kidneys, nerves, or heart. Type 2 diabetes is a very serious disease, and it is very common in the United States. Pierre will talk about risk factors for type 2 diabetes, and Min-Ji will give suggestions for reducing risk and living with the disease.

Pierre: Thank you, Marisa. There are many different risk factors for type 2 diabetes, but I'm going to focus on four of them. One risk factor that you can't do anything about is a family history of diabetes. If a parent or brother or sister is diabetic, you are at risk. Another risk factor is a lack of exercise. People who are not active are more likely to become diabetic than people who lead physically active lives. A third risk factor is poor diet. People who have unhealthy eating habits are more likely to be overweight, which is one reason they may be more likely to become diabetic. The fourth factor is high blood pressure. It's important for people who have risk factors to take whatever actions they can to reduce their risks. Min-Ji will talk to you about that.

Min-Ji: I'm going to discuss things people can do to reduce the risk of becoming diabetic or to help control diabetes. Pierre mentioned that poor diet and lack of exercise are risk factors for diabetes. The good news is that people can control these things. Regular exercise and a healthy diet can help prevent diabetes. If your blood pressure is too high, reduce your use of salt and alcohol, and take any medications your doctor prescribes to help you lower your blood pressure. Doing these things will help prevent diabetes, and if you already have it, they will help you control the disease.

Marisa: This ends our presentation. Diabetes is a big problem for many people. There is no cure. However, if you know you are at risk, you and your doctor can work together to try to reduce your risk. If you are diabetic, you can do things that can help you live longer and better with diabetes. Are there any questions?

UNIT 7

Page 134, Listen

Jim Peters: Welcome to *America Rising* on KXYZ. Our guest today is Professor Susan Klass from Haymond Community College. Dr. Klass will be talking to us about the process of lawmaking. Welcome, Dr. Klass.

Professor Klass: Thank you, Jim. It's a pleasure.

Jim Peters: And it's a pleasure to have you here. So tell us, how is a federal law made?

Professor Klass: Well, basically a law starts as an idea. Anyone can think of the idea for a new law. Then they get others to sign a petition supporting the idea. If the petition gets signed by enough people, it goes to a congressperson. If the congressperson likes the idea, he or she sponsors it—introduces and supports it in Congress.

Jim Peters: OK, so someone has an idea, finds enough people to support it, and the idea gets sponsored by a senator or representative. Then what?

Professor Klass: Well, the idea is proposed as a bill in the House or Senate. The bill gets sent to the appropriate committee. For example, if the bill is about school reform, it gets sent to the Education Committee.

Jim Peters: Right.

Professor Klass: The bill gets voted on by the committee. If it gets approved, it goes back to the full House or Senate.

Jim Peters: Depending on whether the bill came from a senator or representative.

Professor Klass: Yes. It goes back to the sponsor's part of Congress. If it passes there, it moves to the other part of Congress, which then votes on the bill. The bill either gets approved or rejected, or it goes back to the original committee for revision.

Jim Peters: So, for example, if a bill starts in the House of Representatives, and it passes there, it goes to the Senate, which then votes on it.

Professor Klass: Yes. And if the bill is approved, it goes to the president, who can sign or veto it. If the bill gets vetoed, Congress has three choices. It can make changes to the bill and try again, it can give up on the bill, or vote to override the president's veto.

Jim Peters: You mean the president's decision isn't final.

Professor Klass: Not necessarily. It requires a vote of two-thirds of both houses of Congress to override. That means 67 senators and 290 representatives. If one house or the other doesn't get a two-thirds majority, the president's decision stands and the bill will not become a law. But a two-thirds majority in both houses of Congress is more powerful than the president's veto.

Jim Peters: Well, this is all wonderful information. This is why it's so important to contact our representatives about important legislation.

Professor Klass: Exactly. Our elected officials can't represent us unless we speak up. And they are under constant pressure from big business and from special-interest groups. Individual citizens need to know what bills have been proposed, and we need to let our representatives know how we feel. If we have an idea about a law that we believe should be passed, we should understand that it may remain an idea unless we do something about it.

Jim Peters: Thank you, Professor Klass, for this valuable information. We'd like to take some calls from our listeners now, about bills that are currently being considered in the United States Congress . . .

Page 138, Listen, Exercises A and B

Good morning and welcome to your Citizenship class. I'm Ms. Miller, and I'm looking forward to being your instructor.

As many of you know, to apply for citizenship, you need to fill out documents from United States Citizenship and Immigration Services. After you submit the documents, you have an interview with a USCIS official, who will check the information on your forms, ask you questions, and confirm that you are telling the truth. It's extremely important to tell the truth because if anything is found to be untrue, you will not be admitted as a citizen and will not be able to try again for five years. You will also need to speak and understand English well enough to pass a simple dictation test. You'll also need to pass a civics test, which includes two sections—one on U.S. government and a section on U.S. history. If you make it through all of this, you will take an Oath of Allegiance and be sworn in as a United States citizen.

So . . . let me go through each of the major requirements for citizenship in a little more detail.

First, there's an age requirement. Applicants must be at least 18 years old.

Second, there's a residency requirement. You need to have been lawfully admitted for permanent residence. This means you need to produce an I-551 card—the card that used to be called a green card . . . because it used to be green. You need to have lived in the United States for five years, and you need to have been physically present for thirty months of those five years. You can't have left the country for more than a year at a time.

Requirement number three is one that we will discuss in later classes. Basically, an applicant is required to demonstrate good moral character. This means you are ethical, that you behave morally. The government has identified things that indicate that a person does not have good moral character. Some examples are if you have been convicted of a serious crime, have been convicted more than once for gambling, or have been involved with smuggling aliens into the country. This is just a partial list.

The fourth requirement is that you must show attachment to the Constitution. You must convince government officials that you value the ideas expressed in the United States Constitution and support them.

The fifth requirement is the language requirement. You must speak, read, and write everyday English. There are some exceptions for people over 55 who have lived in the country fifteen years or more, or people who are over 50 who have lived here twenty years or more.

The next requirement, the sixth, is that you demonstrate knowledge of the government and history of the United States. You do this by passing a civics test.

Finally, you have to take the Oath of Allegiance. You promise to support the Constitution, to give up any allegiance to any other country, and to bear arms in the armed forces or perform non–military services for the government, if required.

For most people, these are the seven general requirements, although there are some exceptions, for example, for people who are married to U.S. citizens or people who are in the military. For those of you who have access to a computer, you can read about these requirements and find study materials on the United States Citizenship and Immigration Services website. I'll give you a handout with the URL—the address for the site. You can find the forms you need on the site. In this class, you'll be studying all of the information that you might need to include on your forms. You'll practice listening, speaking, and dictation to make sure you have the English skills needed to pass the test. And you'll spend a lot of time learning about the United States government and history.

Page 141, Listen, Exercise A

Today, we'll be talking about the expansion of the United States—not about states and the dates they became states, but about larger territories, because most of the land was acquired that way.

We still have states today with the names of the original thirteen colonies, but before independence, Britain owned essentially all of the land from the East Coast to the Mississippi River. After Britain lost the Revolutionary War in 1783, all of that territory became the United States of America.

If you look at your map, you'll see a large territory just west of the Mississippi River. This area was the Louisiana Territory, and although it had been claimed at one time by Spain, it was controlled by France in December 1803, when the United States purchased it. Thomas Jefferson, the president at the time, was very happy about this purchase, which almost doubled the size of the United States and guaranteed free movement along the Mississippi River.

East Florida, West Florida, and a small area at the southeast of the Louisiana Territory were all part of Spanish Florida after the Revolutionary War. All of these areas were added to the United States in 1819, by a combination of negotiations and military actions.

Territories including Texas and California became part of the United States after wars with Mexico. The area that was then Texas was acquired in 1845, and a large area including present-day California was acquired in 1848.

Spain, Great Britain, Russia, and the United States had all originally claimed the Oregon Territory, but in the end, the United States acquired it from Britain. The two countries reached agreement in 1846. Alaska was purchased from Russia in 1867. Russia was having financial difficulties, the profit from trade in the Alaskan settlements was low, and it did not want to see Alaska fall under British control. The purchase was unpopular with American citizens at the time, but later the discovery of gold and oil in Alaska would prove that the purchase had been a good one. Although acquired by the United States in 1867, Alaska waited until 1959 to become a state.

Hawaii was annexed to the United States in 1898 and became a territory two years later, but it didn't become a state until 1959.

UNIT 8

Page 146, Listen, Exercise A

Today we're going to discuss one of the most famous Supreme Court cases—*Miranda* v. *Arizona*. Many of you have probably heard the *Miranda* warning on TV—when a police officer reads a suspect his or her rights. This is basically the warning:

"You have the right to remain silent. Anything you say can and will be used against you in a court of law. You have the right to have an attorney present during questioning. If you cannot afford an attorney, one will be appointed for you."

Sound familiar? In some states, police officers are supposed to check to confirm that the person understands. In these states, a longer version is used, such as this one:

"You have the right to remain silent and refuse to answer questions. Do you understand? Anything you say may be used against you in a court of law. Do you understand? You have the right to consult an attorney before speaking to the police and to have an attorney present during questioning now or in the future. Do you understand? If you cannot afford an attorney, one will be appointed for you before any questioning if you wish. Do you understand? If you decide to answer questions now without an attorney present, you will still have the right to stop answering at any time until you talk to an attorney. Do you understand? Knowing and understanding your rights as I have explained them to you, are you willing to answer my questions without an attorney present?"

So that's the *Miranda* warning—the short version and the long version.

Page 146, Listen, Exercise B

OK. Now I'm going to give you a little background . . . tell you a little about the *Miranda* case. And then I'm going to describe a common misunderstanding related to the *Miranda* warning. First the case.

The Constitution gives rights to people suspected of a crime. The people who wrote it knew that governments could be unjust—government authorities could do whatever they wanted to people if they accused the people of being criminals. The Constitution tries to protect people who could be wrongly accused. The right to remain silent and the right to an attorney are two protections.

In 1963, Ernesto Miranda was accused of kidnapping and raping an 18-year-old woman. He was brought to the police department for questioning, and he admitted that he had committed the crime. However, he was not told about his right to remain silent, and he was not told about his right to have an attorney present.

At the trial, his defense attorney tried to get Miranda's confession thrown out. It was the only evidence against Miranda. But the confession was not thrown out, and Miranda was found guilty.

Miranda's attorney took the case to higher courts, and in 1966 the Supreme Court decided that the statements Miranda made to the police could not be used as evidence, since Miranda had not known his rights.

Since then, police have been required to read or tell criminal suspects their rights before interrogating them.

Miranda did not go free. New evidence was found against him. He was found guilty at a second trial, and he went to prison.

TV has helped make the *Miranda* rights well known. But TV has also contributed to some misunderstandings. On TV, you often see police officers stopping someone on the street, and you hear them reading the person his or her rights. Actually, police are required to read these rights only to people they take into custody—people they are going to question at the police station, in the police car, and so on. The police can arrest someone without asking questions, and in this case, the police don't have to read the person any rights. Also, police don't have to read someone his or her rights to ask for personal information such as the person's name and address.

Page 158, Listen, Exercises A and B

Professor: I'm going to be talking briefly about infractions, misdemeanors, and felonies. These are the three types of crimes recognized under our state law. We've already talked about infractions. These are things that don't stay on your criminal record and that don't carry a jail or prison sentence. These are usually civil offenses like minor traffic violations or littering. Today, I want to focus on the two more serious types of crimes—misdemeanors, which are more serious than infractions, and felonies—such as robbery and illegal drug use, which are the most serious. I'll start with misdemeanors. . . Give me some examples of misdemeanors. Yes, Shannon.

Shannon: Trespassing?

Professor: That's right. Trespassing is a misdemeanor. Have you ever seen fences out in the country that have "No hunting or trespassing" signs on them? Well, it's a crime to climb the fence and go onto that property. It's a misdemeanor. Another one. . . Justin?

Justin: Um, vandalism.

Professor: That's right. One more. Emil?

Emil: Is shoplifting a misdemeanor?

Professor: Yep. In this state it is. Good. Now, does anyone know what kind of penalties people can receive for misdemeanors?

Justin: Fines.

Professor: That's right. Often the penalty for a misdemeanor is a fine. There can be jail time, too. Up to one year. But the time would be in a county jail, not a state prison. Or sometimes a person who commits a misdemeanor might get probation— a person on probation does not have to go to jail but must demonstrate good behavior and must report regularly to a probation officer. Another penalty might be community service. This is common for a first offense, especially for young people. Now for a felony, you can receive a large fine, but you can also go to prison. Felony charges carry prison sentences from one year to life. And some states have the death penalty for the very worst crimes. In some states, if you commit first-degree murder or another terrible crime, you will receive the death penalty. A person who is found guilty of a felony can still have to pay a fine, too. Sometimes a very big one. In addition to murder, felonies include arson, burglary, and rape. That's it for today. Any questions?

Shannon: What if someone can't pay a fine?

Professor: Oh, I think the courts often set up payment programs. The person can pay a little each month.

Barbara: How long will a misdemeanor stay on a person's record?

Professor: Forever. So don't do anything stupid. OK. That's it for today.

UNIT 9

Pages 170–171, Listen, Exercises A and B

Ross Simon: Welcome to *Focus on Green*, on KXYZ. Our guest today is Councilwoman Janine Frank, from West Burbank. Councilwoman Frank will be telling us about one particular effort to make her city a greener one, and how each of us can do our share—and make a difference. Good morning, Councilwoman Frank!

Councilwoman: Good morning, Ross! It's so nice to be here.

Ross Simon: I know you're very busy, Councilwoman, so we really appreciate your being here. Now, we're very interested in all of your city wide environmental projects—especially one that relates to carpooling. But first, can you tell us a bit about how you're greening your city?

Councilwoman: First Ross, I have to tell you that none of my work would be possible without the good people of my city, West Burbank. And I also have to say that my hard work is shared by all; this is truly a team effort.

Ross Simon: Well, it seems to be a great team! So tell us about how your program got started.

Councilwoman: Well, the first step, of course, was to educate people about the consequences of not doing certain things. In this case, that means showing them what will happen if we don't start conserving our resources. The next step was to offer solutions. Of course, there's no single solution to every problem, but once we start brainstorming, you'd be amazed at what we can think of.

Ross Simon: Right. Can you give us some examples?

Councilwoman: Let's take carpooling, for example. Everyone knows that we should do it, but how can we implement a successful program? My committee and I proposed a city wide ride sharing program that is a big success. It's also simple to use. People can register online; they just need to enter their starting point and destination, and then they will be put in touch with similar travelers.

Ross Simon: Sounds great, Councilwoman. But what if someone's shy or doesn't feel comfortable doing that online?

Councilwoman: Good point, Ross. Well, we also have "casual carpooling." People can call our carpool hotline or go online to find a specific meeting place. Then they can join others in their commute to work.

Ross Simon: That's great!

Councilwoman: Yes. And there's a third option; other groups— several, in fact—who travel longer distances have joined together to form a "vanpool." They share the cost of renting a van, plus gas and any other related expenses.

Ross Simon: Talk about a team effort!

Councilwoman: Yes, Ross—it's always interesting to me how people can work together to find so many wonderful solutions to a problem.

Ross Simon: That's certainly impressive. And tell us, Councilwoman. What are the consequences of *not* carpooling?

Councilwoman: Well, Ross, I must tell you that I was surprised to learn these facts. Did you know that if every commuter car in the U.S. carried just one more person, we'd save up to 600,000 gallons of gas and 12 million pounds of carbon dioxide every day?

Ross Simon: Wow! That is surprising—and yet now I'm sure my listeners will join me in being excited about the fact that we can do something—like ridesharing—to make a difference. Thank you again, Councilwoman, for joining us, and we wish you all the best!

Councilwoman: Thank you, Ross. And I'd like to invite interested listeners to check out my website, at www.councilwomanfrank.com, to find out how they can start this kind of program—or any of the initiatives we've started—in their own city.

Page 176, Listen

Joseph and his family have recently moved to a new community. Hector is one of his new neighbors.

Hector: Good morning, Joseph! How's it going?

Joseph: Hey, Hector. Great. I'm just trying to get this recycling thing straightened out.

Hector: What? No recycling back in your old town?

Joseph: No, we had recycling. It's just the rules were different! Here it seems a bit more complicated—not that I'm complaining because honestly, I do think it's important!

Hector: I know—it can be confusing! Here's a tip: Look in front of Tony's house; he's always the first one to put out his recycling. You'll always know what day it is if you check in front of his house!

Joseph: Ah! Thanks. If I'd known that before, I wouldn't have had trouble. Between Tony and the calendar, I should get it straight soon! Well, I have to tell you, I just wish we had had these types of regulations where I used to live. So much of our garbage was just thrown away without being recycled.

Hector: That's a shame. I wish we had started recycling years ago. Hmmm. I can't tell you the amount of junk we threw away without sorting!

Joseph: I can imagine. Believe it or not, my thirteen-year-old is great at helping us keep the trash sorted. He's the one who makes sure we have all of our paper, plastics, and metals separated and sorted correctly. He's like the recycling police!

Hector: Yeah, well, they do talk about it in school these days. My daughter taught me the three Rs: reduce, reuse, and recycle. I wish they had taught us about the environment back when we were kids! Actually, I wish we had all been more educated about the amount of waste we produced.

Joseph: Come on, Hector! Back in those days they were just thinking about using, not conserving! I think if our parents had been aware of the damage they were doing, they would have done things differently.

Hector: Well, I guess we're moving in the right direction then! You know, the best thing would be if everyone in the whole country could sort their trash. Maybe if we had more kids around like your son, we wouldn't have a lot of the problems that we currently have!

UNIT 10

Page 186, Listen, Exercises A and B

Our topic this week is the growth of the Internet. Like many important advances in technology, the Internet did not start with an invention. It started with an idea and a vision for the future. And that idea and vision came from a man named J.C.R. Licklider. Today, I will talk about Licklider's vision.

First, you need to understand something about Licklider's background. Unlike others who worked with early computers, Licklider was not an engineer. He started his career in the 1940s as an experimental psychologist. In his work, he used computers to collect and analyze data. Most engineers of the time saw computers as not much more than very powerful calculators. And, in fact, that's what most computers were in those days. But as a psychologist, Licklider saw computers very differently. He was interested in using the computer as a communications tool.

Licklider was frustrated by the slow progress of his research, so he decided to keep a record of how he spent his work time. He discovered that he spent 85 percent of his time putting together the data he needed to make a decision or to learn something that he needed to know—even with the help of computers. In other words, he spent most of his time finding information. But once he had the information, he could often understand what it meant and make a decision very quickly—sometimes in just seconds.

Because of his own experience, Licklider wanted to find a better way for humans and computers to work together.

He thought they should be equal partners because they each had different, but equally important, strengths. By "thinking" together, Licklider believed that both computers and people could do far more than either could do alone. This is how he explained it in an article he wrote in 1960:

"…Human brains and computing machines will be coupled together very tightly, and . . . the resulting partnership will think as no other human brain has ever thought and process data in a way not approached by the information-handling machines we know today."

He also described how in ten to fifteen years computerized "thinking centers" would exist. These "thinking centers" would be used to store and find information, like libraries, but would be much, much larger. And they would be connected to each other and to individual users through a network.

Not new ideas today, of course, but Licklider, who was trained in psychology, not computer science, wrote these words in 1960. Amazingly, he had come very close to describing *today's* Internet.

That's all we have time for today. Next time, we will talk about how Licklider's vision became the reality of today's Internet.

Page 190, Listen, Exercises A and B

Michelle Allen: Good afternoon, Dr. Knowles, and welcome to *Technology Today*.

Dr. Knowles: Thank you, Michelle. It's nice to be here.

Michelle Allen: So, Dr. Knowles, lately we've been hearing a lot, both positive and negative, about the effects that the Internet has had on human communication. Let's start with the positive.

Dr. Knowles: Well, there are many positives. We all know that the Internet has made it incredibly easy for people to stay in touch with family, friends, and business contacts who are far away. With the Internet, we can also reconnect with people from our past. And we're able to make new friends and contacts with people we would never have even met before. For example, the Internet has given people who live in isolated areas the chance to communicate with others who share their interests and concerns. For people with disabilities that prevent them from going out and meeting others face to face, the Internet has opened a whole new world. And, of course, the Internet has made it possible for scientists to share information instantaneously. The sharing of scientific ideas was the original reason for the creation of the Internet. It remains one of its most important uses today.

Michelle Allen: That's a pretty impressive list . . .

Dr. Knowles: Yes, it is . . .

Michelle Allen: Why, then, are there so many warnings about the Internet harming human communication?

Dr. Knowles: First of all, let me say that I strongly believe that the Internet has done more good than harm. However, I do have some concerns about heavy Internet use, especially among young people.

Michelle Allen: Such as?

Dr. Knowles: Well, when young people use online communication to replace or avoid face-to-face interaction, I think that's a problem. For example, a naturally shy person who spends all of his or her time online won't develop the social skills he or she needs to feel comfortable communicating in person. Humans are sociable by nature. We need emotional, intellectual, and physical contact to be truly happy. Although you might be able to get the emotional and intellectual contact you need online, you can't hug a computer or see the effect that your words and actions have by looking into its eyes. Body language and eye contact are a huge part of human communication, but they don't exist in online communication.

Michelle Allen: Well, people do use emoticons, you know, smiling faces, and so on . . . Isn't that a form of body language?

Dr. Knowles: Oh, I don't think you can compare the two. People express hundreds, even thousands of emotions with their eyes and bodies. There are only a handful of emoticons.

Michelle Allen: Very interesting . . . well, let's bring some callers into the conversation . . . Our first caller is Mike from Ontario . . .

Page 196, Listen, Exercises A and B

Nick: I've always thought of myself as an up-to-date kind of guy. And as a writer, I was also pretty certain that I understood the English language. Until yesterday, that is, when my 13-year-old daughter gave me a little language quiz . . . And I failed miserably. As I pointed out to her, however, it wasn't really a fair quiz, since it was in a foreign language—sort of. Foreign, that is, to a middle-aged not-as-up-to-date-as-he-thought-he-was kind of guy. What I'm talking about, if you haven't guessed already, is the language for sending text messages, or "texting," as they call it.

Now, I'm not talking about the shorthand that has been used for years in business—things like ASAP (*as soon as possible*), or FYI (*for your information*). Those abbreviations are still used, and even old guys like me know what they mean. I'm talking about something much newer than that.

To help me here, I've brought along a native speaker, my thirteen-year-old daughter Tiffany. Actually, I should say native *writer*; this language is mostly a written one at the moment, although more and more expressions are making their way into the spoken language.

Nick: Hey, Tiff, 'sup?

Tiffany: NM.U?

Nick: AAS . . . Did you understand that? Well, neither did I yesterday, but as you can see, I'm a fast learner. Tiff, can you translate that for our audience, please?

Tiffany: Sure, Dad. You asked me 'sup', which means "What's up?" Then I answered NMU—which means "Not much. How about you?" And you answered AAS, which means "Alive and smiling."

Nick: Alive and smiling indeed . . . OK, so Tiffany has agreed to give me a second chance on my quiz, and I've been up all night studying. So . . . here goes.

Tiffany: Okay, Dad, the first one is easy: BFF

Nick: No problem! BFF means "best friends forever."

Tiffany: WTG, Dad! Oh, sorry, that means "Way to go!" OK, number 2: P911.

Nick: Parent emergency? Like if your father is having a heart attack or something?

Tiffany: No, Dad. It means "Parent alert," like when your parents come into the room, and you have to stop texting . . . Okay, here's another easy one: H&K.

Nick: Hugs and kisses.

Tiffany: Yes! Now you're going to translate the shorthand, OK?

Nick: K. (That means OK, for anyone over 20 in the audience today.)

Tiffany: How do we write "sleepy"?

Nick: Hmmmm . . . let me think . . . ah . . . S . . . no, no, CP, right?

Tiffany: Yes! Here's one you'll like: How do we write "Do not be late?"

Nick: DNBL8 . . .

Tiffany: I knew you'd remember that one! OK, just one more. What does "gratz" mean?

Nick: Congratulations!

Tiffany: Gratz, Dad. You did XLNT!

Nick: THX, Tiff. For *What's on Your Mind*, I'm Nick Amado . . . ADBB, my friends!

Tiffany: That means "All done, bye-bye!"

Glossary

absorb *v.* take something in through the surface

adapt *v.* change your behavior or ideas in order to fit a new situation

adjust *v.* gradually become familiar with a new situation

agriculture *n.* science or practice of farming

alleged violation *adj.* an action that breaks a law, rule, or agreement, which is believed to have happened but has not been proven

allergy *n.* condition that makes you sick when you swallow, touch, or breathe a particular thing

aluminum *n.* type of metal

ambitious *adj.* having a strong desire to be successful or powerful

amend *v.* make small changes or improvements, especially in the words of a law

amputation *n.* cutting off a part of someone's body for medical reasons

approach *v.* move toward or near someone or something

aptitude test *n.* test used for finding out what someone's best skills are

arrangement *n.* something that has been organized or agreed on

artery *n.* one of the tubes that carries blood from your heart to the rest of your body

assemble *v.* come together in the same place

atmosphere *n.* mixture of gases that surrounds the earth

automatically *adv.* without thinking about what you are doing

bail *n.* money exchanged so that someone can be let out of prison while awaiting trial

bear arms *v.* carry guns and other weapons for self-defense

biodegradables *n.* materials, chemicals, and so on that are changed naturally by bacteria into substances that do not harm the environment

branch *n.* a part of government or other organization that deals with one particular part of its work

break *n.* a period of time in which you stop what you are doing in order to rest, eat, and so forth

bridge *n.* upper part of your nose between the eyes

bruise *n.* mark on the skin of a person or piece of fruit where it has been damaged by a hit or a fall

calculation *n.* act of adding, multiplying, or dividing numbers to find out an amount, price, and so forth

category *n.* group of people or things that are all of the same type

cell *n.* smallest living thing

central *adj.* in the middle of an area or an object

chemical *n.* substance used in chemistry (the science of studying substances and the way they change or combine with each other) or produced by a chemical process

cholesterol *n.* substance in your body which doctors think may cause heart disease

citation *n.* official order for someone to appear in court or pay a fine for doing something illegal

civic leader *n.* authority figure working for the local government

collapse *v.* fall down or inward suddenly

colony *n.* group of people who have left their home country to live in a new place

comfortable *adj.* relaxed or not worried about what someone will do or what will happen

commercial *adj.* relating to business and the buying and selling of things

commitment *n.* promise to do something or to behave in a particular way

comply *v.* do what you are asked to do or what a law or rule tells you to do

computer screen *n.* flat part of a computer on which you see words, images and so on

concentrate *v.* think very carefully about something you are doing

confidential *adj.* secret and not intended to be shown or told to other people

conserve *v.* prevent something from being wasted, damaged, or destroyed

continuously *adv.* without stopping or being interrupted

crash *v.* suddenly stop working

criteria *n.* facts or standards used in order to help you judge or decide something

crop *n.* plant such as corn, wheat, and so on that farmers grow and sell

current *adj.* happening, existing, or being used now

customer *n.* someone who buys things from a store or company

damaged *adj.* physically harmed

data *n.* information or facts

decay *v.* be slowly destroyed by a natural chemical process, or to destroy something in this way

detection *n.* the process of detecting, or the fact of being detected

diabetes *n.* a disease in which there is too much sugar in the blood

discourage *v.* persuade someone not to do something, especially by making it seem difficult or bad

discrimination *n.* the practice of treating one group of people differently from another in an unfair way

disease *n.* illness that affects a person, animal, or plant, with specific symptoms

display *n.* part of a piece of equipment that shows information

distracted *adj.* unable to pay attention to what you are doing

ditch *n.* long, narrow hole in the ground for water to flow through, usually at the side of a field, road, and so on

diverse *adj.* very different from each other

document *n.* piece of paper that has official information written on it

draft *v.* order someone to fight for his or her country during a war

electrical appliance *n.* piece of equipment such as a stove or washing machine, used in people's homes

eliminate *v.* get rid of something completely

embarrassed *adj.* ashamed, nervous, or uncomfortable, especially in front of other people

emergency flashers *n.* hazard warning lights

emit *v.* send out gas, heat, light, sound, and so on

employment agency *n.* business that makes money by finding jobs for people

energy-efficient *adj.* energy-saving

enforce *v.* make people obey a rule or law

engineer *n.* someone whose job is to design, build, and repair roads, bridges, machines, and so forth

environment (the) *n.* land, water, and air in which people, animals, and plants live

equipment *n.* tools, machines, and so forth that you need for a particular activity

establish *v.* start something such as a company, system, situation, and so on, especially one that will exist for a long time

evolve *v.* develop and change gradually over a long period of time

exercise your rights *v.* use your legal freedoms and advantages

factor *n.* one of several things that influence or cause a situation

faucet *n.* thing that you turn on and off to control the flow of water from a pipe

federal *adj.* relating to the central government of a country which consists of several states

fee *n.* an amount of money that you pay to do something

fertilizer *n.* substance that is put on the soil to help plants grow

financial security *n.* enough money to live on comfortably

flag down *phr v.* make the driver of a vehicle stop by waving at him or her

flexible *adj.* able to change easily

foreign policy *n.* politics, business matters, and so on, that affect or concern the relationship between your country and other countries

former *adj.* having a particular position in the past, but not now

fossil fuel *n.* resource such as gas or oil that has been formed from plants and animals that lived millions of years ago

foster care *n.* supervised care in an institution or temporary home for delinquent or neglected children

found *v.* start an organization, town or institution that is intended to continue for a long time

furnish *v.* supply or provide something

general public *n.* ordinary people in the community

generation *n.* all the people in a society or family who are about the same age

global warming *n.* increase in the world temperatures, caused by an increase of carbon dioxide around the earth

goods *n.* things that are produced in order to be sold

greenhouse gas *n.* a vapor, especially carbon dioxide or methane, that traps heat above the earth and causes a warming effect

guidance *n.* helpful advice about work, education, and so forth

harsh *adj.* unkind, cruel, or strict

hazard *n.* something that may be dangerous or cause accidents, problems, and so on

health insurance *n.* an arrangement in which you pay a certain amount of money each month to a company with the promise that this company will pay a certain amount of money toward your medical bills

highway patrol *n.* police who make sure that people obey the rules on highways in the U.S.

hormone *n.* substance produced by your body that influences its growth, development, and so on

Human Resource (HR) Department *n.* section or division of a company that deals with employing, training, and helping people

imagination *n.* ability to form pictures or ideas in your mind

immerse *v.* to be or become completely involved in something

impact *n.* effect or result of an event or situation

impact *v.* have an important or noticeable effect on someone or something

impartial *adj.* not giving special support or attention to one group; unbiased

impose *v.* introduce a rule, tax, or punishment, and force people to accept it

impression *n.* the opinion, belief or feeling you have about someone or something because of the way she, he, or it seems

in demand *adj.* needed or wanted by a lot of people

in exchange *adv.* in return for something; in payment for something

inform *v.* formally tell someone about something

inhale *v.* breathe in air, smoke, or gas

injury *n.* physical harm or damage that is caused by an accident or attack, or a particular example of this

innovation *n.* introduction of new ideas, methods, or inventions, or the idea, method or invention itself

insulation *n.* the material used in order to cover or protect something, especially a building

insulin *n.* a substance produced naturally by your body that allows sugar to be used for energy

interior *n.* inner part or inside of something

interstate *n.* road for fast traffic that goes between states

intrusion *n.* unwanted person or event that interrupts or annoys you

issue *v.* officially make a statement or give a warning

know by sight *v.* recognize by seeing

learning permit *n.* official document that gives you permission to learn to drive

lease *v.* use or let someone use buildings, property, and so forth, when he or she pays rent

martial art *n.* sport such as karate in which you fight with your hands and feet

master *v.* learn something so well that you understand it completely and have no difficulty with it

material *n.* things that are used for making, doing, or learning something, for example, books or school supplies

measurable *adj.* able to be measured in terms of size, length, amount

medical history *n.* your past illnesses, doctor visits, vaccinations, and so on, that have been documented by your doctor

mentor *v.* teach, advise, and encourage people in order to help them succeed at work or in school

merchandise *n.* things that are for sale in stores

mobile home *n.* type of house made of metal, that can be pulled by a large vehicle and moved to another place

moist *adj.* slightly wet, in a pleasant way

natural resources *n.* all the land, minerals, energy, and so on that exist in a country

nausea *n.* feeling you have when you think you are going to vomit

neglect *n.* failure to take care of something or someone well

normal behavior *n.* usual way of acting

notify *v.* tell someone something formally or officially

novice *n.* someone who has just begun learning a skill or activity

numerous *adj.* many

obstacle *n.* something that makes it difficult for you to succeed

occupation *n.* job or profession

official *adj.* approved of or done by someone in authority, especially the government

operate *v.* if a machine operates or you operate it, it works or you make it work

outcome *n.* final result of a meeting, process, and so on

overdue notice *n.* written or printed statement telling you that something that was supposed to be completed or handed in is late

overturn *v.* turn upside down or knock onto its side

penalty *n.* punishment for not obeying a law, rule, or legal agreement

permanent *adj.* continuing to exist for a long time or for all time

personal computer (PC) *n.* small computer that is used by one person at a time, at work or at home

personnel *n.* people who work in a company or for a particular kind of employer

petition *v.* formally ask someone in authority to do something

physician's assistant someone who is trained to give basic medical treatment, in order to help a doctor

pollute *v.* make air, water, soil and so on dangerously dirty

population *n.* the number of people or animals living in a particular area, country, etc.

power line *n.* large wire carrying electricity above or under the ground

power plant *n.* building where electricity is produced to supply a large area

prescription medicine *n.* drug that can be obtained only with a written order from the doctor

principle *n.* moral rule or set of ideas about what is right and wrong, that influences how you behave

priority *n.* right to be given attention first and before other people and things

procedure *n.* way of doing something, especially the correct or normal way

professional *adj.* skilled, trained, or expert at something

promotion *n.* move to a better, more responsible position at work

protest *v.* say or do something publicly to show that you disagree with something or think that it is wrong or unfair

public transportation *n.* buses, trains, and so on that are available for everyone to use

pull over *v.* drive to the side of a road and stop your car, or to make someone do this

pulse *n.* the regular beat that can be felt as your heart pumps blood around your body

racial prejudice *n.* unfair feeling against someone who is of a different race

reconstruct *v.* build again

records *n.* information about something or someone, which is either written on paper or stored on a computer

registration *n.* official piece of paper containing details about a motor vehicle and the name of its owner

regulation *n.* official rule or order

reference letter *n.* letter containing information about you that is written by someone who knows you well, usually to a new employer

referral *n.* act of sending someone or something to another place for help, information, and so on

rejection *n.* situation in which someone stops giving you love or attention

represent *v.* do things or speak officially for someone else, or express his or her views or opinions

research institution *n.* large establishment or organization devoted to the study of a particular subject

resident *n.* someone who lives in a particular place

restrict *v.* limit or control something

restriction *n.* rule or set of laws that limits what you can do or what is allowed to happen

retail *adj.* referring to goods sold in a store for personal use

retaliation *n.* action against someone in order to pay them back for something they have done

rinse *v.* use running water and no soap to remove dirt, soap, and so on

rotating *v.* turning around a fixed point

screening *n.* medical test that is done on a lot of people to make sure that they do not have a particular illness

sentence *v.* legally punish someone who has been found guilty of a crime

share credit *v.* share the approval or praise doing something good

shoulder *n.* area of ground beside a road where drivers can stop their cars if they are having trouble

simulator *n.* machine that is used for training people by letting them feel what real conditions are like

solar energy *n.* power from the sun that is used to produce heat, make machines work, and so on

specialist *n.* doctor who knows more about one particular type of illness or treatment than other doctors

spreadsheet *n.* computer program that can show and calculate financial information, or a printed version of this information

standard *n.* level of quality, skill, or ability that is considered to be acceptable

statistics *n.* numbers which represents facts or measurements

sturdy *adj.* strong and not likely to break or be hurt

substance *n.* a particular type of solid, liquid, or gas

supplement *n.* something added to improve your diet, especially a vitamin

supplies *n.* things necessary for daily life, especially for a group of people over a period of time

suspect *v.* think that something is probably true, especially something bad

suspend *v.* officially stop someone from working, driving, or going to school for a fixed period, because she or he has broken the rules

switch *v.* change from doing or using one thing to doing or using something else

symptom *n.* physical condition that shows when you may have a particular disease

take (someone) by surprise *v.* surprise or shock someone by happening or doing something in a way that is not expected

take the initiative *v.* be the first one to take action to achieve a particular aim or solve a particular problem

team player *n.* someone who works well as a member of a group or team

testify *v.* make a formal statement of what is true

tornado watch *n.* checking an area in order to warn people about the danger of a tornado

tow truck operator *n.* someone who drives a strong vehicle that can pull cars behind it

toxic *adj.* poisonous

traditional *adj.* following ideas, methods, and so on that have existed for a long time

transportation *n.* system for carrying passengers or goods from one place to another

treatment *n.* method that is intended to cure an injury or sickness

turbine *n.* engine that works when the pressure from a liquid or gas moves a special wheel around

twister *n.* a tornado

uniformed *adj.* dressed in a uniform

unjust *adj.* not fair or reasonable

uproot *v.* pull up a plant or tree and its roots out of the ground

upset *n.* unpleasant, disturbing feelings

vehicle *n.* thing such as a car, bus, etc. that is used for carrying people or things from one place to another

victim *n.* someone who has been hurt or killed by someone or something, or who has been affected by a bad situation

violation *n.* action that breaks a law, agreement, principle, and so on

violently *adv.* happening in such a way as to be liable to hurt people, destroy property, and so on

warrant *n.* official paper that allows the police to do something

work ethic *n.* idea or belief that hard work and persistence are morally good

working conditions *n.* situations or environments in which someone works

Index

Credits

Photo credits

All original photography by Richard Hutchings/Digital Light Source. Page 5 Hamiza Bakirci/Shutterstock; 8 Ron Chapple Stock/Corbis; 12 Image Source Pink/Alamy; 14 Courtesy of the St. Lawrence County One-Stop Center in Canton, New York; 15 (1) iStockphoto.com, (2) Bill Bachmann/Alamy, (3) Terry Harris/Alamy, (4) Imagebroker/Alamy, (5) Redchopsticks.com LLC/Alamy; 16 Photos 12/Alamy; 21 Somos Images/Corbis; 24 Blend Images/Jupiter Images; 25 Simon Marcus/Corbis; 27 Gregor Schuster/zefa/Corbis; 30 Shutterstock; 32 GoGo Images Corporation/Alamy; 34 (top) Adam Gregor/Shutterstock, (middle) Shutterstock, (bottom) Jupiterimages/Thinkstock/Alamy; 38 Radu Razvan/Fotolia; 44 Image100/Corbis; 45 Juice Images Limited/Alamy; 48 Shutterstock; 50 Shutterstock; 52 Mediacolor's/Alamy; 53 Randy Faris/Corbis; 55 Don Smetzer/Alamy; 60 Shutterstock; 64 Shutterstock; 65 Eric Nguyen/Corbis; 66 (left) Mike Hill/Alamy, (middle) Rick Doyle/Corbis, (right) iStockphoto.com, (bottom) AFP/Getty Images; 70 Rick Wilking/Reuters/Corbis; 74 Photo Network/Alamy; 75 Alexander Hafemann/iStockphoto.com; 76 (left) Joe Bator/Corbis, (middle) Zooid Pictures, (middle left) Luis Camargo/iStockphoto.com, (bottom left) iStockphoto.com, (bottom right) Ted Pink/Alamy; 80 (left) Joe Belanger/Alamy, (middle) Mark Higgins/iStockphoto.com, (right) Shutterstock; 84 Pacific Press Service/Alamy Stock Photo; 85 Moodboard/Corbis; 90 Tetra Images/Newscom; 94 (left) Lars Zahner/Fotolia, (middle) Arclight/Alamy, (right) Blend Images/Alamy; 100 (left to right) Peter Casolino/Alamy, Peter Casolino/Alamy, Jim McIsaac/Getty Images, Jupiterimages/Polka Dot/Alamy, Christian Petersen/Getty Images; 104 Shutterstock; 105 Charles Gullung/zefa/Corbis; 108 (left) Arena Creative/Fotolia, (right) Image Source Pink/Alamy; 111 iStockphoto.com; 113 Bill Aron/PhotoEdit; 115 (left) Shutterstock, (middle) Blend Images/Alamy, (right) Tetra Images/Corbis; 118 Jupiterimages/Brand X /Alamy; 119 Nucleus Inc./Photolibrary.com; 120 (left) Sue Bennett/Alamy, (middle) RubberBall/Alamy, (right) Tina Chang/Solus-Veer/Corbis; 124 Push Pictures/Corbis; 125 Jim West/Alamy; 129 Bettmann/Corbis; 134 Imagebroker/Alamy; 135 (top) Stephen Chernin/Getty Images, (middle) Alex Wong/Getty Images, (bottom) Alex Wong/Getty Images; 136 Jeff Greenberg/Alamy; 138 Chris Hondros/Newsmakers/Getty Images; 144 (top) Peter Gridley/Taxi/Getty Images, (middle) ClipArtGallery.com, (bottom) Robert Harding World Imagery; 145 RubberBall/Jupiter Images; 146 Kim Kulish/Corbis; 151 (top) Bettmann/Corbis, (bottom) Bettmann/Corbis; 153 Shutterstock; 156 Bonnie Kamin/PhotoEdit; 160 Jeff Greenberg/Alamy; 164 Africa Studios/Fotolia; 165 Jupiterimages/Brand X /Alamy; 166 (top) Shutterstock, (bottom) Shutterstock; 170 (top) Somos Images/Corbis, (bottom) Sally and Richard Greenhill/Alamy; 172 Shutterstock; 174 (top) Doug Wechsler/Photolibrary.com, (bottom) Peter Arnold, Inc./Alamy; 176 Jason Knott/Alamy; 177 GoGo Images Corporation/Alamy; 180 (top) Mike Theiss/Ultimate Chase/Corbis, (bottom) Shutterstock; 184 Mark Scheuern/Alamy; 185 Chad Baker/Getty Images; 187 (top) Bettmann/Corbis, (bottom) M.I.T. Museum and Historical Collections; 190 Paul Hudson/Getty Images; 192 Alexander Caminada/Rex Feature; 194 Wong Maye-E/Associated Press/ PA Photos; 196 (top) Ned Coomes/Zooid Pictures, (bottom) Michelle D. Bridwell/PhotoEdit; 198 Detlev Van Ravenswaay/Science Photo Library; 204 Shutterstock; 211 Tim Pannell/Corbis.

Illustration Credits

Luis Briseño pp. 46, 188; Laurie Conley p. 33; Deborah Crowle pp. 58, 61, 68.

Text Credits

Pages 166–167, Taking the Green Route: "Water Conservation Facts" downloaded on 2/4/09 from http://www.chnep.org/MoreInfo/water_conservation_facts.htm; "Conserving Water Means Big Savings for the Pocket and the Planet" downloaded on 2/4/09 from http://www.p2ad.org/files_pdf/cwmbs.pdf; p. 174, How Daily Life Is Changing Our World: "Waste Reduction and Recycling," downloaded on 2/4/09 from http://www.kab.org/site/PageServer?pagename=Focus_Waste_reduction; p. 180, The Greening of Greensburg, Kansas: "Tornado-Ravaged Kansas Town Rebuilds 'Green'" downloaded 2/4/09 from http://www.usatoday.com/news/nation/2008-05-01-greensburg_N.htm "Tornado's Gifts: Greensburg Rebuilds, Revitalizes," downloaded 2/4/09 from <http://www.npr.org/templates/story/story.php?storyId=90167618; "In Wake of Twister, Kansas Town Is Rebuilding Green" downloaded on 2/4/09 from http://www.cnn.com/2008/TECH/05/02/greensburg.green/index.html; pp. 186–187, 198, The History of the Internet: "J.C.R. Licklider and the Universal Network" downloaded on 5/20/08 from http://www.livinginternet.com/i/ii_licklider.htm; "The History of...The Internet" downloaded 5/19/08 from http://www.fcc.gov/cgb/kidszone/history_internet.html; "The Internet: A Short History of Getting Connected" downloaded on 5/19/08 from http://www.fcc.gov/omd/history/internet; "All About the Internet: History of the Internet" downloaded on 5/19/08 from http://www.isoc.org/internet/history/brief.shtml; "Internet Pioneers: J.C.R. Licklider" downloaded on 5/20/08 from http://www.ibiblio.org/pioneers/licklider.html; "The Birth of the Internet" downloaded on 5/19/08 from http://www.fcc.gov/omd/history/internet/documents/newsletter.pdf; "The Computer as a Communication Device" and "Man-Computer Symbiosis" downloaded on 5/19/08 from SRC Research Report #61 at http://gatekeeper.dec.com/pub/DEC/SRC/research-reports/abstracts/src-rr-061.html; p. 192: Virtual Driving: Brown, Joe. AutoWeek, August 27, 2007, p. 26. "Virtual reality check: The road can be a dangerous place, and simulator technology can provide a safer place to learn" downloaded from Lexis Nexis Academic on 5/23/2008; Description of *StreetWise* downloaded on 5/23/2008 from http://www.roadreadyteens.com/index.html; Free Drivers' Ed Game Teaches Safe Habits, downloaded on 5/23/2008 from Educational Games Research website, http://edugamesblog.wordpress.com/2008/02/27/free-drivers'-ed-game-teaches-safe-habits/; Yount, Lisa. Virtual Reality, Chapter 3 Lucent Books: Chicago, 2005, downloaded on 5/23/2008 from http://www.scienceclarified.com/scitech/Virtual-Reality/The-Virtual-Classroom-Virtual-Reality-in-Training-and-Education.html.